1968 – Oct. 2 – 1968

Happy Anniversary
To Marian & Ken.

Aunty Sue

THE UNLIMITED POWER OF PRAYER

Design and layout by Sal Lazzarotti

CREDITS

"The Silent Child" by Frances E. Leslie, adapted from *Science of Mind.* "The Vacant Seat" by Don Mott, reprinted by permission of Good News Publishers, Westchester, Illinois. "Last to Be Picked" by Bob Pettit, adapted from the book *The Drive Within Me,* copyright 1966, Prentice-Hall Inc., Englewood Cliffs, N.J. "Barefoot to America" by Legson Kayira, reprinted by permission of Harold Matson Co., Inc. "A Soldier's Prayer" by Gerald Kersh, copyright 1938, reprinted by permission of the Sterling Lord Agency. "A Prayer For Wisdom" by Sister Mary Camille, S.M., copyright 1966 by St. Anthony's Guild, Paterson, N.J. "Prayer When Feelings Are Hurt" by Norman Vincent Peale from the booklet *Prayers for Every Need,* Foundation for Christian Living, Pawling, N.Y. "For One Who Is Tired" from *Songs of Hope* by Grace Noll Crowell, copyright 1938, Harper & Brothers; renewed 1966 by Grace Noll Crowell; reprinted by permission of Harper & Row, Publishers, Incorporated. "Teach Us, Dear God" by Marian Anderson, from *Prayers of Women* edited by Lisa Sergio, Harper & Row, New York, N.Y. "The 'Hold-Up' Prayer" by Lorraine Juliana from *Our Sunday Visitor.* "Prayer For the Complacent" by Robert Raines, reprinted from *Creative Brooding,* by permission of the Macmillan Company, copyright 1966 by Robert Raines. "A Prayer of Thanksgiving" from *Light of the Years* by Grace Noll Crowell, copyright 1936, Harper & Brothers; renewed 1964 by Grace Noll Crowell; reprinted by permission of Harper & Row, Publishers, Incorporated. "Our Prayer of Thanks" by Carl Sandburg from the poem, *Our Prayer of Thanks.* From the book *Aim for a Star,* by Helen Lowrie Marshall, copyright 1964 by Helen Lowrie Marshall; reprinted by permission of Doubleday & Company, Inc. and Hallmark Cards, Inc.

Our Father

which art in heaven, Hallowed be thy name. Thy kingdom come. Thy will be done in earth, as it is in heaven. Give us this day our daily bread. And forgive us our debts, as we forgive our debtors. And lead us not into temptation, but deliver us from evil: For thine is the kingdom, and the power, and the glory, for ever. ✝ ✝ ✝ Amen

About This Book

Millions of Christians across the world *say* the 66 words on the preceding page daily. The question that has been raised, however, is: how many *pray* them?

Pray them, mean them, live them. If the Lord's Prayer were prayed and lived by the army of men and women who call themselves Christians, it is a safe assumption that we would be living in a different world from the one we see about us today.

What is the problem? Are we praying amiss? Have our prayers lost their efficacy? Is our faith weak?

The answers are no different today from when they were asked in our Lord's time on earth. No different from when He gave His model prayer to the disciple who requested: "Teach us to pray." No different from the time He gave His sample prayer to those gathered for the Sermon on the Mount.

We can be sure the people who sought to follow Him were no different from those in His camp today. They had the same misconceptions, the same hang-ups, the same shallowness of understanding about prayer that many of us have. What we need to do is re-read the sixth chapter of Matthew and study the framework in which Christ set forth His prayer.

Among the statements He made were these:

- When you pray, don't be like the hypocrites who pray standing in the synagogues and on the street corners where they can be seen by men.
- But when you pray, pray to your Father in secret; and your Father Who hears you in secret will reward you openly.

- When you pray, don't use vain repetitions as the heathen do, for they think that they shall be heard for their much speaking.
- Your Father knows what you need before you ask.

Remembering these points before going to prayer would be to everyone's advantage, for at times we are all guilty of "vain repetitions," of praying so that others may hear, of using more wind than heart.

The premise of this book is that there is limitless power in prayer. Its purpose is to show through deeply personal illustrations how others have found this to be true. If you sometimes feel that your prayers are earthbound, ineffective, unheard or unanswered, the many examples of power-filled prayer in this book cannot help but inspire and uplift you.

Some of the stories no doubt will have more meaning now than others, because they may speak more directly to your present needs. Regardless, read the book in its entirety; then keep it close at hand for future reference. It is a permanent treasure of life-changing experiences to which you can return again and again for sustenance and succor.

At the end of each chapter, you will find a Spiritual Workshop, one prepared by the editors of Guideposts as a personal experiment in prayer. You may want to attempt one or more of these exercises. A forewarning: as the name implies, they are workshops and only the serious student of prayer, one willing to work, will find much meaning in them.

One other note: Sprinkled liberally throughout the pages of this book are favorite prayers, specific examples of helpful petitions to God. Once again, as in the case of the Lord's Prayer, these are models. Mark them and return to them from time to time; they can help bridge barriers between you and God.

As always, our hope in preparing such a volume is that your life may be blessed and enriched and that through these stories you discover for yourself the unlimited power of prayer.

The Editors

CONTENTS

2. Lord, Change Me

3. Lord, Heal Me—Your Way

4. Lord, Give Me Concern for Others

5. Lord, Fill Me with Gratefulness

6. Lord, Teach Me to Dream Big

THE UNLIMITED POWER OF PRAYER LORD, HELP ME

LIFE always has been and always will be full of the unexpected. At one time or another—we all come nose to nose with an emergency, which calls for quick thinking and quick action.

Unfortunately, we don't always act with prudent decisiveness. Too many of us freeze when we face sudden danger and by the time we regain our senses it is too late to avert an accident. What enables some people to react effectively and others to lock up, immobilized? Scientists have long puzzled over the question without coming to many firm conclusions. One thing we know for sure, proper conditioning can sharpen our reactions and lead to faster, more responsible action.

A lifeguard is trained to react when he sees someone floundering in the water. A soldier trained under live fire knows how to protect himself when he faces battle conditions. Many driving instructors have their pupils purposely put their automobile into a skid on a safe expanse of ice so they can practice recovering control.

In each of the following stories, another form of conditioning is common to all. It is a spiritual conditioning. Because the people involved in these articles knew God firsthand, they knew what to do when emergency presented itself.

Instead of panic, they turned to prayer. Instead of fear, they evoked faith. These dramatic testimonies offer contemporary evidence that God is, indeed, our ever present comforter and guide. For when these people called out "Lord, help me," He did just that.

1

Empty—emotionally and spiritually—the star of TV's Girl Talk recalls the day she gave up on life.

Hand on My Shoulder

by VIRGINIA GRAHAM

AS a child there were many times when I went to bed fearful of the darkness because I was unable to touch and see the things that made my waking hours secure. Then my father would pillow my face in his palm and tell me stories about men and women of the Bible. He made these people come alive and the miracles of faith seem very real.

"God's love will always sustain you," he would say. "It sustains everyone who seeks Him."

One night I asked him, "Papa, you've been up in a plane and seen how small the houses and cars are? Well, how can God have eyes and ears which can see and hear everyone and everything in all those millions of houses and cars?" And then I got to the question that really bothered me: "How can I hear Him?"

And my father replied, "If you stop talking long enough, you can hear Him. God is inside you. He loves you and He is there to help you when things go wrong."

The wisdom of his faith grew in me, like an inner companion, and when Father passed on I felt that my faith was strong enough to help me over life's bumps. The first test came at age 19 when I was in an automobile accident. After surgery and prolonged treatment the doctors said that in all probability I would never be able to bear a child.

At first I refused to accept this verdict. Many prayers later I saw that we can hardly expect to have everything we want, even if we want it very much. Our way, our will, are not as important as God's will.

2

Some years later when I met and fell in love with Harry Gussenberg, I told him that we probably wouldn't be able to have children. Nine months and four days after we were married our daughter, Lynn, was born.

In the years which followed I began to get sudden temperatures and infections without any apparent reasons for them. Yet there was no loss of weight and certainly no loss of energy. I was active and busy, both as a mother and in radio work, and my energy seemed to come not so much from physical strength as from spiritual vitality. The doctors took dozens of tests and found nothing wrong.

One test, however, revealed something they hadn't even looked for in the first place: I was to have another baby. I was the happiest woman alive because the gift of life was going to be mine again.

One night three months later I suddenly felt a terrible pain and was rushed to the hospital. I was taken immediately into surgery. When I awoke the next morning the room was empty and gray, except for the sunlight filtering through the venetian blinds. When my doctor came in, his face told me that the news was not good.

"You lost the baby," he said. Then he added hesitantly, "There were other complications too."

Just then Harry entered. He looked pale and worn. Gently he took my hand. "I want you to go to sleep now," he said.

"I don't want to go to sleep," I said, miserably. "I want to go home."

"You've got to go to sleep," Harry insisted. He turned his face away and then left the room.

I turned to the doctor. "Why is he acting so peculiar? I'll be going home tomorrow, won't I?"

"No. We're going to have to do a little more surgery."

"What do you mean? What surgery?"

Then for a while time seemed to hang in suspension. When my heart and mind began working again, I looked imploringly at the doctor and asked, "Do I have cancer?"

He is one of the sweetest and gentlest and finest men in the world, but he couldn't erase the answer I saw in his eyes. In agony of spirit I clutched his sleeve, "I'm not going to die! You told me I had no cancer!"

"Virginia," he pleaded gently, "Virginia, that was a preliminary test. I thought you were intelligent enough to understand. . . ."

"Intelligent!" I shouted. "A woman of 36 with a child and a husband and the glorious experience of living. How do you ever get intelligent enough to accept cancer?"

Harry came back into the room and on his anguished face was the same knowledge that was now mine.

After a while they quieted me with sedatives.

A day later the parade of doctors and tests began. On the second day I told myself, "This is not going to be. I cannot inflict this pain on my husband and child too. I cannot kill them."

And my heart cried out, "I have tried to love where it was needed. God, why have You failed me? How could You betray me like this? You do not love me."

I was angry and for the first time in my life I knew the terrible emptiness of being alone.

My head was whirling. I picked up the phone and called Harry and said, "I am not going to put you and Lynn through this suffering. Thank you for all the wonderful years we've had. I want you to know that what I am going to do is best."

I hung up, got out of bed and walked to the window. The day was bleak, gray and sunless. Deliberately I raised the window and swung one leg over the sill. I turned to swing the other leg out. But suddenly there was a powerful grip on my shoulder. It was real, very real, as real as my breath. I knew who it was.

"Papa," I said. "Papa, you told me that God is in me. What happened?"

His voice was clear, as if he were talking to his small child: "Don't let anger and fear talk. Listen. Listen to His voice. God is in you. His love will sustain you."

The voice diminished to a whisper, then faded. "Don't go, Papa, don't go. . . ."

But the strong grip on my shoulder was gone. I looked up. The sun was beginning to probe through the gray overcast and light was pouring through the window. I put my hand to my face and realized it was wet with tears. I knew I could not take my life. Only the Giver of life could be the Taker. I could only accept His will, not mine.

I swung my leg back over the sill into the room. A flood of relief swept over me, as if cold water had been poured over a burning person.

The next morning I was taken to the operating room for ten hours of surgery. I was ready for it—and for the 35 radium treatments in the weeks that followed. The strength to go through this was given me as I needed it.

Fifteen years have passed and my doctor still talks about that experience and says, "There was always something in you that made me feel you were going to make it. Your recovery was a kind of miracle."

And I tell him—and the world—that what he calls a miraculous recovery was only God in me—or me in Him. This is stated better in His Book: *For in Him we live, and move, and have our being.**

* Acts 17:28

A Prayer Under Pressure

Our Father, when we long for life without trials and work without difficulties, remind us that oaks grow strong in contrary winds and diamonds are made under pressure.

With stout hearts may we see in every calamity an opportunity and not give way to the pessimism that sees in every opportunity a calamity.

Peter Marshall

The violent wind shook the tree in which this family of five had taken refuge. The water rose higher. There was only one hope.

Hurricane!

by FRANK EIFERT

LUCINDA SEARS stared out over Lake Okeechobee with a troubled light in her eye. The sky was darkening and the wind was whipping dust about the sides of her cabin.

It was September 16, 1928, a day that southern Florida will never forget. A monstrous storm was on its way, but people like Charles and Lucinda Sears and their three children—people who lived just off Florida's biggest lake—had no warning of its approach.

A tall, proud woman, Lucinda had worked hard with her husband to make a living and build their small home. When the storm came, she closed the windows. Then she and Charles watched the dust whipping around the cabin. The wind increased and soon their roof blew off as if it were a piece of cardboard.

The terrifying storm had boiled up out of the Caribbean, intent on destroying everything within its 500-mile range. The monster slashed its way through Miami, roared across the Everglades and up the peninsula, leaving behind destruction and death. The dead were everywhere: among the timbers and masonry of demolished homes, in city streets and on highways.

As soon as the roof had blown off their cabin, Lucinda grabbed her daughter, Effie Ann, not quite two years old, while her husband, Charles, reached for their two sons, Cleofus, almost five, and Charles Jr., three. They ran outside looking for shelter.

All they could see was an old bent tree which had withstood an earlier storm. The nine-foot mud dike around the lake had burst with the pressure of the flood. The rising water drenched them and made everything so slippery that Cleofus dropped from Charles' arms and disappeared for a moment. Charles, balancing the other boy in one arm, finally pulled Cleofus from the watery muck. Then carrying the children, Lucinda and her husband climbed into the tree's sheltering branches.

Silently they watched as their cabin broke into pieces. Parts of a chair, a dishpan, blankets, shoes, lamps—everything they owned—washed by them in one enormous wall of water.

Cleofus was limp; he had swallowed too much water. Was he gone? The father, his arms aching, worked on his small son. Soon he felt the child's breath faintly against his ear. Just the slightest breath, but it was enough to start him working more frantically to drain the water out of his son. Soon Cleofus was joining his little brother in whimpering: a blessed sound now.

The fury of the storm grew. As the water level rose, the frightened family climbed higher into the tree until they were clinging desperately to the top branches which were thrashing wildly in the mighty gusts of wind. The water slowly began to creep up around their bodies. They could climb no higher.

Night came. The enraged wind tore unabated at the family in the tree. Torrents of rain stung them. And the water inched relentlessly higher, slowly reaching muddy hands of death toward them.

Once Charles slipped and he and the two boys were nearly swept away. Lucinda made Effie Ann lock her little arms around her neck and then, legs wrapped around a branch, Lucinda reached down and one by one pulled the boys up with her. She held all three children until Charles could get back into the tree and again help her.

After a while even breathing became a struggle. Charles called through the screaming wind:

"Cindy, we're all gonna die."

Her voice rang back across the tempest.

"No, honey, we're not gonna die. God's right here with us!"

The water was almost up to her neck. She was straining to hold Effie Ann's head above the water. How could she believe they would live?

"Cindy, if I could just get closer to you. . . ."

"You just hold on to those boys!" she called back.

Praying for a little more strength in her almost paralyzed arms, she painfully lifted Effie Ann a fraction higher. Faintly she heard her husband's voice again.

"Not much more time."

She lifted her eyes to a stygian sky, to One Whose quiet command had stilled another tempest in Galilee. Then she began to sing, accompanied by the gurgling of water and roar of the wind:

> *Father, I stretch my hands to Thee,*
> *No other help I know;*
> *If Thou withdraw Thyself from me,*
> *Ah, whither shall I go. . . .*
> *Author of faith, to Thee I lift*
> *My weary, longing eyes;*
> *O may I now receive that gift;*
> *My soul, without it, dies.*

As Charles Wesley's old hymn was carried away on the wind, it seemed to Lucinda that she could hear a great chorus of angels singing with her. And as she reached higher for the everlasting arms of faith, she saw three flashes of light streak across the eastern sky in perfectly timed succession.

"Thank You, God. Thank You," she murmured. She knew without a doubt that the flashes of light had been a sign from God.

It was no surprise to her at all when the water began slowly, very slowly, to recede.

The wind slackened, spent, decreasing with the reluctance of an ebbing tide. The storm drifted back to the sea to hide its face. Then it was quiet once more.

The family in the tree, muscles aching, chilled to the bone, hungry and thirsty, clung to the branches, waiting through the long hours of the night.

The children whimpered low and then, too tired to even whine, they were silent, half-sleeping burdens to be held close. It was well into the next day before the waters were low enough for the parents to climb from the tree and wade to safety. They stumbled to an aid station in a state of shock. Tender hands ministered to them and put them to bed.

Their night of terror had passed. But that's not all the story. Not for tall, proud Lucinda who, within inches of death, sang a song of faith into the teeth of one of the worst hurricanes on record.

For, eight days after the storm, Lucinda bore her fourth child—a healthy girl.

A Prayer For Strength

Oh Father, Whose voice I hear in the winds and Whose breath gives life to all the world, hear me. I am a man before You, one of Your many children. I am small and weak. I need Your strength and wisdom. Let me walk in beauty, and make my eyes ever behold the red and purple sunsets. Make my hands respect the things You have made, my ears sharp to hear Your voice. Make me wise so that I may know the things You have taught my people, the lessons You have hidden in every leaf and rock. I seek strength, Father, not to be superior to my brothers, but to be able to fight my greatest enemy, myself. Make me ever ready to come to You with clean hands and straight eye, so that when life fades as the setting sun, my spirit may come to You without shame.

Chief Tom White Cloud
Ojibway Indian

"After an air crash, you're supposed to stay with the plane. But we had no food or water and I was the only one who could move."

Nightmare Mountain

by MAJOR THOMAS D. SMITH III

IN those terrifying moments when our airplane began to disintegrate I had time for just three thoughts. I was sure that all 10 of us in our Air Force C-47 were going to be killed. I hoped that it would be quick and painless. And I knew that, spiritually, I wasn't ready. I felt like a student abruptly faced with a final examination for which he isn't even remotely prepared. And this frightened me far more than the prospect of mere physical extinction.

The date was January 13, 1966. We were flying from Izmir, Turkey, to our home base in Wiesbaden, Germany. As a passenger, I was feeling relaxed and cheerful. I had just enjoyed a leave in Turkey that had left me in excellent condition. I was wearing a summer flight suit and light leather jacket; the weather had been pleasant in Turkey.

But it was far from pleasant in Greece. Around the peak of 7,800-foot Mount Helmos a blizzard was raging. We flew too close and ran into what we pilots call a windshear, two layers of high speed winds moving in opposite directions. Like a pair of demonic hands those winds seized our transport, spun it like a toy, flung it tail-first toward the jagged, snow-covered rocks. Even before it hit the ground the aircraft was apart. The metal fuselage split open just where I was sitting. I felt myself catapulted into a white, freezing emptiness.

I fell at least 200 feet, but I landed at an angle, on a slope. And instead of crashing into the rocks, I hit deep snow. I don't remember the impact because I blacked out.

10

Slowly I came back to a world of cold, of pain, of darkness. My first thought was that I was blind. My hands were numb, but when I raised them to my face I realized that my whole head was encased in snow, ice and frozen blood. When I clawed it all away, I could see.

About 400 feet distant was what was left of the aircraft. The largest remaining piece seemed to be the tail section lying a few feet from a great chasm in the ice. I could hear moans: there were other survivors.

Despite the pain in my neck and shoulders I could move. The cold was unbelievable. It seemed to drain all my strength and willpower, yet I staggered to the place where the wreckage lay. I sank to my knees and asked God why He had allowed me to live to endure this horror.

At that moment I heard someone cry out for help. Then I knew why I had been saved. Two of the men were dead. Two had vanished. One man died as I carried him to what was left of the plane. The four others were badly hurt but somehow I managed to get them into the shattered tail section. Then I had to do something to keep out the wind or else the snow would bury us all.

I began to try to bend the jagged metal skin of the plane. My hands were almost useless; I didn't seem to have the necessary strength. And yet, all the time, I had the most extraordinary feeling that I was not alone, that God was with me, literally beside me, helping me. So whenever my strength seemed to fail, I would say, "God, I've done all I can by myself; now I must have Your help." Then I'd try again, and I would succeed.

My hands were really the worst problem. I put them under my flight jacket, next to my skin, in an effort to thaw them out. But as soon as I went outside to do anything they would freeze again. Finally, I just began using them like hooks. I collected as many parachutes as I could find—I think I found nine altogether—and clawed them open. I covered the survivors, tried to seal out the wind that coated us with ice and kept nudging the tail section toward the ice chasm.

Darkness fell. The temperature dropped to 10 degrees Fahrenheit. One man screamed all night; he died the next day.

I knew that rescue planes would be looking for us. But I also knew they would have no chance of finding us in the dark. And when daybreak finally came, fog and freezing mist still covered the top of the mountain where we lay. One survivor tried cranking a portable transmitter in an effort to signal to the planes whose engines we sometimes heard. As the hours passed I knew I would have to make a move. After an air crash, you're supposed to stay with the plane. But we had no food or water. I was the only one who could move. If I waited much longer I might be too weak to do anything. Besides, the wind seemed stronger than ever and the tail section kept getting closer to the crevasse.

My plan was simple: I would try to slide, stagger or crawl down the mountain until I got below the overcast. There I would try to signal a plane. I set out, dragging a red parachute to use as a signal.

Somehow, mostly sliding on the seat of my pants, I worked my way down the mountain. And here again God was surely with me, because without knowing it I was actually sliding down the crest of a ridge. On either side were precipicies, sometimes a 3,000 foot drop.

At last 1,000 feet below, I broke into the clear, spread out my distress signal and lay there exhausted. It was about 3:30 in the afternoon. Within 15 minutes the crew of a C-130 spotted me. The pilot flew low over me, dipping his wings. Feebly I signaled our location. I knew his radio would summon rescue.

Then came the thoughest part of all: the climb back. The short January day was ending. I could not survive a night in the open; besides, I wanted to tell my friends that help was on the way. But moving up those wind-tortured slopes was almost more than flesh and blood could stand. Once I slipped and slid back 100 yards. I lay there, not caring whether I lived or died. The C-130 was still circling, and the pilot seemed to know how I felt. He came zooming in as close as he dared, gunning his engines and dipping his wings. "Come on, boy," he seemed to be saying, "You've come this far. You can make it."

I was really out of my head most of the way back. I remember trying to sing, "I'll Walk with God," and it seemed that all the angels in heaven joined in. At other times I babbled parts of the 23rd Psalm, fragment prayers and phrases about faith moving mountains. In a few patches of mental clarity I remember telling myself that if I gave up now I'd be leaving my wife, Lee, the finest wife in the world, with five orphan children. Today I'm sure of one thing: I didn't make it back to that plane all by myself. Somebody was helping me— the same Somebody Who had spared my life so I could help others survive up there on Nightmare Mountain.

When I got back, I was frozen delirious babbling incoherently. It took the others three hours to get some semblance of warmth back into me. All that night we had to huddle there, sleepless—in fact, I didn't sleep at all for the whole 72 hours of our ordeal. But the next day a rescue team of Greek mountaineers reached us.

Later, helicopters from the carrier *Forrestal* landed on the mountain despite the fierce winds and flew the other survivors to a hospital. I was the only one in good enough shape to go directly to my family.

Looking back, it seems to me that the Lord had been preparing me for this crisis for a long time. My interest in pistol shooting had taught me the importance of concentration, and without a fantastic degree of concentration I would never have made it back up the mountain. To keep my eyes keen and my pistol hand rock-steady, I had given up all stimulants: no alcohol, no tobacco, no caffeine. I was in top physical condition when that plane broke apart; otherwise, none of us would have survived.

To feel that your life has been spared for a purpose like this leaves a man feeling very grateful and very humble. I know that the little irritations and problems of life bother me far less than they used to. I try harder to build a solid Christian relationship with our children; nothing in the world is as important to me as passing along the faith and gratitude I feel for the gift of life.

Finally I wish to state that this experience has not made a picture-book Christian out of me. Unfortunately, I still must battle the same weaknesses as before. However, I am trying harder to live each day so that if death opens the door again, suddenly, and says to me, "T. D., are you ready?" this time I'll be able to answer, "Yes. Yes, I am."

In the midst of the halocaust, her children cried hysterically, "We'll die, we'll die." Yet, this mother did not panic.

That Bad Good Friday

by MRS. LOWELL THOMAS, JR.

IT began as such a happy day, that Good Friday in 1964. The snow which had been coming down for two days let up suddenly which meant that my husband, Lowell, could fly to Fairbanks, Alaska, and get back in time for us to have all of Easter weekend together.

The children and I waved good-bye as he drove off to the airport, then shut the door quickly because it was still below freezing outside. About five o'clock, feeling lonesome for him, Anne, eight, David, six, and I went upstairs to watch TV. Anne and David were wearing blue jeans and cotton T-shirts; I had on a wool dress and nylon stockings. We took off our shoes so we could sit on the bed.

It was half an hour later that I heard a rumbling sound. Although we frequently hear a similar roaring—the firing of guns at a nearby Army base—I knew instantly that this was the sound of an impending earthquake.

I leaped up, called to the children to follow, and raced for the stairs. By the time we reached the front hall the whole house was beginning to shake. We ran outside into the snow, David crying, "Mommy, I'm in bare feet!"

We were about 10 feet beyond the door when the world around us fell apart. We were flung violently to the ground which was jolting back and forth with unbelievable force.

The hallway through which we had just run split in two. We heard the crashing of glass, the ear-rending sound of splintering wood. In front of us a great tree crashed full length onto

15

the ground. Our garage collapsed with a sharp report.

Now the earth began breaking up and buckling all about us. Suddenly between Anne and me a great crack opened in the snow. I stared in disbelief as the trench widened, apparently bottomless, separating me from my child. I seized the hand she stretched out to me in time to pull her across the chasm to my side.

By now the whole lawn was breaking up into chunks of dirt, rock, snow and ice. We were left on a wildly bucking slab; suddenly it tilted sharply, and we had to hang on to keep from slipping into a yawning crevasse. Though sobbing, Anne had the presence of mind to hang on by herself, thank God, for I was holding David with one hand, our bit of ground with the other.

Now the earth seemed to be rising just ahead of us. I had the weird feeling that we were riding backward on a monstrous Ferris wheel, going down, down toward the water (our house had stood on a high bluff overlooking Cook Inlet). When the worst of the rocking stopped, I looked around and saw that the entire face of the bluff had fallen to sea level. A few feet away, at the water's edge, lay the roof of our house.

All I could think of was that the water would rise as earth tumbled into it and we would be trapped. The cliffs above us were sheer, with great sections of sand and clay still falling.

The children both were hysterical, crying and saying over and over, "We'll die! We'll die!" I realized we'd have to find a way up that cliff but the children were too frightened to walk.

I suggested that we say a prayer asking Jesus to take care of us and guide us. Both children stopped crying, closed their eyes and fervently pleaded with Him to come and help us. This had an extraordinary effect on them and on me, and we set out with the first real stirrings of hope.

The next 20 minutes were one great nightmare as we clambered up and down the great slabs of earth and snow, our bare feet raw and aching in the cold. I found a large tree leaning against the cliff and thought for a few moments that we might be able to shinny up it, but we gained only a few feet. We kept moving to the right, trying to avoid holes at our feet and rubble still falling from the cliff.

Suddenly a man appeared above us. "Help!" we called to him. He shouted down that he would hunt for a rope, then disappeared. As we waited we were aware for the first time that we were soaked to the skin from lying in the snow; the children were shaking and their lips were blue.

At last six or eight men appeared at the top of the cliff. One of them, a stranger to us, started down toward us, finding one less steep spot. The children threw their arms around him as he reached us. He took off his black wool jacket, put it around Anne, then boosted David into his arms and led us all back up along the rope.

At the top there was a steep, sheer rim which I doubt I could have scaled by myself. But willing hands hauled us up and tucked us into a waiting car. When I turned to thank our rescuer he had gone. But nearby I saw the strained, white face of our neighbor Wanda Mead. Someone told me that two of her five children were missing.

We were driven to the home of friends who lived well away from the devastated area. They wrapped us in blankets, but there was no heat in the house nor any way to make a hot drink.

The children were offered beds but refused to leave my side where I huddled with the others over the portable radio; but the children finally curled up in sleeping bags on the floor. Sleep for me was impossible until two questions were answered: had Fairbanks, where Lowell was, felt the quake, and how could we get word to him that we were all right?

The radio reported all the homes along our street destroyed, and that the two Mead children were still missing. I winced at the frequent pleas, "Urgent to Dr. Mead . . . needed immediately at Providence Hospital."

Perry Mead, Alaska's only neurosurgeon, spent the next 24

hours going from bed to bed at the hospital, tending to the needs of others while tears for his children streamed down his face.

The radio listed tremendous damage in the downtown area. We, living in Anchorage, watching it grow day by day, had felt personal pride in each new building that rose. Now the tally of damaged schools, stores and office buildings mounted by the hour.

There was a continuous stream of "Tell John his father and mother are at the Stewarts," or "The Johnson family wants to know the whereabouts of daughter Ann." It seemed an eternity to me before radio contact was reestablished with Fairbanks and we learned that it had felt merely a strong jolt. Planes were arriving from there with doctors and supplies, and I knew Lowell would be aboard one of them.

Then suddenly the announcer's voice said, "If anyone knows the whereabouts of Mrs. Lowell Thomas and family, please contact us immediately." I ran to the telephone and was so overwhelmed to find it working that I could hardly talk to the person who answered. But I got the essentials through, and just half an hour later Lowell walked through the door.

Words cannot describe our reunion. The kids and I were tremendously relieved, but Lowell's emotions were those of a man who had not known for many hours whether his family was dead or alive.

Next morning, Easter Sunday, Lowell, Anne, David and I rose early. We put on the same clothes we had been wearing for two days: Anne the coat provided by our unknown rescuer, far more meaningful to her than any Easter bonnet; David a pair of pants too small to button, me some men's corduroy trousers.

Many in the Easter congregation wore similar misfits, and the air in the heatless church was so cold that our breaths hung white above us as we sang "Hallelujah!" But it was an Easter service to remember.

At the rear of the church the minister had pinned two sheets of paper, one to be signed by the "haves"—those who had clothing and household goods to contribute—and one where the homeless could write down what they needed. At least 20 families there that morning had lost everything, yet as we left the church I saw that not one person had signed the "have not" list.

For what was there that we did not have? We had new gratitude for the gift of life and for the fact that, in one of history's worst earthquakes, loss of life had been as small as it had. We had a state to rebuild with a new love for the word "Alaska" born the night we watched our neighbors rise to heroism. Above all we had the Easter message ringing in our hearts.

For the first Christians, too, lived through a sorrowful Friday, a Friday when their dreams collapsed, their hopes lay in ruins, when by every earthly standard these people had lost everything. And then on Sunday morning they were the first to whisper the news that has transformed every loss from that day on, the news that love had won, that God had the final word, that death was overcome, that He had risen.

The empty boat, its motor still running, moved slowly away from the water-treading couple. Death seemed to be only a matter of time.

Overboard!

by BENNIE SHIPP

I REMEMBER how badly our kids wanted to go fishing with us that November morning. The two boys tried to talk us into letting them skip school, and even the little girl was for it. But of course we said no.

My wife and I always went fishing Mondays. I'd shut down my filling station and we'd haul our outboard to Lake Chickamauga. This particular Monday was gray and raw. But that meant good fishing, and we'd have the lake to ourselves.

Sure enough, when we reached the beach there wasn't a car or boat in sight. We pushed the boat into the water, I got the motor going, and we were off, without so much as a frown over the fact that Vivian couldn't swim a stroke and wasn't wearing a life jacket. Funny how you figure some things just won't happen to you.

Vivian had brought a coat for me to put on, but I couldn't take time before starting. Seems like I couldn't wait to get to a spot I knew where I could just smell those big black bass waiting for us. Out on the water, though, it was a lot colder. We were moving along pretty well, maybe 18 miles per hour, and the wind was fresh.

"You'll catch cold!" Vivian hollered over the noise the outboard was making.

Well, I reached for the coat, and I guess I gave the tiller a twist, because that boat gave a terrific lurch. I was holding on so I didn't fall. But Vivian was thrown from the seat into the water.

I choked the motor down, never taking my eyes off the spot where she went under. Then I dived in. I swam straight down, looking for her through the brown water. I saw her, got my arm around her and started kicking for the surface. We broke water just when I thought my lungs would burst.

Vivian was wonderful. She didn't fight me or grab me the way some people would, just lay back on my arm and I saw she was praying. I looked around for the boat. I couldn't hold her up much longer with our heavy clothes soaked with water.

I couldn't see the boat. I turned around the other way, figuring the dive had mixed me up. I made a complete circle in the water. There was no boat. Then I saw it. It was 200 yards from us and moving away fast. In my hurry to get in the water I hadn't shut off the motor all the way. the boat was gone and so were we.

I saw Vivian had seen it now, too, but she just whispered, "God's going to take care of us, Bennie."

Well, I knew I couldn't take care of us much longer, that was sure. The shore looked a million miles away. There wasn't a sign of anyone else on the beach, and even if someone came right now, by the time they could put a boat in the water and get out to us, it was going to be too late.

It was the weight of our clothes plus the ice-cold water that made it so bad. I knew we had to get Vivian's coat off. I got my arms under her shoulders and she wiggled and tugged at the heavy, clinging thing, and we both swallowed a lot of water. But at last she broke free of it.

But getting my boots off was a different thing. I had on the highlaced shoes I wore at the filling station and they got heavy as iron and dragged me down. I tried to get one hand down to undo the laces, but Vivian and I both got ducked. She had had all the water she could take.

She wasn't scared, though, not even now. "God's going to help us," she said, over and over.

Well, Vivian seemed so sure I began to figure how maybe God could do it. Perhaps He could send a sea plane and set it down on the water beside us. But the only thing in that gray winter sky were a few birds.

I was too tired to hold my head out of the water all the time. I sank down below the surface where I didn't have to kick so hard in those iron boots, holding Vivian up above me. Every little while I climbed up and got a swallow of air. Each time it seemed as if I wouldn't make it.

And then I knew I was dying because I could see my whole past life. And it wasn't much to look at. Not until two years ago, anyway. I saw the years I'd spent stock car racing, the money I'd wasted, the heavy drinking, the close calls racing a car after a few drinks.

And I saw Vivian, the way she'd been all those years. She'd never given up on me, she'd just kept on praying for me. No matter how late or how drunk I'd come home, she'd have dinner hot and waiting. And no cross words either, just:

"God loves you, Bennie. He's waiting for you."

Then one night, two years ago, I'd come home at 2:00 a.m. when the bars closed, and there was Vivian just sitting and waiting as she always was. And suddenly I knew she was right about God because no one could be as good as Vivian on his own. I got down on my knees then and there and gave my life to Him. . . .

I swam up to the air and breathed for a while, remembering these things and the wonderful family life we'd had ever since. I hauled one of my boots up as far as I could and clawed at the laces again, but they were hard as steel. I sank back below the water. I didn't think I'd make it to the top again. My arms ached with holding Vivian above me.

Well, it was God's life now and it was all right for Him to take it anytime. I just didn't like to think about the kids, coming home from school, and us not there. I was too tired, too tired to keep struggling. I thought I could sleep—except that Vivian was pulling at me, tugging my arm. She was shouting:

"The boat! The boat!"

Now I saw something moving on the lake. I couldn't make

out what it was at first, but it looked as if it was coming nearer.

"It's the boat!" Vivian said.

It couldn't be. But it was, our own empty boat, somehow turned around and headed straight for us. I knew it couldn't happen. But I was seeing it. And even then I didn't dare hope I could grab it. I didn't have any swim left. That boat would have to come to the very square foot of water where we were for it to do us any good. If it was even three feet away it was going to pass us by.

I watched it come, moving straight as if a sure hand were on the tiller. And suddenly I knew—sure as I'd ever known anything—that boat was coming right to us.

I just lifted up my hand and my fingers closed over the side of it. It was the last strength I had. I couldn't do any more for a long while than just hold on. Vivian had more strength than I had by then. She climbed aboard and shut the motor down, and for a long time I just hung on. Then, when I was rested a bit, I climbed in too.

Well, we sat there, water streaming off us, and we just shouted for joy. Then we sang for joy. Then we prayed for joy and just magnified God in every way we knew. Vivian saw I was rubbing my arms and she said:

"Bennie, it wasn't God alone. You held me up till He could come."

But I shook my head. "You've held me up too, Viv. I was thinking in the water how you prayed for me all those years when I couldn't. Well, I was just swimming for you, when you couldn't."

And I guess that's about all we can do for each other, just hold one another up, until God provides the help we need.

"When I came to after the crash, a scrubby bush was all that stood between me and a 150-foot fall."

Pinned to a Canyon Wall

by GERTRUDE IDA LONG

HARD to tell what all was going through my mind that afternoon in September, 1962, as I drove down that narrow mountain road in Southern California, taking an occasional glance down into the shimmering hot canyon which lay 350 feet below.

There was a chain-link fence along the edge of the road; rather puny, I remember thinking. But really, I imagine my mind was mostly on other things. Widowed a year before, I had begun doing ironing and housecleaning to supplement my income, and it was such a job that had taken me up the canyon this day.

How I miss Ralph! I thought to myself. I was nearly 60 and with Ralph gone my life didn't seem very important.

I was suddenly brought up straight in the seat when I realized the brake pedal was going way down to the floor. I pushed harder, but instead of slowing down the car seemed to lurch ahead faster. I pulled on the emergency brake but nothing happened.

A sharp curve was coming. I knew I would never get around it. The car careened into the fence; the iron links snapped like a paper chain, and in that incredible instant I knew that the car was going over the edge of the cliff.

The car turned over. My head hit the windshield. And then suddenly I was falling through the air, outside the car, tumbling down the almost vertical wall of the canyon. I clawed and grappled but the sand and rock slid with me. And then the world went as dark as night.

24

How long it was before I became conscious I don't know. I was leaning on my back almost in a standing position because the slope was so steep; my feet braced against something. Blood was trickling into my eyes from a cut on my forehead. My right side ached terribly.

I called out "Help!" but that made the blood come faster. Painfully I moved my head, trying to see where I was. My feet, I discovered, were wedged against a mesquite bush, one of those tough little desert trees that had somehow got a grip on this rock face. One hundred and fifty feet below me was the jagged floor of the canyon. Except for that mesquite bush I would have plunged the rest of the way to certain death—and still would if it pulled loose.

I twisted my head and looked up. Two hundred feet above me I could see the line where the road cut into the cliff. And below that, directly over my head, a sight that made me catch my breath. Up there, somehow suspended on the sheer canyon wall, was my car. I stared in astonishment, wondering why it did not come rolling down on top of me.

Surely it could not balance there much longer. And then as I looked farther up and down the canyon an eerie feeling crept over me. This mesquite bush which had stopped my fall was the only growing thing on the entire cliff. Everywhere else only the bare rock shimmered in the heat. A few inches to either side and I would have been killed instantly.

If God had spoken aloud I could not have known more surely that this was His bush, that it was He who held the car above me, as He held my life itself and all it contained. This thought kept me sane as the growing horror of that day began to unfold.

The worst of it was the sun. It beat down blinding and burning and there was no hiding from it. Once in desperation I tried to escape the sun by climbing the cliff, leaving my foothold on the mesquite bush and inching backward up the almost perpendicular wall. At once a landslide of sand and dirt ran away from beneath me and I started sliding, staring in

terror at the rocks far below. The bush, when my feet touched
it again, was like a haven in a strange land.

When the bleeding on my head stopped, I screamed again
for help. The sun was directly overhead now, pressing down
on me like an iron hand. I screamed until my tongue swelled
from dryness and my lips cracked.

The uncanny thing was the sounds: music, laughter, voices.
I heard radios playing, cars starting up, children shouting. For
all along the canyon rim, above the road, were homes, out of
sight but not hearing. Some strange trick of the wind or the
slant of the rocks sometimes brought the sounds so close I
started. And yet shout and shriek as I would I could not make
them hear me. My voice, too, followed the air current down
into the canyon.

And so the long, incredible day dragged on. My skin blis-
tered from the heat. Sometimes I think I fainted. And yet,
conscious or unconscious, I was aware that God was holding
me, talking to me, telling me something if only I could hear.

Then the hornets found me. All at once they were everywhere, swarming over my face, my legs, into my ears, their
buzzing like a high-pitched scream. And they stung. Each
sting was a knife jabbed into me. I shrieked like a crazy
woman. I waved my arms, I writhed this way and that, every
minute afraid I would lose my balance. Then as suddenly as
they had come, the hornets went away.

It was perhaps an hour later when the first shadows began
to move up the canyon walls. In an instant the shimmering
oven had become a dim, chill cavern. And it was more than
the cold which set me shivering. Suddenly I knew how dark
and lonely and fearful this deep canyon would be at night. It
was hard to force my dry lips open, but once more I cried out,
"Help!"

Far away, somewhere above, a man's voice answered.

"Where are you?"

"I'm here!" I yelled. "Down here!"

"Where are you?" he called again.

It was a long time before the crazy air currents let him hear me again; after that it was another hour before the fire truck arrived. And while I waited I heard at last what God was saying.

Life was precious. Even to me, who that very morning had valued it so little. Who had been tired of living as I rode along strong and healthy. Look at you now, He seemed to say; broken and battered and burned—but clinging desperately to life. Life is precious because it is filled with His work for us.

The firemen who lowered themselves on ropes past my incredibly balanced car couldn't believe I was alive. The man who had heard me shout couldn't believe it. "I was cleaning out my storm drains," he kept saying when they had hauled me in a basket stretcher up to the road. "I don't know why, but I never go down there to the edge of the yard."

The doctors who put 17 stitches in my scalp and set my broken ribs couldn't believe it. "Nobody could survive that fall," they said. "Nobody could hang onto a cliff that long."

"No," I agreed with them all. "Nobody could." And then I told them Who held me above the abyss, and Who brought me out, and Who will do the same for us all.

Keep Me Safe, Lord

Lord, be Thou within me, to
    strengthen me;
Without me, to keep me;
Above me, to protect me;
Beneath me, to uphold me;
Before me, to direct me;
Behind me, to keep me from straying;
Round about me, to defend me.
Blessed be Thou, our Father for ever
    and ever.

                    Lancelot Andrewes

*When the man climbed into the car beside Jean Kling-
er, she screamed and pushed the horn, but no one
heard. She was alone—almost.*

The Protecting Power

by CATHERINE MARSHALL

IT is an obvious fact that fear is growing each year among
women in our country. Every week we read about some
new violence to our sex, such as the murder of the eight young
nurses in Chicago several years ago. We're told what to do:
keep away from dark streets, carry a squirt gun filled with
ammonia in our purse, put special locks in our house or apartment, and so on. Some of these are wise precautions.

Yet there are times when all the safeguards man can devise
cannot stand between us and the raw evil in this world. At
these times we need a surer protection—what is perhaps the
only real protection we can have. Let me tell you how this
helped a friend of mine in Florida.

One bright sunny morning Jean Klinger started out in her
car for Delray Beach to take her final Montessori teacher's
examination. As she turned her car from Military Trail down
Fourth Street, she noted the time on her watch. It was 8:50.
Good: she'd be at school by nine.

Fourth Street near Military Trail is a lonely stretch of road
until it runs into the residential area. There are few houses;
the terrain is dotted with farms and sand flats.

Just ahead of Jean Klinger was a light colored pick-up truck.
It slowed down, then pulled over to the side of the road. An
arm out the car window signaled to Mrs. Klinger to pull over
too. She did so instinctively, wondering if something were
wrong with her car.

A big burly man wearings a sports shirt open at the neck

strode up to her window. "Lady, can you tell me how to get to Dixie Highway?"

Mrs. Klinger was unsuspecting. After all, it was broad daylight. "I'm so sorry. I don't live in Delray. I'm just on my way to school here. Afraid I can't give you directions."

The man was looking at her intently. He glanced about him, then suddenly jerked open the car door and pressed a hard metal object into Jean's back. When she sat there, paralyzed, he shoved her to one side and climbed in beside her.

Instinctively she screamed and, reaching over, pressed hard on the horn. But there was not a car or pedestrian around; no one to hear.

"Don't try that again or I'll kill you," the man growled, pressing the metal object harder into her back. Fear, panic, terror washed in waves over her. . . .

Jean admits that she has always had many fears. Sensitive, intense, vivacious, she feels deeply. Long ago she determined to face up to her fears and to search for ways to eradicate them. Her search led her to God and asking for His help in freeing her from these shackles. She even dared to ask that in certain circumstances He would help her to be willing to do the thing she feared. This led her to apply for a teaching position at the Unity School of Christianity.

During an early session there she confided to her instructor that she had not yet learned how to deal with her fears. The instructor gave her a copy of a prayer that became part of the fabric of Jean Klinger's life.

> *The Light of God surrounds me.*
> *The Love of God enfolds me.*
> *The Power of God protects me.*
> *The Presence of God watches over me.*
> *Wherever I am, God is.*

Upon arising that June morning, as every morning, she had prayed that prayer of affirmation. Then at the crisis moment,

sitting beside the threatening man in the car, when panic and
terror almost overcame her, she was forced back on this
prayer resource. Jean cannot remember the exact words she
used, but she knows the essence of them.

"How can you force yourself on me this way?" she cried.
"You are a child of God. You do not want to hurt anyone. God's
love is in you. God wants you to be a good man. He cares about
you. And I am His child too. And completely under His protection. His love and protection surround me. . . ."

As she spoke the words, she felt warmed. There seemed to
be a kind of aura around her—like a soft light. Then into her
mind there came the clear picture of the face of the janitor at
the Unity School, one of the kindest, most gentle men she had
ever known, beloved by everyone who knew him. It was as if
God were saying to her, "You told the man sitting beside you
that he is a child of Mine. True, but now to help you really see
that, superimpose the janitor's face and image on the other
man."

Jean followed directions and, sure enough, after that, she
could actually sense God's love enfold her abductor.

The result was immediate. The lust seemed to leave the
man. He removed the object from Jean's back. Jean saw that
it was merely a key case.

The man started Jean's car, drove on in silence for a while,
little trickles of perspiration running down his face. He seemed
more and more confused. Then he drew over to the side of the
road and stopped. "Get out," he ordered. Quickly Jean opened
the door and jumped out. The man drove off, the car careen-
ing down the road.

Later, Jean Klinger found her car undamaged at the spot
where she had first been stopped. The man and his pick-up
truck had disappeared.

Despite the ordeal, Jean Klinger went back to the school,
took her examination, passed it. She is glad, she told me, to
share her experience because she believes it may point to the
most important protection of all for women.

And I agree with her. "I am the light of the world," Jesus told us. Usually we have thought this to be some kind of oriental imagery. I wonder! The experience of an increasing number of women would indicate that in His contemporary presence, in His name and His person, there is literal light, protection, power—largely unrealized, untapped, unresearched.

Jesus goes on to make another common sense observation: *For everyone that doeth evil hateth the light, neither cometh to the light, lest his deeds should be reproved.** To me it is significant that Jean Klinger felt an aura of light around her and that her attacker either could not or would not penetrate it. By repeating the prayer of protection so regularly she had bathed herself in this light; it was there the moment she called out for help.

It probably has never occurred to most life-long Christians that in the light of Jesus Christ there is such help and protection. We tend toward materialism, let us admit it, so we believe in the efficacy of material protection: guns, locks, police, sirens. While all these means are valuable, obviously they are not enough, for never have assaults on women been so high. There are times when, like Jean Klinger, we may have no protection left other than the spiritual: *Let us then cast off the works of darkness and put on the armor of light.***

But dare we believe that spiritual resources are real armor? The Scriptures give us a resounding "Yes!" True stories like Jean Klinger's certainly verify this.

Yet something is required of us. We must take some step of faith to put on that armor of light and practice walking in it every day. Furthermore, whoever heard of putting on a clanking suit of armor silently or unobtrusively? That is why, at the crisis moment, Jean Klinger had to speak out in ringing tones Christ's own authoritative words.

* John 3:20
** Romans 13:12

FOR SAFETY'S SAKE

Much has been written about precautions women can take to protect themselves. Here are some of the safeguards that law enforcement agencies recommend.

At Home

1) *When alone at night keep home locked.*
2) *Have locks installed by specialist.*
3) *Never leave keys in mailbox, under mats, etc.*
4) *Make callers identify themselves through peepholes, or use door chain.*
5) *If awakened by intruder, be still. He may not disturb you.*
6) *In summer, open windows from the top.*
7) *When alone, keep light on in hall or living room all night.*

Away From Home

1) *Don't walk alone in dark places.*
2) *Don't accept rides from strangers or casual acquaintances.*
3) *At night, travel with a friend whenever possible.*
4) *When driving alone, keep car doors locked and windows closed.*
5) *Don't wear suggestive clothes. One girl-watcher could be your deadliest enemy.*

In the middle of a raging hotel fire, this man—trapped and ready to panic—seemed marked for death. Then, he turned to his only refuge and an incredible peace swept over him.

The Safest Place on Earth

by GREGORY VOJAE

FOUR days after the fire in the Winecoff Hotel in Atlanta, one of the worst blazes in history, I went with the building superintendent back up the 10 floors to my old room. The frame of the hotel was concrete and had not burned. Water from the fire hoses still stood in puddles. Sodden ashes, inches deep, lay over everything.

The room had been totally destroyed.

One hundred and twenty-one people died in that fire in 1946. I often have wondered why I should have been saved while others perished. I still have no answer to that question. But if I do not understand *why* I was spared, there is no doubt in my mind as to *how* I was saved. The principle is one anyone can use in any situation in which he finds himself in danger.

How vividly I remember the first moment I knew something was wrong. I sat up in bed, instantly awake. The lights were out in my room, but my bed and the desk and the walls were glowing with a strange reflected light coming from the window. "A fire somewhere!" I said to myself as I threw off the covers.

The minute I leaned out the window I knew where the fire was. From the window directly below me came a cloud of choking smoke and that eerie, pulsing red light. The wail of a fire truck drew closer. Other sirens joined it. A woman below me began to scream. A man put his head out the window and cried, "Help us! Help us!"

The stairs! Why didn't they run down the stairs! I dashed to the door of my room, yanked it open and staggered back coughing. The air must be better near the floor. I put my face right down on the old red hall carpet and began to crawl for the stairway. Tears came to my eyes, my lungs burned; the air on the floor was as poisonous as the rest. A few yards farther on I heard a roaring, crackling sound like a giant chimney on fire. The stairway was a seething inferno of flame. I got up, swaying in the poisoned air, dashed back to my room, and slammed the door.

A fire escape! Where was a fire escape? I'd been at the Winecoff for six weeks now; my mind raced through its halls. There was no fire escape. A sprinkler system? No. Fire doors? Every door I could remember was made of wood.

A sheet rope! I'd make a rope of by bedding and go out the window. And then? All my sheets and blankets and spreads tied together might reach two floors, and I was 10 floors up.

I was trapped. I could feel panic welling up in me.

I had to stop that fear. I turned back into the room and my eye caught sight of my Bible on the night table by my bed. There was a Psalm, the 91st, which we Christian Scientists often used to help people who were afraid. I'd used it myself. Christian Science has taught me that dwelling "in the secret place of the most High" is being in communion with God, and this is the safest place on earth. Could I enter it now, that safe place? Could I be there at the same time I was in this burning building?

I closed my eyes and started to say the Psalm to myself.

He that dwelleth in the secret place of the most High shall abide under the shadow of the Almighty. . . .

Even as I said the words all sense of unreasoned fear left me. I knew I would not be alone.

"What is it you want me to do, Lord?"

And suddenly I knew I had received an answer. I was to put on my clothes. I did not argue with myself about the logic of the command, I simply got dressed.

A man above me screamed. But as long as I was saying my Psalm I was surrounded by peace. And while I was there in that center of calm I could hear the soft, quiet words that God whispered in answer to my questions.

"What shall I do now, Lord?"

"Make a rope out of your sheets."

So I made a rope. I had to work by the window to get any air at all. I'd run to my bed and jerk off a piece of sheeting and dash back to the window to knot it. I was a traveling accountant, going from city to city for Columbia Pictures; it had been years since I had worked with knots. I prayed that I could remember how to make a hitch that would not slip.

. When I had finished my rope I tied it around the center post of the double window in my room and prepared to start down.

"No, not yet."

The command was crisp, clear. I had to obey. But I couldn't see the reason for it. People all around me were crying and screaming now. An object plunged past my window. It took my mind a long time to accept what my eyes had seen: a child.

Once again I made a move to let out the rope.

"No."

I pulled it in and waited. The paint on the door to my room began to boil. Great blisters formed. I fled back into my safe place.

Because thou hast made the Lord . . . thy habitation; there shall no evil befall thee. . . .

To make God my habitation. That was the trick. But it was hard: the roar was coming closer.

"Now, Lord?" I asked.

"Not yet."

Another minute passed. The door began to smoke. And then, suddenly, came the command:

"Now. Climb out."

I played the rope out the window. Slowly I put my foot over the sill, out into the night. My heart was pounding. I slipped my other leg out and balanced with my waist on the window sill. Then, inch by inch, I edged myself backward into the swirling gases, 10 stories above the ground. Even as I was grabbing my sheet rope I saw the flames break through the door and come reaching, lapping into the room. The heat was so intense the backs of my hands were scorched as they clung to the window sill. I stiffened for a moment, glanced down into the volcano and fled back into my safe place.

For He shall give His angels charge over thee, to keep thee in all thy ways. They shall bear thee up in their hands . . . .

No sooner had I slipped out of that room than it became a blast furnace. Where I was for the moment, hanging below my window, was safe. What I was going to do when I got to the end of my sheetrope I didn't know. My job was to live in the center of my safe place and to obey, one step at a time. Totally unafraid, fully trusting God, I clung steadfastly to my improvised rope.

And then, slowly coming into view through the smoke, I saw the tip end of a ladder. Two floors below me and off to my right I saw a fireman just coming to the top of the ladder. He was looking around.

Did he see me? I called out and he turned. But how was I to get to him? There wasn't time for him to go down and move the fire truck. Any minute now the heat in my room would weaken the strands in my sheet and I would fall.

Then I saw that God had prepared the answer to this prob‑ lem too. The fireman was holding something in his hand. It was the end of a hemp rope. The other end was tied to the window of the room next to mine. The fireman started the rope swinging. I let go of my rope with my left hand and reached out into space . . . and missed. How much more time before my own rope burned through? The fireman swung his rope again. And this time my fingertips closed around it so that I had a rope in each hand.

Carefully I transferred my weight to the new rope, and then let go of my sheet.

Slowly I swung myself into the arms of the fireman.

Four days later when I was back in my room with the building superintendent, I went to the window and looked down to the ground, 10 dizzy floors below. Sticking to the inside of the window post were a few shreds of charred sheeting: my rope must have burned through only moments after I left it. How perfect God's timing had been! He kept me waiting in that room until the very moment the fireman would come up his ladder. He gave me just enough time on my own rope to be seen by the fireman, to reach out for the new rope, to miss, to try again, to climb to safety.

The superintendent came over and looked out of the window too.

"You're a brave man," he said.

But I wasn't brave. I wasn't brave at all. I just knew how to dwell in the secret place of the most High. For as long as I stayed there, I was in the center of the safest place on earth.

*Have you ever had a sudden, startling urge to pray for
someone, though you had no special reason why? That
prayer may be more important than you dream. Such
a prayer was for this young couple.*

Out of the Depths

by SHIRLEY-JO JESSUP

THE day had started out so happily, for it was the day, six
years ago, that we were heading for Los Angeles. There
my husband, Bryce, was to go back to school for his master's
degree in religion. We were sorry to leave the church in Oregon where he'd been minister for two years, but he wanted
the extra education.

Our plan was to leave after supper that night, when we
could put our two little girls to bed on a mattress in the back
seat, and to drive straight through to Bryce's parents' home in
San Jose, California. It was 700 miles of straight driving but
easier, we thought, than dragging three-year-old Jerri and six-
month-old Janni in and out of restaurants and motels. Besides,
we told ourselves, it was July; driving at night would be cooler.

We didn't know, then, how fatigue can numb the brain and
slow the muscles. All through that hot summer day we carried
things from the parsonage to the big U-Haul trailer we had
rented. It was happy work. Our belongings were like a résumé
of our five wonderful years of marriage: my wedding dress,
Bryce's theological library collected book by book, dishes,
furniture, albums of precious photos. Many of our wedding
gifts had never left their boxes, waiting for that dreamed-of
day when we would have "a permanent home."

By 6 p.m., car and trailer were loaded. After supper at a
friend's house and a dozen goodbyes, we tucked Jerri and
Janni into their back-seat bed and started out.

The heat and the hauling and the emotion of leaving good friends had taken their toll. From the start it was a struggle to stay awake. Because of the trailer, Bryce didn't want me to drive. It was my job to keep him alert. But as the miles passed my head would snap up with a jerk and I would know I had been asleep.

At four a.m. we pulled into a gas station in Klamath Falls, Oregon, and bought soft drinks, then walked back to check the trailer. In the gray, pre-dawn light the little red rocking chair looked strangely comforting strapped to the top of the load. It had been my mother's as a little girl and then mine, and now it was Jerri's.

Through the rear window we peeked in at our sleeping children. To find a motel at this time of night and get out bags and baby food and all the rest seemed almost harder than to keep going.

And yet we knew that just ahead lay the hardest driving on the trip: the treacherous straight stretch of road south of Klamath Falls, with a deep ditch running along the right-hand side and on the left a main irrigation canal 12 feet deep and 25 feet wide. But by now the cold drink was reviving us. We climbed back into the car. Fatefully, we made the decision to keep going . . .

Ten minutes later and 400 miles farther south, Bryce's father sat up in bed.

"The children are here," he said to his wife.

Bryce's mother squinted at her watch. "They can't be," she said. "They weren't going to leave till after dark. They couldn't get here till mid-morning at the earliest."

But Bryce's father was already on his way to the front door. When his wife joined him he was standing outside, staring into the empty night. At last, reluctantly, he went back inside.

"You dreamed it," she said.

"It wasn't a dream," he insisted. "It was something much stronger."

Back in bed, they both offered silent prayers, not really

*knowing what they were praying for or why. But both felt a
compulsion to pray.*

At the moment that Bryce's father awoke, I, too, was startled
from sleep. I must have dozed off almost the minute we left
the gas station. Now I was wakened by a cry from Bryce:

"Hang on!"

He was wrestling with the wheel. The car was rocking
sickeningly on the rim of the steep ditch at our right. For a
horrid moment we swayed there. Then at last the headlights
swung left and we felt pavement beneath the tires again.

Now Bryce spun the wheel the other way. But the car continued a slow, relentless arc to the left. We were heading
straight for the deep water canal on the other side. Bryce
threw all his strength against the wheel. But the heavily-
loaded trailer, jackknifed behind us, was forcing us off the
road. We were crossing the shoulder. And then we plunged
down the incline into the canal.

For an unbelievable moment the car floated there in the
early morning darkness, then sank.

"Roll down your window!" Bryce yelled.

I heard the handle crank on his side as icy water gushed
over us. Bryce was leaning into the back seat. I saw him drag
Jerri forward and then, like figures in an underwater ballet,
float out the window.

It had happened so fast that only then did I rouse myself
from my stupor. I seized the window handle on my side, but
it was jammed. I threw my shoulder against the door but the
water outside pressed it shut.

The window's open on Bryce's side. That was the thought
I held in my mind as I groped for Janni in a floating debris of
diapers, bottles and blankets. The water was cold and thick
with slimy moss. There was a pain in my back and my lungs
were straining against my chest. The mattress had floated to
the ceiling but I couldn't find our baby.

I found a tiny air pocket at the top of the car and pressed
my face into it, but soon the oxygen grew short and my lungs

seemed to be on fire. For the first time I realized I was screaming. All that seemed to matter was to keep the slimy water from
touching my face.

"Dear God," I prayed, "let me faint first. Don't let me be
alive when the water covers me."

I felt a hand take mine. It was Bryce. At least I would die
holding his hand, I thought. But he was pulling at me, dragging me away from the roof. I struggled to get free. He was
pulling me; I was swallowing the slimy water. He wouldn't let
go.

And then suddenly, unbelievably, fresh air was in my face.
My lungs were swelling, filling with it. My hand touched
something solid and I held on.

"Janni!" Bryce was screaming at me. "Where's Janni?"

While I coughed, unable to speak, he dove back beneath the
dark water. From somewhere I heard crying. Then in the gray
light I saw Jerri standing on the bank, shivering in her
drenched little nightie. I saw that my hand had closed on the
rocking chair.

Bryce's head appeared a few feet away. He was treading
water, gasping, too winded to speak. Then he disappeared
again. This time he was gone a long, long time. When he came
up he was holding Janni. I didn't want to look at that tiny limp
form. His feet found the roof of our car and he stood on it,
water up to his chest, our baby in his hands. Her head fell back
and I knew she was dead.

From the bank came an anxious little cry. "Don't drop Janni,
Daddy! Don't drop Janni!"

Bryce lifted Janni's face to his own and blew into her mouth.
He took a breath, then blew again, and then again and again.
At last, her chest shuddered and she let out a tiny wail.

"She's breathing!" Bryce shouted.

He splashed with her to the bank while I followed. Jerri
threw herself into my arms, and a few minutes later an early
motorist found us.

At the hospital in Klamath Falls doctors assured us there

was no damage to Janni's brain. X-rays showed three crushed vertebrae in my spine which would quickly heal: the only injury to any of us.

From the admitting room Bryce put through a call to his parents. For the first time the wonder of our being alive and well swept over me. How had Bryce ever gotten us all from that car? How had a man who was exhausted, who was only a novice swimmer, who knew nothing about mouth-to-mouth breathing—how had he done all the right things at the right times?

"Hello, Pop," I heard him say into the telephone.

"What's wrong, Bryce? Are you all right?" his father interrupted.

"Don't be alarmed—we've had an accident but everyone's fine."

"Thank God," said his father. Then he asked, "Was it at four o'clock this morning?"

Bryce stared at the phone in surprise. "How did you know? Did somebody tell you?"

There was a little pause at the other end. "Yes, Somebody told me," said his father.

Are You Afraid?

An experiment to help you deal with your fears, based on the writings of Norman Vincent Peale.

IS fear a constant companion in your life? If it is, something is wrong. Normal fear is a built-in preventative, for it keeps us from doing hazardous and foolish things, but abnormal fear is a mortal enemy which siphons off energy, destroys inner peace and makes people ineffective and powerless.

"How do I know if my fear is abnormal or not?" you ask. Norman Vincent Peale gives a good example of abnormal fear in the story he tells of a businessman who came to his office and stated:

"I think I am losing my mind. I cannot make the simplest decisions. Throughout my business career I have handled matters of large importance which have involved vast sums of money, but now the smallest decisions cause me no end of struggle. I am haunted by the possibility that I will make a mistake. Whether it's selecting a green or a brown tie in the morning, taking the bus or my car to work, eating in the office or out, I fear I will make the wrong choice. Often I have trouble making any decision at all."

Obviously, the businessman's fear was abnormal. But often the line of distinction is more finely drawn. If you are in doubt, test yourself on the following questions:

Is my sleep disturbed by one or more fears? . . . Do I stop in the middle of work because my mind is taken over by fear? . . . Does fear often make me listless and ineffective? . . . Do I avoid social gatherings because of my fear? . . . Does fear keep me from enjoying the little things of life?

43

If you answer yes to any one of these questions, it is time for you to confront this fear openly and make an effort to rid yourself of it. The following procedure was recommended by Dr. Peale to his friend who found it helpful in dealing with his problem. See if the plan doesn't prove effective for you. Before you begin find a quiet place and a comfortable chair. You will need a Bible, paper, pencil and a pair of scissors for this Workshop.

1. SPELLING IT OUT

Begin by drawing a line lengthwise through the center of your paper. On the left hand side write down in detail the fears that trouble you. "Why must I put them on paper?" comes the question.

There is a great therapy in trying to write out what it really is that bothers you. In the case of a deep fear, you need to see it laid out before you. Once you begin to describe it to yourself on paper, it may suddenly take on a different shape. A fear that may seem enormous bottled up in your mind can assume quite normal proportions when put in words on paper.

2. BODY RELAXATION

Psychologists report that fear produces tension which can block creativity. So it follows that you need a relaxed body before you can have a relaxed mind. And it will take a relaxed mind to enable you to rid yourself of fear.

Sit down in an armchair. Stretch your arms out as far as possible. Then allow them to fall limply on the arm rests. Relax your fingers. Stretch your legs out as far as they go and let them fall limp too. Take a series of deep breaths, slowly letting the air out of your lungs. Open and close your eyes by letting the eyelids drop laxly. Conceive of your entire body as being inert and totally yielded to the chair. Spend several minutes picturing in your mind some peaceful scenes: wheat waving in the wind, a lake full of soft ripples, green moss in the middle of a forest.

Continue this exercise until you are sure the tension has drained out of you.

3. MIND RELAXATION

If your body is sick, you go to a physician and receive a prescription for medicine. Since abnormal fear creates an unhealthy condition in the mind, a prescription for another kind of medicine is needed. We suggest it can be found by searching your Bible. On the right hand side of your paper write down some of the verses that speak to your need. Passages like these:

For God hath not given us a spirit of fear; but of power, and of love, and of a sound mind. II Timothy 1:7

Be not afraid, neither be thou dismayed: for the Lord thy God is with thee withersoever thou goest. Joshua 1:9

Lo, I am with you alway. Matthew 28:20

The verses go on and on—all assurances that God can handle your fear, that He wants you to be free of it and to have a sound mind. He asks, yes implores, you to give Him your burden.

Read through the Psalms for further comfort, ending with the 23rd Psalm.

4. THE ACT OF TRUST

All the steps taken so far will be inadequate to rid you of fear unless you can now do one important act. It is perfectly described in Proverbs 3:5:

Trust in the Lord with all thine heart; and lean not unto thine own understanding.

If you really do not think that God has your best interests at heart, then it is pointless to pray to Him for help. Your negative attitude will block the channel; prayer, Bible-reading and churchgoing thus become meaningless routines.

The key then is *trust*. You trust God. Regardless of all that goes wrong, you believe He loves you and cares about what happens to you.

How can a person full of doubts do this?

It takes an act of acceptance, of becoming childlike in your faith.

A pastor called on a young mother who was afraid for her husband who was traveling in a foreign country. She reached a state of near panic as she imagined the things that could happen to him. The pastor noted a child playing nearby. "How old is your daughter?" he asked.

"Carol's four."

"Is she upset and worried too?"

"Of course not."

"How do you explain Carol's lack of fear?"

The woman hesitated. "Carol's just a baby. Besides, I'm here with her. I suppose she puts her trust in me and that's that."

The pastor suggested to the mother that she take the child in her lap. "Now, just as Carol puts her trust in you, I suggest you transfer the picture and think of yourself as a child in relationship to God. Put your trust in Him. Believe that He is looking after Jack. Every time you feel a sense of panic sit in this chair and picture yourself, Carol and Jack all safe in God's hands."

5. INTO THE WASTEBASKET

One final action is needed. Go back to the sheet of paper on which you wrote out in detail the specifics about your fear. Offer up a prayer something like this:

"Lord, I have brought this matter to Your attention. I know now that while I am unable by myself to throw off this fear, You are totally adequate. I put my trust in You."

Now take a pair of scissors and cut your sheet of paper in two, leaving your fears on one side and the Scripture verses on the other. Take the half which lists your fears and tear it up and throw the pieces into the wastebasket. As you let them fall, say to yourself, "It is done." Then take the list of verses and place them in your Bible to reread whenever you need strength. A good spot to place the list is near Proverbs 16:20 which says:

He that handleth a matter wisely shall find good: and whoso trusteth in the Lord, happy is he.

A Soldier's Prayer

Stay with me, God. The night is dark,
The night is cold: my little spark
Of courage dies. The night is long;
Be with me, God, and make me
  strong. . . .
I know that death is but a door.
I knew what we were fighting for:
Peace for the kids, our brothers freed,
A kinder world, a cleaner breed.
I'm but the son my mother bore,
A simple man, and nothing more.
But—God of strength and gentleness,
Be pleased to make me nothing
  less. . . .
Help me, O God, when Death is near
To mock the haggard face of fear,
That when I fall—if fall I must—
My soul may triumph in the Dust.
                    Gerald Kersh

THE UNLIMITED POWER OF PRAYER **LORD, CHANGE ME**

THE fact that we are all creatures of habit is proven many times in the course of a day. We go to bed at a pretty regular hour and get up at about the same time each morning. We eat about the same foods at about the same place about the same time, whether we are hungry or not. We read the same newspapers each day, listen to the same radio programs and watch the same television shows. If our schedule is tampered with, even slightly, some of us become highly irritable and distraught.

Though schedules and patterns can work to our advantage and can help discipline us to get our jobs done, many habits are ruinous and debilitating. We are prisoners to them. The question we pose to ourselves is, "How can I change?" Trying to change ourselves, pull ourselves up by our own strength, is, for the most part, an exercise in frustration. We try, but seldom seem to engineer any noticeable gains.

When and under what conditions can change occur? Often, it comes only when we take someone else into our confidence, making a commitment or promise or statement of intention to that person.

For people seeking a more fulfilling spiritual life, the beginning often comes with the admission, "I have sinned and fallen short of the glory of God."

In this chapter, you will read 10 different examples of people who turned from old destructive patterns and traded them for a new life in God. Each one in his or her own way said in effect, "Lord, change me."

2

*A hasty marriage, an illicit romance and the "Hound
of Heaven" are the ingredients of this dramatic story*

Profile of One Woman's
Search for God

by ROBERTA LEE

A S I look back now I wonder how differently things would
have turned out if I had gone ahead and dropped the
letter from my pen pal, Rebecca Ward,* into the wastebasket.
But I didn't and therein lies the story.

It began with a too-hasty marriage. My husband and I went
in different directions from the beginning. We tried to put on
a good front for the sake of our two children, but behind the
facade was boredom and indifference.

My ideas of marriage, I know now, were gleaned from romantic movies and magazines. When my husband did not
measure up to these juvenile fancies, I felt full of self-pity. In
this mood, I suppose it was inevitable that I be tempted into
an extra-marital affair. The man turned out to be our next door
neighbor, Ralph Carlson.

My husband and I spent occasional evenings with the Carl-
sons. Betty Carlson was a critical, discontented person, constantly holding her husband up to ridicule, while Ralph and
I got along beautifully. His compliments were music to my
ears.

Soon the liaison started, with all the lies and furtive meetings and whispered phone calls that go with this messy sort
of thing. My conscience bothered me at first, but I rationalized
my actions. Betty had made it clear she did not like her husband, and it was quite obvious that my husband did not

* All names in this story, including the author's, have been changed.

care for me or he would have been more attentive and romantic.

Caught up in this new "love," my interest in all else waned, including my hobby of writing letters to pen pals all over the world. Thus, when I received a letter from Rebecca Ward, one of my correspondents, I considered dropping it into the wastebasket.

With the letter poised over the basket, I for some reason did not let go. I put it back on my desk, thinking, "It's only polite to answer her." And I did.

Our correspondence increased and soon I looked forward to hearing from her. I liked her sense of humor and her enthusiasm for life. What I didn't like were the prayers and tracts that she often enclosed. She knew nothing of my infatuation for Ralph: how was it that these enclosures were often uncannily apropos?

Meanwhile, I was being an attentive and loving mother, salving my conscience by throwing myself into activities with my children during the day. It was the nights I began to dread. My husband worked the late shift and I slept alone. Only I wasn't doing much sleeping.

For, increasingly, I was consumed by a restlessness, a sense of Something hounding me and leaving me no peace. I tried reading a novel at bedtime but couldn't concentrate on it. I'd turn out the light determined to sleep, only to toss and turn all night.

One lonely night in sheer desperation for something to read, I picked up a Bible and idly leafed through it. I read a verse here, part of a Psalm there . . . then the first verse of the 51st Psalm caught my interest when it spoke of God's mercies blotting out our transgressions. I could use some of that, I thought.

As I read the fourth verse I felt a sudden pain in my heart! I read it again: *Against Thee, Thee only, have I sinned, and done this evil in Thy sight. . . .*

For the first time I was filled with a sense of shame. Always before I had thought that sin was wrong because it hurt other people. That I could have hurt God, Himself, by my sin was a horrible shock!

I remembered how I felt when somebody hurt me; then I realized how much greater God was than I, and so how much greater His hurt. Stunned, I slid to my knees beside the bed. I couldn't pray. All I could do was moan "Oh God" over and over as He opened my eyes to my shallowness and selfishness.

This was the beginning of an all-out battle, with my bed the battleground. I didn't surrender easily. Night after torturous night, I argued with the Hound of Heaven. I would go to bed and the only book I *could* read was the Bible. I was afraid to read it, yet I couldn't leave it alone.

Sometimes the struggle lasted till dawn and I'd have to drag myself out of bed to attend to the children. I avoided people as much as possible. Days would go by without my ever combing my hair because I couldn't stand the sight of myself in the mirror!

The truth was I did not want to change. I liked the way I lived, or told myself I did. All I really wanted was to get rid of the overpowering guilt connected with my affaire. And so I worked through the Psalms, sticking up for my rights, arguing my case. After weary hours of battle, I'd cry, "I am weary with my groaning . . . I water my couch with my tears." *

One evening, after tucking the children in bed, I sat at the dining room table in no hurry to go upstairs to bed where I knew I would be in for another tussle with the Lord. My eye caught sight of the last booklet Rebecca had sent to me. Leafing through it, I saw the words *born again.* Instantly the old red flag was up, but I read on, just to prove to myself that it made no sense. Satisfied that it didn't, I tossed the booklet down and went upstairs.

There I opened my Bible again. "Bet it doesn't say a word in here about being 'born again,'" I muttered. But there, in the

* Psalm 6:6

third chapter of John, mentioned in the pamphlet, were Jesus' own words: "Ye must be born again."

Feeling a little betrayed, I switched out the light and tried to go to sleep.

Then God was there again! It was not an audible voice, but sort of a voice in my mind. Yet I knew that it wasn't my own voice or even my own mind forming the words.

On this particular night my "conversation" started with Him explaining that this second birth, with me cleansed and free from my former sins, is what He gives to those who give themselves to Him. I recalled all the awful things I'd done and offered the excuse that I was not "good enough."

He reminded me that no one is "good enough." It is a free gift.

I balked at this. It couldn't be that simple!

He informed me it was.

I wanted what He had to offer but I was afraid of all it might involve. He agreed that it wouldn't be easy, but He reminded me of His promise to be there always and to help me along the way.

I was torn in two, part of me wanting desperately to surrender my will to Him and the other part fighting tooth and nail to live as I pleased. Why did I have to go through all of this? If God wanted me changed why didn't He just change me? He was more powerful than I!

The answer came that He wanted me of my own free accord. I could refuse Him if I wanted.

I pleaded for Him to help me, to make it easy for me, but no answer to this came.

He was waiting.

I couldn't stand it any longer. I knew I couldn't go back to what I had been, and without Him there would be nothingness.

I cried, "I can't fight You anymore! Do with me as You will!"

Almost immediately peace came to me and soon I fell asleep. It was then I had the dream.

I was running down a lonely road in a dense fog. I was afraid. Then I came upon a beautiful staircase leading up into a thick mist. After a short pause, I started up the stairs. They were wide and not steep; there were bowers of flowers on either side giving off sweet fragrance.

After I had climbed some distance, I noticed that the flowers were gone and the stairs were narrower. I thought about going back, but there was only the fog below.

I continued climbing. The stairs were now curving. But the stairs seemed endless. Although now desperately tired, I somehow felt that life would not be worth living if I did not gain what lay at the top.

I was crawling now, one step at a time. The stairs were only as wide as my body and making sharper curves. Finally, completely exhausted, I could go no further.

In utter despair I cried out, "Jesus, help me!" My head was in my arms and I lay sobbing on the stairs. So it was that I sensed a Presence rather than saw it. I lifted my head and saw bare feet several steps above me. There was a large scar on the instep of each foot.

I reached up for His hand and rose to my feet, all exhaustion leaving me. His face was gloriously beautiful to behold. Joy beyond understanding flooded over me and I awakened to find myself sitting upright in bed.

I sat unmoving a long time, savoring the memory of the love that shone from that face. I was loathe to go back to sleep for fear it would fade as dreams most often do.

Yet, morning came and the dream remained fresh in my mind. Also a resolution of things to do.

First of all, I had to make a clean and final break with Ralph, although for some months I had been avoiding him.

Then the children and I began going to church regularly every Sunday. They enthusiastically helped me set up a family devotional center, using my cedar chest as an altar.

Surprisingly, one day my husband brought home a lovely wooden cross. He mounted it on a mahogany base, and as I watched him working I knew that this relentless love of heaven was pursuing him as tirelessly as it had me, down the avenues of his particular resistances and defenses. We set the cross on our altar, along with candles and the Bible, and here the children and I kneel for evening prayers.

The wonderful, exuberant glow of conversion when I felt washed and free lasted only several weeks. Then came a series of tests, doubts and difficulties. And it was then that I saw the significance of my dream.

The pleasant, flower-strewn first stage of my climb was like the exhilaration of those first weeks after my rebirth. But then the stairs got steeper and narrower. Trying to heal bruised and broken relationships is a painfully slow process. But it is when the Christian walk seems too difficult that we can lift up our eyes and catch a glimpse of the One who has gone this way before.

A Prayer of Self-surrender

Lord, empty me of me,
That I may fill up with Thee.
Every minute I've spent on me,
Lord, I now dedicate to Thee.
The more the world takes from me,
The more will I produce for Thee.
The more perfect my confidence in Thee,
The more special Thy Providence to me,
And whatever may happen to me,
I say, Blessed be the Name of Thee.

Susan Anthony

"An eye for an eye, a tooth for a tooth" is what society demanded from this convicted killer. His story may challenge your thinking about capital punishment.

Bill Bowen's Finest Hour

by JAMES S. CANTRELL*

WHEN I was first asked to go to see Bill Bowen in his penitentiary cell I resisted. I live in Birmingham, Alabama, almost 100 miles from Kilby Prison. Surely, I said to myself, there are good chaplains at Kilby. Surely there are plenty of fine ministers in nearby Montgomery. Perhaps, also, something in me was reluctant—although I hated to admit this even to myself—to become involved with a man convicted of murder. But someone had given my name to Bill Bowen's mother. She asked me to go, and I went.

I don't know exactly what sort of man I expected to meet. All I knew was what I had read in the papers. Bill Bowen, crazed by drink or drugs or both, had killed a woman with a knife, fled from the scene, later came to his senses and turned himself in to the police. At his trial, he said that he deserved to die for what he had done. The judge and jury agreed.

The man I met on death row was a stocky, blue-eyed individual with thinning blond hair—not remarkable in any way. He was sharing a cell with another condemned murderer. Already the long series of stays of execution and postponements was under way; the dreadful cat-and-mouse game that most prisoners finally come to regard as worse than death itself.

But there was a remarkable serenity about Bill Bowen, and it did not take me long to find out why. Someone had preceded me there on death row, a Person who Himself long ago had

* Mr. Cantrell is the pastor of the Third Presbyterian Church of Birmingham, Alabama.

56

died between two condemned felons. And He had wrought the miracle that St. Paul describes, *Therefore if any man be in Christ, he is a new creature: old things are passed away; behold, all things are become new.**

Let me quote from some of the letters I received from this man during the long, harrowing months that followed; letters filled not with bitterness or fear or despair but with a kind of joyousness that under the circumstances is almost incredible.

"When a person first comes to death row he feels pretty low," Bill wrote. "In my case, I knew that what I did was a terrible thing; that's why I gave myself up, because there was no excuse for it. When I came here, I felt that no one would ever love me again, not even God. I didn't think He would forgive me. I was as low as a man could go. But many friends began to write and some good Christians came to see me. I began to pray and read the Bible, and after many weeks I found my Lord. He came to me here on death row, He forgave me, He gave me peace of mind and heart, hope and faith in Him and others. This is wonderful; I can never thank Him enough."

I suppose there is always the chance that a condemned man will pretend to have a change of heart in order to obtain clemency. But such deception would include repeated appeals for mercy. Bill made none. Besides, such pretense would be based on a terror of dying and, as the end approached, Bill showed no such terror.

"I have no fear of death anymore," he wrote, "because I have come to know Jesus and He took away my fear. I know a real happiness now, and I am firmly convinced that nothing can separate me from God; not if my life ends in a few days or if I live for many years."

This newfound happiness did not mean that Bill tried to make excuses for the way he had lived and the things he had done:

"Tomorrow I will be 32 years old, and what have I done for my Lord, my fellowman? If I have done anything good, it is

* II Corinthians 5:17

small compared to the wrong I have done. Why? What will make a man live the best part of his life for the devil when he could live for Christ? I cannot understand it now; you see, Christ has been so wonderful to me in the last few months that I cannot see why I haven't had this joy all my days. Isn't Jesus wonderful?"

Actually, Bill did what he could for his Lord and his fellow man while he was in prison. One day he wrote to me with excitement:

"I have some great news in which you can rejoice with me to the glory of God. There was a friend of mine here who said he did not believe in God. Since my time was so short, I wrote him a letter telling him I was glad to have his friendship and, also, of my faith in God. Well, today the chaplain told me that this man came to his office with tears in his eyes, wanting the chaplain to pray for me and for himself! So if I die now, I will feel better because Christ used me to plant a seed of faith in this man's heart. Who knows the outcome of it? Only God. The glory is all His."

Soon after, I got a message that Bill urgently wanted to see me. It turned out that he had heard, if executed, that he could before his death arrange to donate the corneas of his eyes to blind persons whose sight might thereby be restored. Could I make the arrangements with the doctors to have this done? I could and did.

Several times the date of the execution came very close, then was postponed at almost the last moment. Someone told me that the Governor was heard to say wearily that such responsibility was too much for one man, that there ought to be a board of experts to pass on such things. But the ponderous machinery of the law clanked on.

Bill's cell mate's time ran out. This man also had turned to Christ, and showed the same remarkable serenity and control. Both men asked me if I thought our church would receive them into membership, even though they were on death row. I asked my people about it. When the congregation agreed to accept them, the men's joy and gratitude were touching to behold.

Now Bill was all alone in his cell. Another letter came:

"Mr. Cantrell, this is my hour. I seem to feel it in all my mind, body and soul. It may be the will of God that I come home, and by dying I may be able to do more than by living. If in my hour I can show some people that the love of God will reach even the lowest of men, that He comes to death row as well as any place else, then I will have done the will of God and will go happy.

"Let me put it another way. I have failed God so many times in my life that it may not be His will that I live. But I have this chance to prove His love. If in that hour someone can see a little of Christ in me, if only for that moment before death, then it all will be worthwhile. Pray that I can overcome the fear of the flesh on that night and go home to Him with a word of cheer. Let my heart, soul and mind be on Christ in that hour. Everyone of us has his hour; this is mine, and I accept it as such."

The final night came. When I arrived at the prison the first thing Bill said to me was, "Did you bring the doctors for my eyes?" I told him that the doctors were ready.

When I went upstairs to the execution chamber with the warden I noticed he was carrying a length of rope. I asked him why and he shook his head grimly (few if any of the men who run our prisons believe in capital punishment). "Sometimes they struggle," he said. "Sometimes we have to tie them."

No one had to tie Bill Bowen. He came in quietly, led by his guards. There was no tension in him at all.

He spoke to the warden, urging him not to feel badly for what he had to do. He walked over and sat down in the chair under the harsh overhead light. The straps and the headpiece were adjusted. He pointed out calmly to the guards that the straps over his left forearm were loose. They came back and tightened them.

Before the hood was slipped over his head he made his last statement to us all. "I am now ready to pay for the crime I committed. I have no malice for anyone. God has forgiven me; Christ has saved me. This chair will not send me to my death, but to my home."

The warden gave a signal. I kept my head bowed. When I raised it, Bill Bowen's brief and troubled hour on this earth was over.

The next day I met a friend on the streets of Birmingham. "Well," he said, "I hear you were with Bill Bowen at the end. Is that right?"

The answer seemed to be waiting, deep inside me. "No," I said. "I was with him at the *beginning*."

A Prayer for Wisdom

Lord, that I may see . . .
not so much through the encompassing
darkness of night
as through the enmeshing
distractions of noon.

Lord, that I may see . . .
that I may look above and beyond
the things that clutter life,
that confuse it, obscure it,
wrench it from You.

Give me light
to economize my love . . .
not to crush or squander
but to channel it
so that duties and circumstances
get what they deserve
and people get what they need. . . .

So often I see nothing
because I fear the light
that would make me see
myself.

Sister Mary Camille, S.M.

*"I thought my life would be completely transformed.
Then I discovered conversion was only the beginning."*

The Anatomy of Change

by JOHN L. SHERRILL

FOR a short while after I became a Christian, I thought my
life was going to be completely changed. The Bible itself
encouraged me in this. *If any man be in Christ,* wrote Paul,
*he is a new creature: old things are passed away; behold, all
things are become new.**

Yet as time passed I found many old and destructive patterns still with me. And all around me I saw that this is too
often the case with Christians. I knew one faithful church-
goer who had a bitter distrust of Jews. Another had an over-
weening pride. A minister I knew had a deep antipathy for
his own son. Even those closest to Christ felt the sting of the
enigma: James and John vied for honors in heaven; the Christians at Corinth slid from glorifying God into debauchery.

Are we all hypocrites, then, who say we are Christians and
lead imperfect lives? Don't we know from experience that we
are much the same after conversion as before?

Shortly after I began grappling with this problem in Christian living, I met a dynamic minister who supplied what, for
me at any rate, has been the key to the answer. This young
man, a Southerner by the inheritance of generations, felt that
as a Christian he must take a positive stand in the current
civil rights struggle. He, therefore, continued to send his son
to his newly integrated school, although it was being boy-
cotted by most of the white community.

He acted this way, as I say, because of his Christian convictions. But ironically, some of the angriest criticism of him came

* II Corinthians 5:17

61

from members of his own church. These were the people I
wanted to know about: "What did he think about their Christianity?" I asked. His answer always has stuck with me.

"It is my feeling," he said, "that we are converted in different areas at different times in our lives. Many of my
parishioners are simply not yet converted to Christ's view of
brotherhood. But I do not question the genuineness of their
conversion on other levels."

Now, I don't know what the theological status of this idea is;
I only know it describes something that I see. It is as though
Christ converts those areas of our lives which we surrender to
Him, but will not force from us what we do not freely give.

It has been so in my own life. I did experience a conversion
to the knowledge that God came down to earth in the form of
a human being. In this area—the beginning point—I am truly
in Christ, as Paul says, and here it is clear to me that I am a new
creature.

But if I expected to find the habits and attitudes of a lifetime swept away and a new and Christ-like character substi-
tuted for the one I had been feeding through the years, I was
due to be sadly disappointed. And I believe now that Christ
rarely works in this way. Conversion seems to be more of a
process than a status.

Well, how do we get on with this growth process, we par-
tially-converted Christians? I decided to pick some recalci-
trant area of my own behavior for an experiment in pinpoint
conversion.

Before choosing, I set up some ground rules. I would select,
I decided, some attitude or habit or preoccupation which consumed time and energy that properly belonged to God or to
other people.

Next, I'd face up to my helplessness in the grip of this sin.
By myself I could not beat it. I could only confess that this
was so, and pray the prayer of every man who is asking
for a healing: *I believe; help thou mine unbelief.**

* Mark 9:24

Then from what I knew of the pattern of most conversion, I would have to take some public step, parallel to going forward to the altar at a Billy Graham revival or going to the bishop for confirmation. Some step which would serve to commit me publicly to the new pattern.

And after that I felt I should relax. My effort would no longer be the negative one of trying to combat a failing; it would be the positive one of keeping my attention centered on Him.

The area that I finally settled on for my own experiment was a destructive and time-consuming concern for money. For some people this is a minor vice. Not for me. It was as much of a preoccupation as hatred or the thirst for revenge can be for other men. It got in the way of relations with other people by occupying the front of my mind even when I was away from my checkbook. And, of course, every minute that we spend being anxious about money or anything else is a moment spent in isolation, separated from God.

Serious as these preoccupations were, however, I soon began to see that they were only symptoms of a far more pervasive disease. I once heard a psychiatrist say that he was surprised how many of his patients' troubles were traceable to the traditional "root sins": pride, gluttony, sloth, covetousness, anger, lust and envy. Behind my symptoms, as I defined them, I saw very clearly the evil figure not of covetousness, which I might have expected, but of gluttony.

It came as a surprise. Me, a glutton? But as soon as the suggestion was there I began to see the sprouts of this root sin everywhere. I tended to overdo in a dozen areas, not to taste life but to gulp it. In some areas, such as work, I even tried to make gluttony a virtue. To ask for the conversion of this one trouble area might be biting off more than I had counted on.

But eventually, on a certain afternoon, in the presence of two friends, I did take the step of confessing that I believed Christ to be Lord over this area of my life too. One year has passed since that afternoon. What at first I believed to be a simple weakness has continued to show new faces. Almost daily now I recognize some varied growth of the hungry, insatiable root below. It will take many more months, perhaps years, to recognize all the damage done in my life by this single sin.

Yet this is not the whole story. For along with horror at its size and destructiveness, I also sense a healing going on deep in my being. Like most healing, it is slow. I still have moments of gluttony. But they are rarer. More frequent are days and even weeks together when to sip, taste and enjoy is my pleasure.

I don't know why it has taken me so long to see that this new creature the Bible promises, like all creatures, has a growth process. If a man is *in Christ* all things are indeed new. But the observable fact is that we do not join Christ all at once. We hold on to areas of ourselves that seem too dear, too dangerous or even too trivial to give up. The process of letting them go is a slow and often painful one.

But once they are truly surrendered, a new and mysterious element enters: Christ steps in between our weakness and our enemy, just as He did at Gethsemane when He intervened with the Roman soldiers on behalf of His followers: . . . *let these go their way*, Jesus said, surrendering Himself, *that the word might be fulfilled which He spake, of those whom Thou hast given Me I lost not one.**

* John 18:9, New English Bible

*The all-pro quarterback for the Green Bay Packers
tells about the man who saved him from mediocrity.*

Confidence Is Contagious

by BART STARR

THIS is the story of how a small city in Wisconsin—and a team of football players—were hit by lightning. The lightning I'm referring to is Vincent Lombardi, a stocky Italian-American whom many consider the best football coach in the world. The city happened to be the town where I live, Green Bay, where the Packers come from.

In case you are not a sports' fan, the Green Bay Packers are a professional football team. They are one of the fabled teams of the game with a history of excellence going back to 1919. In that post-World War I year the first players trotted out on the gridiron wearing jerseys that said "Packers" on them, and this was for the nearby meat packing plant which put up the money for the jerseys. The Packers won 10 games out of 11 that season and started on their way towards making themselves one of the resounding stories of sports.

When my wife, Cherry, and I came up from the University of Alabama in 1956, all eager and dazzled by the prospects of my being quarterback on so illustrious a team, the Green Bay Packers had fallen upon some dismal days.

My first year in Green Bay we lost twice as many games as we won, and in 1957 we lost three times as many. In pro ball, records like those are something you don't joke about. Winning with us is a serious business, our bread and butter.

Pro football is a sport—and a clean one—but it is very much a money-making venture. Not winning, therefore, is like not selling the product you've manufactured. It's a science, too, involving hundreds of plays, both for offense and defense.

For a player like me, who wanted to be in pro ball more than anything else in the world, the season of 1958 was frightening. In all that long "history of excellence" the Packers' '58 season was absolutely the bottom. Out of 12 games on our schedule, we tied one game and won—just one. Ten losses: sheer disaster.

In December our coach resigned. The danger signals were up for me and I knew it. I hadn't exactly sparkled out there on the field.

And then the lightning struck!

We were a squeamish group who gathered to meet our new coach and general manager that day in 1959.

"Gentlemen," Coach Lombardi said that day, "we're going to have a football team. We are going to win some games. Do you know why? Because you are going to have confidence in me and my system. By being alert you are going to make fewer mistakes than your opponents. By working harder you are going to out-execute, out-block, out-tackle every team that comes your way.

As the coach talked, you could see the guys straightening up to take a closer look at this intense man.

"But first of all," he went on, "you are going to prepare yourself up here." He put his finger to his temple. "You can't win if you're not ready to win mentally. Therefore, I expect you to think about only three things while you are part of this organization: your family, your religion and the Green Bay Packers."

I for one walked out of that meeting feeling 10 feet tall—and I hadn't played a lick for him!

All of us caught his enthusiasm. Just as he said we would, we started working harder on the field.

I know I worked harder too. It reminded me of the summer I was waiting for my tryout with the Packers. Cherry's folks had a big yard around their house and there I set up a large A-frame. Day in, day out, from morning to night I threw passes into the opening of the A-frame. High, low, on the run, standing still, I worked away at those passes from every conceivable motion and angle. I believe that that total concentration helped get me the job. And that same spirit of hard work was re-ignited by Coach Lombardi.

We started our pre-season games. The tempo rose. Suddenly we won a game and our spirits soared. They kept on soaring. By the end of the 1959 season, we had won seven out of 12 games with virtually the same players who had lost 10 games the year before. In 1960 we won a Division title, then in 1961 a World title, and after that the sky always seemed to be our limit.

How had Coach Lombardi accomplished these things?

You can say, of course, that he did it with his particular genius. But that's not an explanation. Having played for him for nine seasons, I think I have reason to say that his "genius" consists of some very simple things. These are ideas available to all of us and useful in any undertaking if we but have the mental toughness to weld them together into a way of living.

Coach Lombardi doesn't make a secret of those principles. Wherever he is they come out in the way he lives his own life and in the way he thinks. We get plenty of his thoughts. Not only verbally, but in writing. Every week he tacks up fragments of home-grown advice on the locker room bulletin board.

At the start of the training season this year we found this typewritten notice, "Fatigue makes cowards of us all. High physical condition is vital to victory."

This was supplanted the next week by, "The harder a man works, the harder it is to surrender;" followed by, "Pride is what causes a winning team's performance." And so it went week after week.

I can never forget, nor will I ever stop being grateful for, what Coach Lombardi did for me. As I look back to that first question mark of a year under him, I am quite sure he had never seen a three-year veteran who knew less than I did. But he was a patient teacher and he brought out something in me that changed my career and my life: confidence.

Mind you, I was always sure of my talent. I never really doubted that I could play good football, but I lacked the kind of confidence that Coach Lombardi himself had, the kind that oozes out to others. A quarterback is in a position of command; it is he who calls the plays. He must be alert and ready to adjust to the sudden and the unexpected. He has got to have a high boiling point because opponents are going to try to rattle him and he's going to get a lot of whacking around.

Coach Lombardi started building my confidence by first giving me the enthusiasm to work harder, the way I had done with the A-frame. He spent a lot of time just talking to me, examining the "hows" and "whys" of the game. Then he began to bear down on my thinking.

"Treat mistakes with a vengeance!" he'd pound at me. "Don't brood over them, profit from them. If you think about mistakes, you'll make more mistakes. Just come back wiser and harder."

Through it all, the coach repeated his theory that winning is a habit. "It's contagious," he'd say, "and so is losing."

Coach Lombardi won't permit losing thoughts. He contends that pro football has reached a point of such sophistication, that the opposing forces are now in such complicated balance, that on any given afternoon any team can defeat any other. To him there are only two or three plays in a game that decide who wins or loses and if you are not ready for them at all times, you're in serious trouble.

In 1966 we won the Western Division championship even before we had played our last game with the Los Angeles Rams. We were riding high and jubilant. But Coach Lombardi was not. He worried about the last game, even though it didn't affect our league standing. He didn't want us to get out of the winning habit—and we didn't that day!

"If you give anything less than the best of yourselves today," he said to us before the game that Sunday, "you're not just cheating yourselves, or the team, or the millions of fans who are expecting a top-grade Packer performance. No, beyond all others, you are cheating your Maker, the God who gave you your special talent for ball-playing. Such waste is the worst cheating of all."

This was strong and unusual stuff from him and though you may think it a corny, God-in-the-locker-room tactic, you wouldn't think that for long if you really knew Vincent Lombardi. He is a sincere and believing man who goes to church every day of the week, who seldom talks in religious tones, but whose religion is as natural and as integral a part of him as are the prayers we say together before and after every Packer game.

Those prayers are something else I have learned from Coach Lombardi's example. After the week's preparations are over, after the sweat of the practice field and after the groggy hours examining movies and of note-making and of drawing diagrams, after all these things have been completed, the Lord's Prayer said in unison becomes a unifying force pulling all our efforts together. And I have yet to come up from my knees without feeling personally that we were going to do all the things that Coach Lombardi had prepared us to do.

AGE: 22
SEX: Female
RESIDENCE: Skid Row
MARITAL STATUS: Divorced
CHILDREN: Boy 4; Girl 2
HOBBIES: Alcohol

The Woman Who Learned About Love

by REGINA RAMSAY
as told to MYRTH HUDGINS

I HAVE to paint a picture of myself, terrible as that picture is, so you'll understand the incredible miracle in my life.

I was desperate when I married Dave Ramsay. I was 22 years old, my first marriage had been a failure and I was trying rather unsuccessfully to raise two children on the income from my first honest job—waitress in a cocktail lounge.

The children were the only things that gave my life even the vaguest kind of purpose. I'd been dragging along my two-year-old daughter, Terry, like a rag doll from city to city, feeding her hot dogs and bean soup and tortillas only when I, myself, was hungry. I'd left my four-year-old, Mike, with my mother, but I wanted Mike back. The awful thing was that when eventually he came back to me, he'd throw himself on the floor, kicking and spitting and yelling how he hated me. He also stole everything he could get his hands on.

How had I arrived at this mess in my life? It wasn't very difficult. My father, an alcoholic, had died of spinal meningitis when I was seven, so my mother had turned around and married another alcoholic. My mother later committed suicide. When I was 13, I left home and, by the time I was 17, I was on alcohol and dope and mixed up in the rackets of Skid Row. And now, 22 and divorced, I was looking for a way out, an easy way in which my kids could be taken care of too: marriage.

I sorted through all the men I knew. Dave Ramsay was it. He was tall, good-looking, employed and, most of all, peculiar enough to stay home and baby-sit when I wanted to go out drinking. Shortly after we were married I became convinced that he was the biggest sucker in the world. Do you know why? Because he was kind. To me, in those days, kindness was the same as weakness.

We had a daughter, Stacy. Shortly after her birth, Dave learned about my background. But to my amazement he didn't condemn me for it. No, his reaction was totally different. He reacted by working harder, 14 to 16 hours a day, so we could have a home, a car, new furniture. I was bewildered by this man. Yet, little by little, the idea got through that my family wanted something from me. It was love. But I couldn't give it to them.

Rather than get better, things grew worse. Mike was an "F" student, a truant and always in trouble. Dave was going to a therapy group and both our daughters had severe emotional problems. That's the way it was the day before Christmas when I stood in front of my bathroom window thinking of my mother's suicide.

"That's what I want," I thought. "I want to be free."

I grabbed a bottle of sleeping pills and I shook them at the world and cried out, "God, give me the courage to kill myself!"

The instant I said the word "God" something dark came out of my chest. I sensed its movement to my right and out of the window. I know this sounds incredible, but I am reporting exactly what happened. At the time I had never even heard of such a thing as demonic possession. But I believe now that in that instant something evil literally came out of me. I know that I felt as if there were a physical emptiness inside me in the place where the thing had been, and I also felt that the emptiness was being filled by something healing, something good. At the same moment, unbelievably, words came out of my mouth in the form of a song: "I want to walk in the arms of the Lord." I say "unbelievably" because I had never sung a gospel song in my life, and I don't even know whether there is such a song.

I sank into a chair completely bewildered. Then a thought, that was not my own, entered my mind:

"I must confess all my sins."

That day at work the need to unburden myself of the load of sin I was carrying was overwhelming. A fellow at work named Don often talked about his church. Hesitantly, I told him I needed help.

"Regina," he said, "come to our church's revival meeting. You'll learn what you need to know."

When I told my husband that I wanted to go to church, he began to weep.

The following Monday night our whole family attended Don's church. As soon as the revival speaker walked onto the stage and said, "I came here to talk about sin," I identified with him.

We returned on two succeeding nights to hear him tell how he had used people, alcohol and dope and how he had gone forward at a youth rally to confess his sins to Jesus.

"So that's where you go to confess—to Jesus," I thought.

But I couldn't accept the idea that Christ was more than a man. I knew only the story of the Babe in the manger—a fairy tale to me. No one had ever told me the meaning of His death, that He had died for my sins.

In response to the invitation to accept Christ, my little girl and my son rose in front of 150 young people and walked down the aisle. Sensing that this was good, I stepped forward also. Dave followed me.

I knelt on the cold, hard floor, but all I could say was, "God, I give my son, Mike, to You."

After that night he stopped stealing and skipping school. Only a week later, his puzzled teacher phoned to ask, "Mrs. Ramsay, what's wrong with Mike? He's *nice!*"

Mike wasn't the only one who changed. Dave and Terry began responding to me in an especially sweet way. I felt guilty because I still had no love to give in return.

Then Dave persuaded me to attend a Bible class taught by a retired minister who answered my barrage of questions, and said, "Regina, you're never going to understand about Jesus until you ask Him to come into your life."

One night the following week I had a tremendous desire to go out and drink, even though I hadn't had a drink for six months.

In desperation, I prayed, "Jesus, You know that I've done everything sinful short of murder—or suicide. But if You're real and You can forgive my sins and come into my body with Your Spirit, cleanse me."

At once I felt calm, even peaceful. I slept that night. When I awoke the next morning, I knew what being reborn meant. God had touched my life a second time.

Then, God began His "house-cleaning" of my sinful nature. I felt compelled to read the Bible. Knowing that He was speaking to me, I couldn't seem to read it enough. I prayed constantly that I would change, but my struggle was long and painful.

One night, after praying fervently for two days, I read in Galatians about the works of the flesh that war against the Spirit.* "Hatred" sprang out at me from the list. Kneeling, I begged God to take away my obsession to get even with the world.

One afternoon when Stacy came home from school, she looked different to me. For the first time in her life, I wanted to hold and love her. I hugged her so long that she begged, "Mom, please put me down."

Gradually, I began to feel love for Mike and Terry, and my husband. I remember when our marriage began to blend. It was the night that Dave and I knelt together and prayed for the first time.

* Galatians 5:13-26

God has blessed not only our marriage, but He has blessed our children's efforts also. Mike, who is on the football team, made five "A's" on his last report card. Terry was elected secretary of her class this year and Stacy, a second-grader, reads at fifth-grade level.

Perhaps you see now why I believe that no one's life is so hopeless that God can't teach him the meaning of His love. I tell my story to fulfill the covenant I made with God; I'll go on doing it as long as He can use my words.

A Prayer For Humility

Take me and break me and make me, dear God,
Just what you want me to be —
Give me the strength to accept what you send
And eyes with the vision to see
All the small arrogant ways that I have
And the vain little things that I do,
Make me aware that I'm often concerned
MORE with MYSELF than with YOU,
Uncover before me my weakness and greed
And help me to search deep inside
So I may discover how easy it is
To be selfishly lost in my pride —
And then in Thy goodness and mercy
Look down on this weak, erring one
And tell me that I am forgiven
For all I've so willfully done,
And teach me to humbly start following
The path that the dear Saviour trod
So I'll find at the end of life's journey
"A Home in the City of God."

Helen Steiner Rice

Two young girls, both Wycliffe Bible translators, discover in the jungles of Peru that prayer can transcend even the barriers of a strange language and culture.

The Taming of Tariri

by James Hefley

IT was an unbelievable situation. Two young American girls, led by an Indian guide named Guiterrez, had traveled for six hours by canoe through Peru's remote jungle. Now they had reached their destination: the untamed Shapra tribe, whose chief, Tariri Nochowata, was the most feared head-hunter in a vast five-river area. As the canoe touched the bank, a row of savages stared at the girls with dark frowns.

The two slender white girls—Doris Cox and Lorrie Anderson —climbed out to face a big savage who stood before them in regal splendor. Two thick shocks of black hair drooped to his waist. Links of colored beetle earrings hung below his shoulders. Strings of colored beads rattled across his broad chest.

"Him, Tariri, big chief of five rivers," the Indian guide whispered to the girls. Doris and Lorrie tensed. Before them stood the bandit chief who had defied the Peruvian army, a man who beheaded his enemies, then shrunk their heads as trophies of his prowess.

"Great Brother, we have come to live with your people and to learn your language." The white girls spoke in sign language and the few Shapra words they had learned from the down-river trader.

Dirty, naked children pranced excitedly behind Tariri and his warriors. For a long tense silence no one spoke. Then Tariri moved, rattling the beads on his chest, and waved the girls into the village. "Welcome, Sisters," he said, although at the time the girls did not understand what he meant.

Providentially, they had called Tariri "brother"—the one Shapra word which obligated him and his tribe to protect them. Tariri later said, "Had men come we would have speared them on sight. Had a married couple come I would have killed the man and taken the woman for my hut. But two helpless girls came, calling me brother. I was bound to defend them. I felt they were harmless and probably only looking for husbands."

Actually the girls were on an assignment for the Wycliffe Bible Translators* to reduce the Shapra Candoshi dialect to writing for the first time, and then translate it into Scripture portions for the tribe to read. Doris Cox, a Chico, California, girl, and Lorrie Anderson, a resident of Providence, Rhode Island, made an ideal team since both had writing talent, a creative approach to the arts and a conviction that God had called them for missionary service.

Tariri welcomed Doris Cox and Lorrie Anderson to his tribe by giving them a palm shelter and two older women to help them get settled. Many crises followed. One time Tariri's wife became ill and was unable to cook the chief's food. Tariri informed the girls that he was going wife-hunting; a simple matter of killing a husband and bringing the wife back to the village.

"Oh, no," the girls protested. "The God who made the jungle, sun and sky doesn't want this. We'll cook your food until your wife is better."

Tariri grunted in assent, put down his spear and blowgun and motioned to the cooking pot.

Doris and Lorrie knew what they must do. Tariri's food was made by chewing boiled yucca roots and mixing with saliva to become a soupy mixture. But unlike the Indian women who used a communal kettle, the fastidious girls deposited their product in separate kettles. "Our jaws got terribly sore," they said later when they could laugh. "You can't imagine how hard we prayed for the chief's wife to get well."

* 219 W. Walnut St., Santa Ana, California

Tariri's wife recovered and the girls began the tedious work of putting down the Shapra dialect, using methods they had learned at the Wycliffe training center at the University of Oklahoma. They patiently listened to Shapra gibberish, watching how the lips parted to make each speech sound. They symbolized each sound with a letter from the phonetic alphabet. The phonetic translation was then worked into a practical alphabet.

Chief Tariri, intent upon his tribal wars and hunting expeditions, left the girls to their strange activities. But he kept close tab on his new sisters through informers.

After five months, with a two-way radio their only contact with the outside world, Doris and Lorrie noticed that Tariri and his people had become friendly—and curious. "Why do you look at that Book so often?" Tariri asked. "Why do you bow your head, close your eyes, and talk to yourself?" The girls explained that "the Book is the message of the God who made the jungle, sun, moon and sky. When we close our eyes we talk to Him about our brothers, the Shapras."

Three rainy seasons came and went. Doris and Lorrie toiled on in their translation work. The tribe remained committed to savagery and superstition. Wild festivals often were held in the village, sending ripples of fear racing up and down the spines of the girls. The people would drink a weird concoction made from tobacco juice that plunged them into drunken frenzies. When illness struck—as it frequently did—the Shapras would capture a boa constrictor and beg the snake to release the sick victim from its power.

Again and again Doris and Lorrie spoke to the chief about a new life. "The great God loves you, Great Brother. He wants to come into your life."

One day, after hearing this, Tariri impulsively grabbed up his blowgun and stalked off into the jungle to hunt. He said later that as he walked through the thick flora, the battle between the old and the new raged within. He was drawn to the girls' God. Yet tribal customs were a part of his life.

Hours later Tariri returned to the village and stood uncertainly before the girls. Doris asked him shyly, "Will you join us as we talk to God?" Tariri meekly knelt beside her, his beads and earrings jingling in the still jungle air.

Recalling this pivotal point in his life, Tariri now says, "When I prayed to my sisters' God, my heart became joyous. God frightened the devil in me to death. God shot me through with His sun rays."

In the months that followed over 100 Shapras followed their chief in accepting Christianity. In Tariri's life, the change was nothing short of amazing.

He sent jungle runners to the Agurun, Miratos, Huambisas, and Jivaro peoples—his most hated enemies. "My brothers," he said, "I have a murder record on every river. But God has forgiven me. I am a new man. My heart is full of love. Come, see if I am not telling the truth." Hesitantly, slowly, suspiciously, but surely, Tariri's old enemies came to hear the new Tariri speak. They went away puzzled.

News of Tariri's conversion reached America. He was flown to New York. There he saw more people than he ever had imagined existed.

Before returning to the jungle, Tariri asked to meet "the head man from my country." He was taken to the Peruvian Embassy in Washington.

There in the presence of the ambassador and his staff, Tariri solemnly removed his earrings. "Mr. Ambassador," he said meekly, "I give these to you. Please tell people that they came from a chief who once took off heads in the jungle, but has stopped because he loves God."

The story of what happened to a tough-minded intellectual who encountered the Holy Spirit.

The Case of the Skeptical Lawyer

by YAGER CANTWELL

BEATRICE, one of the most beautiful blondes I had ever seen, was looking at me intently. Soft Hawaiian music drifted through the fish net decorations of an exotic Cantonese restaurant. I had only known her a short time, but from the first moment I was more serious about this girl than any other girl I'd ever met.

I had just told her a little of my family background. Then she made the statement that couldn't have shattered my romantic mood any more completely than if she had kicked me in the shins.

"My father is a minister," she said.

I was rocked. As a member of a tough-minded family of lawyers, I had always prided myself on being a scientific humanist, a bit of an intellectual and a militant agnostic. All through college and law school, I had been ready to attack religion as a mish-mash of wish projection, distorted fact, ignorance and irrationality. During my early years of law practice I maintained this same hostile attitude.

In a way, the practice of law had made me even more cynical, because quite often I was thrown into contact with more people who called themselves Christians, yet whose private lives were radically different from the pious masks they wore in church on Sundays. I was not even willing to concede that such hypocrites were a small minority: to me they were an epidemic—and the ease with which they were able to use religion as a cloak of respectability hardly enhanced my opinion of the church.

Not that this antagonism deterred me from finding an oc-

79

casional use for religion. For instance, while still at college and while riding the crest of my arrogant agnosticism, I took a course in the teachings of Jesus. Why? Because I knew that juries are often swayed by pleadings and arguments based on religion. I wanted to be able to outperform any opposing lawyer by Biblically outquoting him. So I figured I had better be prepared.

The teachings of the Man of Nazareth had enormous impact on me—intellectually. No lawyer concerned with communication or persuasion could study what He said and not be impressed by His brilliance of mind, His dialectical thrust, the powers of argument, His use of parables, His astounding narrative ability, His poetic imagery, His magnificent denunciation, even—it seemed to me—His occasional bright patches of humor.

The intellectual "discovery" of Jesus only increased my contempt for the distorted, watered-down image of Him presented by some churches. When anyone asked me for my opinion of theology, I continued to reply that it was the height of concentrated nonsense.

This went on for about 10 years until I met Beatrice. Through most of these bachelor years I had lived by a playboy philosophy in which any pretty girl was fair game and what two consenting adults did in private was no concern of anyone else—as long as no one was hurt. Beatrice had vastly different ideas, however.

Although jolted by the information that her father was a minister, I cared enough about her to take a vacation and follow her all the way across the country to her home. There I met her father, the Reverend Harry O. Nash, of Coronado, California. He was the first man to say to me, "God loves you."

I looked at him in disbelief. I said, "I don't know what you mean by the word 'God,' and I've been trying to define 'love' for over 15 years, and still trying to find out what this 'me' is."

The next day the confirmed agnostic sprained an ankle playing tennis, sprained it so badly that he was laid up for a week with nothing to do but talk to this calm, patient man who burned like a pure blue flame with the love of God. A man who had the guts to lay *his* alleged relationship with the Holy Spirit out on the dissecting table—under the searching scalpel of agnostic cross-examination.

I had known dedicated scientists, doctors, artists, lawyers and tradesmen, I had known what they were dedicated to; but here was a man passionately dedicated to something I didn't understand. From my omniscient viewpoint he was either psychopathic, intellectually debauched or phony, and I intended to find out precisely which.

Meanwhile, an interesting push-me-pull-you developed in my courtship of his daughter: she was beautiful—but Christian; I was vitally attracted to her, but intellectually repelled by her reactions. She was contaminated, I thought, by the bacilli of a long dead and rotting tradition. When I learned that she actually took this Christian stuff seriously, I determined to convert her to the cold, clear beauties of agnosticism. I told her that it "takes stamina to live with truth; it's easy to live with illusion."

When my subtle and extensive campaign finally ran aground, I attempted to enlist the aid of my closest friend, Ernest L. Badenoch, who for years had shared my revulsion for organized Christianity. However, when he met Rev. Nash, within five days he became converted himself, dumped his promising teaching career and went into the ministry.*

This was a severe psychic shock: it put me in a most uncomfortable position. Either Nash was not the phony I had presupposed, or Badenoch was—and I knew this last was impossible. Soon I, the agnostic, found myself wondering if somehow, just possibly, I was missing out on something terribly important, experientially; something that for years I had been too intellectually arrogant to attempt to understand.

Did boy get girl? Did boy marry girl? No, as a matter of fact, Beatrice married somebody else. But a process had been

---

* Presently Rector of St. James Episcopal Church, Bozeman, Montana.

started in me, a process that ended months later with a decision to abandon my god of reason, let go of my common sense and rely on God's. Then, like a frightened child going off a high diving board with eyes shut, I took the final plunge, gave up the faculty I prized more than anything else in the world: my sovereign right to decide for myself—and asked God to come into my life and take charge.

My petition was heard and answered. Very slowly, but unmistakably, I changed. Or rather, I *was* changed. I *experienced* that change. After the leap of faith came personal experience. I found out that the girl's father was right: trying to love God wasn't simply a question of knowing about God; it was knowing God, personally and intimately.

After I made this leap, many areas of spiritual difficulty remained. "Intercessory" prayer, for example, still seemed a wild violation of all the laws of logic. Why should I pray for somebody else? Surely the Power that ruled the universe knew far more about other people's problems than I did, and if He were omnipotent, He could take any necessary action. Why should my words or thoughts affect such actions? In fact, how could they? My verbal and logical approach prohibited experiment with this ridiculous sort of prayer.

Two years later my father became dangerously ill. Not believing in them, intercessory prayers were out of the question for me, but at a church service one morning I was startled to hear the minister pray for my father. Involuntarily, something inside me cried out, "Lord, please help him." And instantly, as if it were written across my mind in letters of fire, an answer came from outside of my own consciousness: *He will be saved.* And he *did* recover.

From that moment on, all argument or verbalizations about intercessory prayer went out the window; I began to experiment in earnest. I found that, with or without verbal logic, intercessory prayer *works*—for me and for others. Things happen that simply cannot be explained by coincidence or accident or fantasy or illusion or any known law of predictability.

Again, the proof is the experience, and no one will admit more quickly than I that until you've had the experience it is hard to believe.

I have much to learn and a long way to grow. But I have discovered that the Holy Spirit can *do* things in loving ways through me, for me and for others which I can't do for myself. He can plan events beyond my imagination and carry out projects beyond my strength. I find that spectacular and unbelievable results occur when I pray as if my life depends on it —as, of course, it does:

"I want only Your will in this situation now, Lord, regardless of consequences—even if it costs me my life. . . ."

This is when things start to happen, when the lid blows off, the roof falls in, life, love and joy begin. This is where the action is, where the excitement starts, where freedom reigns and Power enters.

Prayer for the Complacent

O God, make me discontent with things the way they are
  in the world,
    and in my own life.
Teach me how to blush again,
  for the tawdry deals,
    the arrogant-but-courteous prejudice . . .
    my willing use of rights and privileges
      other men are unfairly denied.
Make me care about the slum child downtown
        the misfit at work,
        the people crammed into the
          mental hospital,
        the men, women, and youth
          behind bars.
Jar my complacence; expose my excuses; get me
    involved in the life of my community,
      and give me integrity once more.

                                    Robert Raines

*Life became so unbearable for this young man that
he went on a suicide mission. Only one thing kept him
from carrying out his plan.*

Case History of a Teen-age Gambler

by Louis Cardone*

I KNEW the top card on the deck was an ace and I wanted
it for myself. Deftly, with a skill I'd spent years developing,
I second-dealed, keeping the ace on top while passing out the
cards under it, until I could deposit the ace in front of me.

And by distracting the players with conversation I had been
able to catch glimpses of most of the cards as I dealt them. I
knew what some of the men were holding before they did. I
knew I was going to win the hand before the betting began.

At the end of the evening I'd won $200, not a bad night for
a 19-year-old kid. I could have won more, but I'd learned
that winning too much discouraged people from inviting me
back. I'd learned, too, that it was a good idea for me to lose
once in a while. After all, I could find a poker game every night
if I wished, and all that mattered was that I had a profit at the
end of the week.

I grew up in a Connecticut town where gambling was the
most popular sport, indoors or out. At ten, I was playing street-
corner dice on Sunday mornings, winning the coins mothers
had given their kids to put in the collection plate at church.
The thought of going to church myself never entered my mind.
My parents didn't go so I didn't either.

Moreover, they separated when I was young, then were divorced. I grew up alternating between their homes, bewildered by what had happened to my family and unable to feel
close to anybody. Maybe the reason I turned to gambling was

* The author's name has been changed.

84

that it seemed to give me an importance in a grown-up world.

At 15 I was working in a gambling joint.

At 17 I was half-owner of the place with an older man. One day as I was crossing the room carrying a box of cards and dice, the police broke in. Had I been caught with the box I would have been accused of operating the place and sent to the reformatory. Knowing this, my partner grabbed the box and claimed to be the sole operator. Being an adult, he only had to pay a $300 fine, while I paid a $25 fine for being a "frequenter." In terms of the life I was leading, I felt my partner had really proved himself to be a true friend. Actually, I never had a friend—just partners in one shady deal or another.

After the raid, I decided to get my military duty out of the way by serving six months and then joining the reserves. I had quit school at 15; while in the Army I was able to earn a high school certificate. Returning home, I found myself wanting to go to college, and I realized that I would have to earn the tuition myself. I did it in the easiest way I knew: gambling.

I also got a job with the man who ran the numbers racket in our city. Soon I was earning so much and having so much fun that I forgot about college. My life probably would have continued that way, perhaps interspersed with more arrests and maybe a jail sentence or two, had I not come into contact with Jack Carpenter.

We met when we were both 16. Jack was a leader of the young people at the Congregationalist church in town. He had persuaded my cousin Ed to join the youth group, and when we met, through my cousin, Jack went to work on me.

Out of curiosity, I agreed to attend a Saturday evening social at the church, but all I got out of it was the unusual experience for me of conversing with girls in my own age group. For this reason, I suppose, I went back four or five times. The evening always ended with a message by the minister, followed by an altar call. One night, to my amazement, I answered the call.

I truly believed I had become a Christian. I dedicated my

life to Christ and made all the promises. I broke off with the
gamblers and racketeers. I quit drinking and smoking. I got
a job with a construction company.

It lasted three weeks. One payday after work I went to a bar
with some fellow-workers. After a few drinks we started a crap
game. Next day I quit my job and spent the afternoon at a
gambling joint. The news of my relapse spread quickly, but I
didn't care. When word reached me that Jack Carpenter said
he would be praying for me I wished him luck.

He must have been praying because there is no other way
to explain what happened to me. At 22, I had everything I
ever wanted—cars, clothes, money, women, an influential job
in the numbers racket. And yet I was growing increasingly
miserable. There was no pleasure for me in anything. I was
always nervous, restless, inexplicably lonely.

For no reason, tears would fill my eyes and I'd have to hide
quickly so that no one would see me sobbing. I was jittery,
short-tempered, always ready to fight, and came close to killing a couple of people. Was I cracking up? Rather than go
mad, I decided to kill myself.

One rainy Monday afternoon I got into my car. I remembered a quiet place in the woods. I headed there, determined
to block the car's exhaust with rags, then lock myself in the
car and let the fumes take my life. But I never reached the
woods. I became confused and lost as though in a fog.

The next thing I knew I was kneeling at the altar of the
Congregational church, sobbing my heart out and pleading:
"Lord God, help me. . . ." For the first time in my life I felt
a strange peace sweep over me and I knew He had heard me.

For a few days, all I was sure of was that the jitters were
gone, the tears had stopped. Yet I needed to talk with someone so I turned to Jack Carpenter, and told him everything.

He listened attentively, then made a strange suggestion:

"I'm sending some kids to the Young Life camp in Colo-
rado. Why not go along?"

I went along and I have been going along ever since. At

this camp I rededicated my life to His service and decided to enter the ministry.

I am now a senior at a college in Minnesota, preparing for the ministry, and just recently I completed four years as a youth counselor and associate pastor at a Methodist church here in Minnesota. I have married, and my wife and I are looking forward to serving God wherever He chooses. For, the way I look at it today, He is the One who rescued me from a hell that I thought had no exit.

Once I tried to follow Him in a superficial way and failed because there was still a great attraction in gambling. The second time I came to Him, all the illusions I had about this kind of life vanished. What a surprise it was to find God still waiting to show me what real life can be like.

A major league pitcher—his baseball career in jeopardy —placed the matter in God's hands and made a life-changing discovery.

The Truth About Pressure

by AL WORTHINGTON

I REMEMBER the occasion years ago in high school when I was asked to give a report before the student body. My heart was pounding so hard I thought I was going to die. Somehow, before a blur of faces, I stumbled through my talk.

Later I discovered that this kind of stage fright is fairly common. According to psychologists, the basic reason for such extreme nervousness is self-centeredness—or a matter of too much ego.

I didn't understand any of this in high school, nor later when I became a professional baseball pitcher. There seemed no connection at all between a speech before a large group of people (which I dreaded) and throwing a baseball for the San Francisco Giants before a big crowd of sports fans (which I enjoyed).

The situation changed when I became a late-inning relief pitcher in 1957. A relief pitcher must be ready to replace the starting pitcher when he tires late in the game. Often he is called into the most pressure-packed moment. It is a long walk from the bullpen across the field. Up to 50,000 fans are shouting at him. Millions more watch his every move on television. No wonder this kind of pressure can make a player's legs go numb and his brain freeze with indecision.

When I took this long walk, it got so that my heart began to pound furiously just as it did during that high school talk. My stomach felt as if it were being jabbed with hot knives. As a result, I often failed to do the job. Soon my stomach hurt so much that there were times when I was physically unable to pitch. The result was that during the next few years I moved from the Giants to the Red Sox, to Minneapolis, and then to the White Sox.

The year of my big inner change was 1958. I was with the Giants then and we were playing at home at the same time Billy Graham was holding his San Francisco Crusade. My wife, Shirley, suggested one night that we attend a meeting. Why not?

When Dr. Graham began to preach, however, an annoying thing began to happen. My heart began to pound harder and harder. In a clear voice the evangelist was asking us to give our lives to the Lord Jesus Christ. Inside I was saying, "He's not talking about me. I'm already a Christian. Why, I've practically grown up in the church. I've even taught a Sunday school class."

Then why was I feeling so much pressure inside? And when Dr. Graham made his final challenge for us to go forward, why did I feel such a strong inner desire to do so?

Just as I was about to get on my feet, another voice said: "Don't do it, Al. Someone might recognize you as a ball player. You can't afford to be embarrassed in front of all those people."

So I stayed in my seat, feeling dissatisfied with myself. Later that night we went to another ball player's home—Bob Speake's—where six of us talked for hours. I was defensive and repeated to them how active I was in the church and—yes—there was that Sunday school class I had taught.

Finally, one of those present turned to me and said, "Al, salvation is not something you earn. It's a gift from God."

That statement stopped me cold. It became clear to me that I was a Christian only in the sense that I had accepted a faith passed on to me by my parents. Never had I on my own made a commitment to God.

Several nights later we went back to the Crusade. This time I did accept the challenge. I told Christ I was turning my whole heart over to Him. I was trusting Him. I was making my break with the old ego-centered life. It was a decision made with my mind, not my emotions.

One morning several days later when our team was to begin a road trip, I awoke with the most amazing feeling of joy. And enthusiasm. It also seemed that all my troubles were in new focus—and I had power to deal with them.

"This is what it is like to be born again," I said to myself. As I was leaving the house for the airport, I picked up our Bible. Eagerly I read it on the plane. It seemed so much clearer to me now.

I thought my troubles were over but how wrong I was. Perhaps I was too zealous; perhaps I just used poor judgment. Regardless, I soon got myself in hot water.

First, it was with some of my teammates: in my new exhilaration for Christ I tried to interest them in Him. They were mostly indifferent or suspicious. One player began to ride me pretty hard.

Then there was the "binoculars" incident. This got a lot of publicity in the papers, and I don't want to dwell on it. Yet it raised a question of honesty which I, as a newborn Christian, felt I had to face.

In major league baseball every team tries to figure out the other team's signals—we call it stealing signs. It's a part of the game, and coaches and ball players on one team watch the players on the other team closely for this purpose.

Someone on the team I was with then came up with the idea of posting a man in the centerfield scoreboard with binoculars to steal the signs of the catcher. He relayed the information to our dugout by pushing a button.

To me, this went too far. I felt it was cheating and said so to the manager. He disagreed and pointed out there was no rule against it. Now I am no "nice Nelly" type. I'll argue strongly with the umpire if I think he's made a wrong decision and I'll brush a batter back with a close pitch if he crowds the plate. Yet this matter of the binoculars fought with my religious convictions.

What was I to do? After much thought and prayer I took a step that even some of my Christian friends thought was wrong. I quit the team. I simply felt that God didn't want me to be a part of what I considered dishonest. So I packed my bags and went home.

It's a wonder my baseball career didn't end right there. The word was getting around in baseball circles that I was some kind of religious nut. So this period was certainly my lowest point. Yet I had taken the step on faith. It was done. I found a part-time job and resumed my studies in a nearby college where I planned to get a degree in education and then a job as a teacher-coach. Shirley and I put the matter of my baseball career in God's hands.

Perhaps in my heart I was not yet ready to give up on the idea of becoming a good major league pitcher. I was in my early 30s, when pitchers usually are at their best. And there was another reason. The change in my spiritual life had made a change in my emotional and physical life.

I first noticed it when I was asked to give a speech before a high school group. I had such a desire to tell these young people about Jesus Christ that I forgot about myself and my pounding heart.

What it proved to me was that the more I centered on Him, the less problem I had with my ego and with pressure. It also told me that I would probably be able to go into those tense, late-inning situations as a relief pitcher and not tighten up and lose my effectiveness.

So when a contract was sent to me from a minor league team, I considered that was my answer and signed it. I pitched well in the minor leagues for two years. It took that long to convince any major league team that I could help them. The Minnesota Twins gave me my big opportunity in 1964.

I wish I could say that the problem of my ego was solved once and for all. The fact is, it has to be dealt with every day. There was one occasion not too long ago when it came back strong again, together with my stomach trouble. I had been pitching well and newspaper stories referred to "Worthington's coolness in tense situations." My mistake was not so much in reading these stories, but in believing them.

We were playing in New York. My stomach felt like someone had used it for a punching bag. I took out my Bible and read this passage in James (5:14): *Is there any among you sick? Let him call for the elders of the church; and let them pray over him anointing him with oil in the name of the Lord.*

I needed prayer. Who to call? I knew some active Christians in New Jersey, but pride made me hesitate. Finally I called Karl Helwig, who is in the automobile business and an active Baptist layman. He listened to my story, then said, "My wife and I will be there in an hour."

When they arrived we went upstairs to my room in the Roosevelt Hotel. We prayed together silently for a few minutes, then Karl stood behind me, hands on my head. I felt the Lord's power flowing through his hands as I recommitted my life to Him.

The test came a few days later in Boston. It was the last of the ninth inning; Minnesota was leading 3-2. Boston had two men on base and there were two outs. I was called in as a relief pitcher to protect our lead and get the final out.

I forgot my stomach, forgot the crowd, forgot television. "Lord, this is just another ball game," I prayed. "Anything and everything I do is for Your glory. That's all I care about."

The count on the batter reached 3 and 2. My catcher signaled for a curve-ball. I was amazed. A curve was my worst pitch. I shrugged, threw the curve. Surprised, the batter swung awkwardly. Missed. We had won another game, and went on to win the American League pennant, beating the New York Yankees for the first time in six years.

A new baseball season is just underway. I hope we win the championship again. But maybe we won't. Baseball is a game of ups and downs. Furthermore, baseball is not *that* important.

What is really important never changes: Christ's love for us. Our need for Him.

This step-by-painful-step process, which helped this popular author * achieve a more meaningful dialogue with God, has enabled thousands of others achieve a more vital prayer life.

When I Leveled With God

by KEITH MILLER

UNTIL that day on the highway in east Texas I had said only mechanical little prayers whenever the occasion demanded. From Christian parents I had inherited the standard kind of faith that included church attendance, grace at meals and the acceptance of a shadowy Father who would help me be good.

The trouble was much of me was pulled toward things that I knew He wouldn't consider good at all: self-centeredness, pride, lust, greed.

This conflict went on until I was 28 years old. I had a wife whom I loved very much and two small children, yet I was empty in my soul and filled with incompleteness and despair. On this particular day I got into the company car (I worked for an oil firm) and took off on a field trip. While driving through the tall pine woods of east Texas, I suddenly pulled off to the side of the road.

I had a feeling of total desolation. Usually an optimistic person who could always say "there is one more bounce in the ball," I told myself that a couple of martinis and a good night's sleep would fix me up. It was no good. I seemed to be a man on a treadmill going no place in a world that was made up of black clouds.

To my surprise tears filled my eyes and ran down my cheeks.

---

* Keith Miller is the author of two highly successful books—*The Taste of New Wine* and *The Second Touch* (both published by Word Books, Waco, Texas).

I looked up in the sky. "God," I said, "if there is anything You want in this stinking soul, take it."

Something came into my life that day which has never left. There wasn't any ringing of bells or flashing of lights, but there was a deep, intuitive realization of what it is that God wants from a man, which I had never known before. And the peace that came with this understanding was not an experience in itself, but was a cessation of the conflict of a lifetime. I realized then that God is not so much interested in having my money nor my time, as much as my will. When I offered Him my will, He began to show me life as I had never seen it.

The process of change that began in my life after that experience has covered every area, but I want to dwell on just one—prayer. For when I set out to live my life for Jesus Christ, I realized I did not know how to find His will for me. I guess I had naïvely assumed that making a total commitment automatically ushered one into a vital prayer life (whatever that meant). But it didn't happen this way to me. Prayers such as "Dear God, forgive me for all the bad things I do," seemed to cover everything, but nothing much happened in my life. Then I began trying to find times during the day for specific private prayer.

I can remember the alarm going off very early. Groggily I would force myself to my feet to grope about in the dark for slippers, robe and my Bible. Many times I would tell God sleepily, "Lord, You know it's not fair for me to wake up my family just to satisfy my selfish desire to have a time of prayer. Deliver me from that kind of legalism." And I'd go back to bed.

Nothing seemed to be working until I posed my problem to a Christian layman who had a dynamic ministry with people. "For me, there is nothing more important than to read the Scriptures every day and to have a specific time of prayer for developing a close relationship with Christ," he told me.

Seeing a man's life with which I could identify did for me what all my "trying" could not. I began getting up again in the morning, using this one specific period each day for prayer and reading Scripture. This prayer time has become the center from which I live the rest of my life.

Soon things began to happen. Since my closest relationships with people were with those who knew the most about me and loved me anyway, to find such a relationship with Jesus Christ, I began to reveal my inner life to Him, *even though I knew He knew already.*

This experience taught me the strange power in prayer of being specific with the Lord. In trying to be totally honest with Him I found a new freedom and sense of being accepted. Instead of saying, "Lord, today I exaggerated a little on my expense account, but You know that everybody does," I was able to say, "Lord, I cheated on my expense account today. Help me not to be a dirty thief."

For a long time I had been disturbed about the problem of my mind wandering during prayer. I would be trying to pray and suddenly my mind would jump to a business appointment I needed to make. For years I forced these things out of my mind to get back to "spiritual things." Then I learned to keep note paper by my side so that when these thoughts came, I would jot them down and then get back to God. Such thoughts during prayer might be His way of telling me of significant people to see or things to do.

The more honest I was in my prayers, the more real He became. I used to start out by saying, "God, I love You" (whether I really did or not that morning). Now I can say, when it is true, "Lord, I'm sorry but I'm tired of You today." But now I can also continue, "You must be sick of me, too, Lord, but forgive me and help me get back on the beam." I discovered that this was a real act of faith because there was no religious feeling involved.

Looking back now, I see that for years I had been a kind of spiritual sensualist, always wanting to have goose pimples in prayer and being depressed when I didn't. I began to feel very tender toward God on those mornings when I would pray on raw faith. I felt this way because at last I was giving back to Him the gift of faith.

The discipline of regular prayer resulted in other changes. I didn't get rid of my problems; I simply began to get a new set of problems. God didn't take things out of my life; instead He brought in a great many new positive things. For example, He filled me with a desire to tell people that life was not a hopeless rat race—that there is the Good News. This led to my teaching an adult Sunday school class, then participation in a prayer group.

As my wife and I began to fill our lives with these new activities, certain old practices seemed to just fall off. God didn't force us to give up anything; He just made the life we were finding such an adventure that many of the activities we had been so busy with now seemed unreal and unimportant.

In conclusion, I have realized that prayer is not a series of requests to get God to help me do the things I think need to be done. Prayer is a direction of life, a focusing of one's most personal and deepest attention Godward. The purpose is to love God and learn to know Him so well, that our wills and our actions will be more and more aligned with His, until even our unconscious reactions and purposes will have the mark of His love and His life.

Prayer no longer seems like an activity to me; it has become the continuing language of the relationship I believe God designed to fulfill a human life.

One Day Can Change Your Life

An exercise in practicing the presence of God, based on the teachings of Dr. Frank Laubach.

WILL you make an experiment and try to spend one complete day with God?

"Impractical," you say. "Unless I try to find some Sunday."

No—not a Sunday. The idea is to take a regular working day, with all your usual routines, and *live it through with God*.

"But how in the world can I be thinking about God and still concentrate on the things I have to do?"

The answer comes from Dr. Frank Laubach, world-famous teacher, author and linguist. Dr. Laubach admits his work was colorless and unproductive until the day he decided to begin such an experiment. The result of "practicing the presence of God" changed his life and launched him on a career which has enabled millions of people throughout the world to learn to read. The principles of his experiment are preserved in a little classic called "Letter by a Modern Mystic" and form the basis for this *Spiritual Workshop*.

HOW TO BEGIN

Decide on a certain day of the week for the experiment—maybe tomorrow. When you wake up, (at least half an hour earlier than usual) begin with a short, simple prayer. "Lord, I will try to stay close to You all day long. Please help me." Then think of yourself as being like a violin in the hands of the greatest artist of all time, producing your best music only when it is the Master who plays music which will also be in harmony with all the rest of the orchestra.

97

Take a few minutes to read a favorite selection from the Bible. The 23rd Psalm, for example. Give yourself at least 15 minutes to absorb God's word into your mind.

LOOK AHEAD

Living a normal day with God certainly does not mean neglecting all other things. It means bringing God into every situation you encounter.

Summarize on paper what you expect the day ahead to bring. Perhaps lunch with an old friend . . . a session at the dentist . . . a report to the boss . . . club meeting . . . a hospital visit . . . shopping. Jot down the events as they come to mind. Then invite God to be a part of each activity. "Be with me, Lord, on the drive to Mother's house. Guide my hand as I write this letter. Be on my lips during this conversation." If you have such a fear, admit it to God. Ask Him to help you be bolder *for this one day.*

AS ACTIVITIES START

A day with God doesn't mean going about with a dreamy look on your face. God doesn't want to distract you from being friendly, smiling, warm and interested in what is taking place. A breakfast table conversation might be no different than usual . . . except you no longer react alone to what is said. If there is any gossip, or negative statements, however, you (and God) will somehow find a way to turn things in a more constructive direction.

The day continues. You are about to make a call. As you place your hand on the telephone, ask God to speak through you.

But God keeps slipping away, you say? Not surprising. Frank Laubach describes his day as follows:

" I have not been very successful so far . . . I started well by finding a rich experience of God in the sunrise. Then I tried to let Him control my hands while I was shaving and dressing and eating breakfast. This was difficult. Then I went to my typewriter and asked God to control my hands as I pounded the keys . . . He keeps slipping away and I keep bringing Him back. . . ."

TALK TO A STRANGER

To prevent this experiment from becoming too introspective, strike up a conversation or make contact with at least one stranger during the day. It should be more than a perfunctory talk, for God will be in on it, too, and He always is sensitive to need. You will be too.

Frank Laubach describes in a memorable way one such encounter. "I was on the boat from Manila to Cebu (Philippines) and saw across from me a woman, whose face was heavily made-up. I spoke to her because she looked lonesome. Three of the ship's officers nearby tittered . . . so I talked loud enough for them to hear too. In our conversation, I told the woman that I was a seeker for God. As naturally as a preacher she replied, 'God is all around us if we only would open our eyes. All the world is beautiful if we would but see the beauty.'"

Then the woman told Dr. Laubach about her act in show business and how wonderfully people had treated her. Her tired eyes were full of life now as she said, "Oh, the world is full of such good people."

When Dr. Laubach rose to leave, he said to her, "I am going about the world trying to find wonderful hours, and I shall remember this as one of them."

LOOK FOR BEAUTY

God loves and enjoys beauty. Therefore, a day with Him will be incomplete without some time spent being aware of what He created. This does not mean a special trip to some scenic spot. It does mean a new, more concentrated awareness of the beauty around us.

Dr. Laubach made this observation. "One thing I have learned today is that everything God made is lovely. The clouds, the tumbling river, the rippling lake, the slender blade

of grass, the whispering of the wind, the fluttering butter-
fly. . . ."

AN EVALUATION

The normal person who attempts this experiment conscien-
tiously, may feel some sense of discouragement at the end of
the day. The total time of association with God may seem
much less than 100 percent. We suggest that you not evaluate
the experiment this way. Ask yourself instead, "Was the day
any different? If so, how? Was it a better day than the average?"

If you felt any increase of love, faith, or just well-being, you
will want to continue the experiment further. Try it for a week,
a month.

After two months of this experiment, Dr. Laubach made this
observation, "This concentration upon God is strenuous, but
everything else has ceased to be so. I think more clearly. I
forget less frequently. Things which I did with a strain before, I now do easily. I worry about nothing and lose no sleep.
I no longer feel in such a hurry about things. Nothing can go
wrong except one thing—that God may slip away from me if
I do not keep on my guard. If He is here, the universe is with
me. My task is simple and clear."

THE UNLIMITED POWER OF PRAYER LORD,
HEAL ME—YOUR WAY

"Why me?" reduces the problem of illness to its simplest form.

Invariably, this is the question we pose to others and to God when beset by some mental or physical malady. From our human perspective, we often accuse life of being unfair—of giving to some and taking from others.

And being logical creatures, we demand an explanation. But like Job, we are often met with silence. There is no one to give us an answer. Oh, our friends may venture a guess as to the root of our difficulty, but they may be as misled as Job's friends.

We avail ourselves of all human resources and knowledge, yet in some cases this is not enough. Our illness lingers. Is there any other recourse?

The following stories are testimony to the fact that there is a power beyond human means. That there is a healing power which can and does lay itself upon the afflicted. Just how and why and when this power manifests itself is one of the mysteries of faith, but it is known that prayer is the instrument through which God is reached.

3

"Dorothy was a retarded child whom they said was unreachable. However, something told me they were wrong."

The Silent Child

by FRANCES E. LESLIE

A S the lady talked, I tried to concentrate on the beautiful room around us instead of her words. For she was telling me about Dorothy, her eight-year-old daughter, the middle one of her five children, a mentally retarded child.

"She's never spoken a single word," the mother repeated. "The doctors say it's hopeless. We took her up to Boston last year and. . . ."

I fixed my thoughts on the green damask draperies framing tall windows that looked out on Park Avenue. How handsome the whole room was, with its crystal chandeliers, its concert-grand piano, its fresh flowers everywhere. What a lovely woman the mother was, an opera singer whose name I had known even before her letter came asking me if I would consider a job with Dorothy.

Yes, a lovely woman—and especially in her love for this little girl whom all the experts said should be put away. The love was the thing to concentrate on. And so while pretending to listen, I closed my ears to the results of reflex tests and encephalograms. In my years of working with retarded children I had discovered that my attention must not go to the lacks but to the special strengths in such children.

That there was strength in each one of them I was sure. I believe that a little of God lives in every one of us, and that to bring it out is the only job of any teacher.

Dorothy and I met the next weekend. With me it was love at first sight: this beautiful, blonde, blue-eyed child—surely a very lovely person lived in such a form. For her part, Dorothy only stared at me with inscrutable eyes.

"It's one of her quiet days, thank heaven," her mother said. "On her wild ones, there's no controlling her." My mind considered those wild days. I liked the sound of them. They told me there was a person here—trapped in whatever chemical or physical prison—but an individual struggling to be seen and recognized. I told her mother I would try the job for a month.

It was a hard one from the beginning. In the afternoons I would take Dorothy to a special class for retarded children. She just sat in a chair, staring straight ahead, making no effort to join in the activities.

"She's unreachable," her teacher told me. "I don't know why they keep sending her."

I gazed around the room at the other children, all engrossed in simple mechanical tasks, and I silently agreed with Dorothy. What was challenging about fitting a square peg into a square hole? With her parents' permission we stopped going there.

Dorothy's problem everywhere, it seemed to me, was the non-expectation of everyone around her. I remember break fast one morning when the other four children and their nurse had come into town. The other quickly finished their cereal but Dorothy, dazzled by the activity around her, hadn't touched hers.

"Just spoon it into her!" the nurse cried impatiently.

"She can eat by herself," I said. "I guess she's just too interested in what's going on."

"Interested?" Nurse gave a snort of contempt. "She doesn't have any more idea what's happening than that canary! It's a shame she's allowed at the table. She just upsets the other children."

It wasn't true. Dorothy's brothers and sisters—especially her older sister Martha—seemed genuinely happy to be with her. But even Martha had fallen into Nurse's habit of talking *about* her ("Dorothy looks nice today." "Dorothy's hair needs combing; shall I do it?") rather than *to* her. It was so easy to assume that because she had no words she had no understanding either.

I understood the problem. It is difficult to keep on talking to someone when there is never an answering voice. I felt it most during our daily walk in Central Park. It was October, warm sunny Indian summer, and Dorothy and I spent hours just walking. When the silence threatened to absorb us both, I sang.

I started with the hymns I remembered from my own childhood back in England. My father had been the organist at our village church and my earliest memory was of him perching me high on the organ console during practice. Dorothy seemed to like the songs, for her feet marched in time to the music and her head nodded rhythmically.

We also brought sketch pads and crayons to the park. I was fascinated by some drawings I had found in Dorothy's room, a pattern of graceful waving lines, drawn over and over again. What it meant I had no idea, but it certainly wasn't "scribble" as Nurse impatiently called it.

And so we would sit on a park bench and sketch. I drew trees and strolling people and the lofty skyline beyond the park, and Dorothy drew pigeons. I saw the very first time what they were, not perhaps the outside of pigeons like other people draw, but the soul of the birds instead, the very way it feels to be a pigeon. Faster than my eyes could follow, her hand moved: the wings in flight, the thrust of the neck, the self-important walk. "Oh Lord," I prayed silently, "what a lovely glimpse of Yourself You have given me today!"

The golden autumn passed too swiftly. Then a day dawned when the rain streamed down the tall windows and wind rattled the doors. So Dorothy sat on the piano bench beside me as I sang the songs I had sung in the park. I started off with one of Fenwicke Holmes' *Songs of the Silence.*

   . . . *I'm singing today and I laugh with joy,*
   And I have not a fear nor care,
   For I feel and know

That above and below
Is the God of the everywhere.

Halfway through this joyous song the miracle happened. One moment I was singing alone, the next Dorothy was singing with me, word for word in perfect tune. Electrified, I played on and on without a break, praying that the spell would not be broken. What a memory! How marvelously her mind had retained the words of song after song—far better than an average eight-year-old!

I heard someone sob. I turned and saw Dorothy's mother in the doorway, tears streaming down her cheeks, unable to do anything but hold out her arms to her child.

From that moment on, life was different for Dorothy. From singing, it was not far to speaking, although words with music always came first. We made up songs for everything.

"Water, a washcloth, see what I mean?
Knees that are dirty will soon be clean!"
"At the planetarium I can watch the stars:
There is Venus, here is Mars."

Other changes took place in Dorothy. Her tensions disappeared along with the frustrations of a spirit bottled up; so did her wildness. The nurse never adjusted to the difference in her and took another job.

As Dorothy continued to learn I lengthened my stay, just another month until she could tell time . . . another until she learned the alphabet. When I left, the month had stretched to five years. Dorothy was a poised, self-sufficient 13-year-old.

Normal? Not if normal means "average." All of us have strong points and weak points and in Dorothy everything is extreme. But this means extremes of knowing and expressing that most of us never reach.

Those wavy lines, for instance, the ones she drew again and again? When she had enough words she told me, "That's what the wind looks like."

Dorothy, your eyes see deep down, important things. Your ears hear silent things, your world is set to music. Oh, if God left something out of you, it was only to fill it with Himself.

Three Months To Live!

by ALMA DEANE MACCONOMY

AS the tall, gray-faced man walked painfully toward the entrance of St. John's Episcopal Church in Washington, D.C., a woman ran up to him. "Are you Dr. Berger?" she asked eagerly.

"Yes, I am."

"Well, I just wanted to see what you look like," she replied. "I've been praying for you for months."

Dr. C. Edward Berger could do little more than murmur his thanks. He had cancer of the pancreas and although he had come that day to a healing service at St. John's, in his heart Dr. Berger did not expect to recover from his painful illness.

Since 1956, Dr. Berger has been rector of All Saints Episcopal Church in Chevy Chase, Maryland. He holds a doctorate in theology and has great respect for the intellectual achievements of specialists in today's society, many of whom are members of his congregation. When, after a biopsy revealed that Dr. Berger's pancreas was made up of the fastest-growing type of cancer cells and his surgeon told him he probably had but three months to live, Dr. Berger believed him.

"In the face of this verdict," Dr. Berger says, "it did not then occur to me to try what some people call 'faith healing.' That would have gone against the habits and beliefs of a lifetime, and I would have had to persuade myself that the surgeon, the pathologist, the internist and the radiologist were wrong. I believe that God works through physicians as well as through bishops, and I heard my very highly-skilled surgeon's voice as the voice of God telling me that in only a little while I would be gone."

108

Although it was the first real crisis of his life, Dr. Berger did not feel sorry for himself. "I simply decided to tidy things up a bit," he said, "and get ready for death, grateful for the happy years of the past. I believed, of course, that Christ *could* heal me, yet despite all the prayers said for me during nine months of pain, I saw no reason to believe that He *would* do so. I was too sick even to ask Him anymore."

But others did continue to ask. Prayers for him began in 1959, when his concerned wife and close friends knew he was in pain. After August 24, the day of an exploratory operation and the surgeon's grave prognosis, people in Dr. Berger's church began offering prayers daily for his recovery.

"Soon I was on prayer lists all over the country and indeed, all over the world," Dr. Berger recalls with awe and gratitude. Masses were offered for him in Roman Catholic churches. Methodist prayer meetings in Washington sent up prayers for his recovery. The Bishop of Tokyo and his clergy had him in their prayers. So did the Bishop of Malaya, the monks of the Order of the Holy Cross, the members of the Order of St. Luke and—he learned recently—the late Pope John.

Dr. Berger admits frankly that he was not aware of any change in his condition because of these prayers. As he began a course of daily X-ray therapy, he knew only that extreme nausea had now been added to gnawing pain and the debilitating effects of sedation. But Dr. Milton Gusack, his personal physician, noticed a change.

"About two weeks after the diagnosis you began to fight like a tiger," he later told Dr. Berger. "You decided to live."

Dr. Berger says he was unaware of this decision. He regards it as a sheer gift of God's grace imparted to his subconscious mind through the prayers of others. As the autumn days slipped by, however, he began to make other decisions. The first was that he would write a book; he began work on it at once. The next was that he would preach on Thanksgiving. The X-ray therapy would be over by then and he could hope to be free enough from nausea to get through the service. Besides, Thanksgiving would be several days beyond his three-month expected life span.

That Thanksgiving Day service at All Saints was unlike any other the church has ever had. All attendance records were broken. As Dr. Berger slowly moved to the pulpit, the pallor of his face, and the loss of 50 pounds made him seem quite gaunt. His usually robust voice was high and thin. His sermon had been written under sedation and now it was being given under sedation. Yet there was something very moving about the man as he stood before his people as much as to say, "Your prayers have made this possible."

The next day he insisted that his wife, Mattie, and his two children, Virginia and Charlie accompany him downtown to have their annual Christmas card photograph taken. Between pain-relieving shots administered by a disapproving nurse, he then started to work on his next sermon. Dr. Berger preached again on Sunday, December 1, and rounded out the day by driving himself downtown to St. John's Church to attend the healing service mentioned earlier.

Several days later he went to his doctor for a regular examination. Afterward, there was an astonished smile on Dr. Gusack's face.

"What are you smiling about?" Dr. Berger asked.

"Your cancer's breaking up," Dr. Gusack replied.

"What! How can you tell?"

"It's getting softer and smaller."

"Are you sure? How long have you known this?"

"About two weeks."

For the first time, Dr. Berger allowed himself to hope.

Six months of pain, weakness, sleeplessness and sedation followed but he preached every Sunday. He began to take part in two worship services each Sunday and extended his office hours. He started calling on parishioners. He was able to face serious parish problems once more. Gradually he lost the gray pallor, he gained weight, the pain lessened. Hope turned to thanksgiving.

Later Dr. Berger questioned his doctor, "I want to know why you think I recovered."

Dr. Gusack, who insists he does not believe in miracles, said that it was one of the very few recorded cases of recovery from pancreatic cancer. He thought three things helped: X-ray therapy; the prayers of thousands of people, though he didn't understand prayer; and finally, Dr. Berger's will to live, the strongest he had ever seen in a patient.

"When I try to add it all up, I don't understand why you recovered. It's a miracle, that's the only way I can explain it."

Today, four and a half years later, the healthy, 228-pound clergyman who preached in England and toured Europe with his family last summer, says, "I don't know why I recovered either, but I believe that God did it, and that He responded to all the prayers of all my family and friends—known and unknown. And I am eternally in their debt.

"One thing I am sure of is that I must tell everyone I meet who faces the pain and the fear which cancer brings, that they must not despair, that God is quite able to effect recovery from even the worst kind of cancer, whether or not the patient deserves it or expects it or prays for it."

J. B. Phillips—whose translations of the Scriptures have illumined them for people the world over—tells of a spiritual illness that threatened his faith.

Dark Night of the Soul

by RAY CRIPPS

TWENTY minutes after I had driven up in front of J. B. Phillips' Swanage, England, home, I was hearing a story from him that I never expected to hear. My image of this great Bible translator was comparable to the solid stones from which his house was built. He was in my mind a spiritual giant, invulnerable and unshakable. My interview revealed another side to this beloved man. But let me start at the beginning.

When I rang the doorbell a woman answered and in spite of the cotton housedress, I knew by the warmth of her smile that this would be Mrs. Phillips.

"Come in, please," she said. "Jack is in his library. He'll be right with you."

"Jack" is what J. B. Phillips is called by his friends. When he came in, moments later, I had the feeling that I was one of them, that I had known this kind-faced man all of my life. He, too, was dressed casually, and his smile was as contagious as his wife's.

"Won't you come out to my hideaway?" said Dr. Phillips. He led the way outside again, and I saw, a little to my surprise, that his library was in a separate building. The library itself was cozy and warm and in my mind's eye I saw Dr. Phillips at work here, translating ancient Greek texts into English as contemporary and gripping as tomorrow's news.

Almost from the first our interview took a direction I could never have anticipated. I had heard about Dr. Phillips' recent illness, of course, and he seemed to want to talk about it. Yet not the physical illness, with its dizzy spells, but the *spiritual* illness.

Was I hearing right?

"It's truly a devastating thing, you know," said Dr. Phillips, "to be ill in your innermost spirit. For the past four years I have been going through what many old-time writers on spiritual matters call 'the dark night of the soul.' That's perhaps too strong a term for it, but I've certainly come to know that the Devil—whom I believe to be real—can make all sorts of devious attacks upon us."

Dr. Phillips' time of testing really began years ago with the quite unexpected success of his writings. Phillips was a parish priest when he began "Letters to Young Churches," his translation of the Epistles. He started the work in 1941, largely for the sake of young people attending his church in London during the dreadful days of the blitz.

"I discovered," he said, "that to many of these young people the Authorized Version of the Bible, and particularly Paul's letters, were completely unintelligible. This was at a time, of course, when the message of them had never been more important."

C. S. Lewis saw a copy of the one to the Colossians, the first translation, and wrote Phillips a congratulatory letter. "It is like seeing an old picture which has been cleaned," Lewis wrote, and urged Phillips to translate the rest of the letters as soon as possible. It took six years to complete the task but the result was an immediate and dramatic success. The number of requests to preach, lecture, broadcast and write mounted alarmingly and the burden of correspondence alone became almost insurmountable to a man with a church to care for as well.

"This was the beginning of a difficult time for me which at first I tried to ignore and then to hide from myself," said Dr. Phillips. "But as pressures mounted I began to be aware as never before of the subtle and insidious dangers of success."

Dr. Phillips got up and walked to the window of his library.

At first, he said, the new life had been exhilarating. His work took him on trips he could never have afforded as a parish priest. There were honors and V.I.P. treatment. There were interviews with the press. There were the ever-growing world sales of his books.

"And all the while something was going on which I did not see until it was too late," said Dr. Phillips, suddenly turning to face me. "Satan was mounting his most devastating attack on me. He was building an *image* of 'J. B. Phillips' that was not Jack Phillips at all. I was no longer an ordinary human being; I was in danger of becoming the super-Christian! Everything I wrote or said had to be better than the last. The image grew and grew until it was so unlike me that I could no longer live with it. And yet the thought of destroying it was terrifying too. It was on this dilemma that I hung."

The first result of Satan's attack was an end to the flow of creativity. "It was turned off like a tap," said Dr. Phillips. Not only in writing did he notice it, but in other areas as well. "One of my hobbies is painting," he said. "I found myself losing all sense of color. Shades which should have taken seconds to mix now took ages."

Then the nighttime battles began.

"Those were the worst of all," said Dr. Phillips. "I found that I could usually struggle on pretty well during the day. But at night it was as if I were the picked target of the Enemy. Irrational fears gripped my spirit, unreal guilt swept over me. Even my sense of God disappeared, though it never reached nihilism nor utter despair. Still, when I turned to God for help, He seemed remote and unapproachable."

I stared at this giant among present-day Christians in astonishment. Faceless fears? Haunting guilt? A God unreachable and far away? Why, he was describing *my* nighttime experience! But I had always imagined that such midnight torment was reserved for people of small faith and small learning like my own. Was it possible that it was the experience of mature Christians as well? And with the question came hope. For it was obvious that the man in front of me had emerged victorious from these lonely struggles.

Dr. Phillips' 20-year-old daughter, Jennifer, put her head in at the door to call us to lunch, and for the next half-hour the four of us spoke of lighter things.

But back again in his library after lunch, he gave me my answer. J. B. Phillips' return from darkness began with what might be called a vision—a vision which centered around a man who had followed much the same earthly path as Phillips himself: C. S. Lewis.

Lewis, too, had become a world-known figure as the result of his Christian writings. He, too, knew what it was to live in people's imaginations as a kind of spiritual hero. His body, too, had succumbed to pressure: he was not well for several years before his death in 1963. Who was better qualified to speak to Phillips' condition?

Dr. Phillips described his experience to me. But he has also written about it in the preface to a new book, which was still in manuscript form on his desk at the time of my visit, and which is the first result of his fresh gift of creativity. This is what he says about the extraordinary occurrence which made so deep an impression on him at a time when he most needed it.

"Many of us," he writes, "who believe in what is technically known as the Communion of Saints must have experienced the sense of nearness, for a fairly short time, of those whom we love soon after they have died. This has certainly happened to me many times. But the late C. S. Lewis, whom I did not know very well but with whom I had corresponded a fair amount, gave me an unusual experience.

"A few days after his death, while I was watching television, he 'appeared' sitting in the chair within a few feet of me. He was ruddier in complexion than ever, grinning all over his face and, as the old-fashioned saying has it, positively glowing with health. I was neither alarmed nor surprised. He was just there—'large as life and twice as natural.'"

And here are the words which C. S. Lewis spoke.

"It's not so hard as you think, you know."

At first, Phillips was baffled. What a disappointment to be visited by C. S. Lewis and to have nothing more important come out of it than an enigma. *What* wasn't so hard as you think? Could it be that Lewis was speaking about death, saying that death was not hard? But why this particular message to him? He was not aware of any special fear of death. And then suddenly he saw that the words could refer to that larger death of which physical death is but a part. And since the self with all its worldly ego and ambitious drives must be relinquished when we leave our physical bodies, how much better to get on with this beforehand.

This was the key that has helped J. B. Phillips emerge from his "dark night of the soul" and regain his creativity and vitality. For this glamorous image of an infallible mentor which had been built up around Phillips was in essence ego-feeding. To destroy it was to destroy the false ego, in a real sense to kill it. C. S. Lewis's words made it easier for Phillips to begin. "It's not so hard as you think, you know," Lewis said.

I wondered suddenly if this very interview was not part of the process: Phillips seemed almost to be insisting that I take him down from any pedestal where my humanness would like to place him.

"In this encounter," Dr. Phillips said before I left, "Dr. Lewis spoke to me as one who is no longer seeing through a glass darkly, but as one who has begun to see the glories of heaven face to face. He was kindly but firmly reminding me of something I knew but had almost forgotten—that the rewards of abandoning self are worth the suffering. Paul said it long ago, 'I reckon that the sufferings of this present time are not worthy to be compared with the glory which shall be revealed in us.' I'm beginning to see that the glories can start right here on earth. It *is* a glorious thing, you know, to be yourself."

I had much to ponder on the way home. I felt that both

Lewis and Phillips had spoken once again to our generation. For who of us does not carry around an image built both of our own pride and the expectations of others?—which is very different from the living man that God made. And who of us is not afraid to shatter that image so that the person God sees shines through? Should we not, with Dr. Phillips, take encouragement from these words:

"It's not so hard as you think."

This Academy Award winning actress recounts her recent struggle with death and the part intercessory prayer played in her recovery.

The Meaning of My Narrow Escape

by DOROTHY MALONE

O NE September morning, in 1965, I awoke to find myself lying on the floor at the foot of my bed, in great pain, unable to move. Much of what happened that morning is hazy now. I was alone in the house with my two small daughters. I know I cried out to them, woke them up, told them to bring me the telephone. I called my mother, and I guess I also called the emergency clinic, because an ambulance was already there when my mother arrived.

The clinic could find nothing wrong with me and sent me home. All that day I lay in bed, the pain getting steadily worse. Finally an internist came, took one look and rushed me to Cedars of Lebanon Hospital.

It was a lucky choice for me. Only three weeks before, the hospital had acquired a new device for scanning a patient's lungs. The device told the doctors that mine were rapidly being closed off by blood clots, that immediate and drastic surgery was necessary.

Yet my good fortune was such that when a team of surgeons was hastily assembled, the man chosen to head it, Dr. Joseph Fields, had himself invented a heart-lung machine that would artificially and miraculously sustain life during the unbelievably lengthy period—11 hours—required for the delicate operation.

I remember nothing of that, of course. But almost as soon as I regained consciousness I can recall my mother telling me that dozens, then hundreds, finally thousands of people were

118

praying for my recovery. My first reaction to this was one of incredulity. I was inclined to think that my mother was saying these things just to encourage me. But when the letters and telegrams poured in, when I saw the newspaper stories that churches of all denominations were holding services for me, I had to believe it, and with belief came a great wave of relief and gratitude.

How does prayer help a person who is desperately ill? I'm sure there are many answers. A metaphysician might say that prayer is a form of love, and that love is a healing force. A devout person might say that God hears and answers—it's as simple as that. All I know is that it brings strength and peace when they're needed most.

People have asked me, "Did your narrow escape from death make you appreciate life more? Did it make you more religious? Did it bring you closer to God?" To such questions, my answer is usually a gentle "No." No, it didn't make me appreciate life more, because I've always loved life, always believed it should be lived as fully as possible. And no, not more religious, because I've always been religious, with an intensity that varies from time to time but never disappears from my life. And no, it didn't change my relationship with God; it just confirmed it.

What my illness did do, in certain areas, was strengthen and deepen convictions I already had. Let me give you just one example. One of the oldest clichés in the theatrical world is "the eternal triangle." Everyone knows what it means. But I've always felt that the most fundamental triangle-situation in human affairs is not a situation involving a man and two women, or a woman and two men. For me, the only truly eternal triangle is the relationship between one person and another person and God—with God at the apex of the triangle.

It's amazing, if you look at your relationship with another person with this in mind, how it changes things. It makes you much less critical, much more tolerant. When someone disappoints or angers you, if you can say to yourself, "I wonder how he (or she) looks to God," you'll find yourself much less likely to judge or condemn. For one thing, you realize that the other person's behavior is affected by all sorts of forces and factors known only to God. For another, you realize that if God loves you, He also loves that other person—and this in itself is a thought that tends to banish anger.

Certainly in the case of the people who were kind enough to pray for me during my illness, this "eternal triangle" was very much in evidence. And I'm convinced that the benefits flow in all directions, on all sides of the triangle, so that those who pray are helped as well as those who are prayed for.

This is not something I "learned" from my illness. It's a conviction that was deepened and strengthened by it. This concept of the eternal triangle has become an inseparable part of my life.

Prayer When Feelings Are Hurt

Kind Heavenly Father, I am a bit ashamed to tell You that I have been hurt. Perhaps I should be less sensitive, but I have been wounded by the action of another and I must admit that I am upset and unhappy by this unkindness. Help me to forget it and to rise above it and not make more of it than the facts justify. Pour Your love upon this wound of the spirit and heal it. Help me not to carry hurt any more. In Christ's name I pray. Amen.

Norman Vincent Peale

This Navy pilot is waging a courageous, uphill battle to become an astronaut—and he's doing it on two artificial legs.

No One Walks Alone

by Lt. Cmdr. Frank Ellis

THERE was no indication of any trouble when I radioed for landing instructions.

"Magu Tower, this is Navy jet 28229 over Los Angeles . . ." I said routinely into the microphone. The time was 3:43 p.m., July 11, 1962.

After a smooth eight-hour flight from Norfolk, Virginia, I was eager to get home to my wife Chris and our two children. (Our third was expected in two weeks.) With luck I would make it to our home in San Diego in time for dinner, I calculated, but it didn't quite work out that way. In fact, I missed dinner by about four months.

As I entered the traffic pattern, I felt an abnormal nose-down on the control stick. I struggled with the stick, but no matter how hard I pulled, the nose pointed down.

Instinctively, I reached over my head for the face curtain that would eject me from the plane. I'd simulated this procedure many times. There was no question but that I had to get out. Then ahead and to the right of the canopy my eyes sighted a mobile trailer park.

Fractions of a second seemed like minutes. Just a few months back at a Squadron meeting we had discussed ejection in populated areas. Now, I was faced with *that* matter-of-life-or-death decision. . . .

Cramming on full power, I raised the landing gear and tried to gain some altitude. No luck. The F9's tremendous sink rate continued, but I was able to alter its heading somewhat. The second I felt I was clear of the trailers, I jerked the face curtain and ejected.

Almost simultaneously, there was a fireball all about me. That's about all I remember of the accident. The Navy investigators later determined that I ejected at about 65 feet above the ground, traveling about 160 miles an hour. I was hurtled through a row of eucalyptus trees, which helped break my fall, and came to rest about 300 feet from the F9's impact point.

An hour after the crash, I was rolled into surgery where doctors worked on me for three hours. In addition to cuts and burns, I suffered broken ribs, a broken back, a left leg broken in several places and a right leg amputated below the knee. Because of the great loss of blood and a brief heart stoppage, my survival chances were poor.

But slowly I recovered. After a week I made it off the critical list. About this time I learned that I was missing one leg. I discovered it myself—there was too much slope to the sheet on the right side of the bed. It was a blow—but I was alive and grateful to God for that. During the second week there came a question about my left leg. The doctors thought there was a 50-50 chance of saving it, but they promised nothing.

I was transferred to San Diego, and two days later Chris entered the Coronado hospital, just across the bay, to keep an appointment in the maternity ward. Dana Angela—eight pounds, eight ounces—increased our family to five and our hospital bed count to three.

Then, things began to settle into a routine and I began to look ahead. One day a doctor asked:

"Well, Ellis, what do you plan to do now?"

"Continue where I left off. I want to become an astronaut."

He thought I was joking, but I wasn't. Before the crash, my chances looked excellent for getting into test pilot school—a step away from space flight work.

"Look, buddy," the doctor said sternly. "I want to set your thinking straight. You may never walk again."

"I'll walk," I said. "And I'll fly again." The doctor shook his head and left the room.

One day not long after that episode I was carrying on one of those talking-to-myself, talking-to-God conversations. Suddenly I was struck by this simple truth: there is a reason for everything, and God can take any mess and make something good out of it. If I did my part, I knew He would do His—He always had in the past. In that one moment, I made up my mind that I was not going to let the loss of a leg change my life or Chris' or the children's. Furthermore, I would prove to the doctors, the Navy and myself that I could still do a job— *the job* I knew best, flying.

With that resolved, I needed a plan, and I was anxious to put one into motion. The first thing I voted for was amputation of my left leg. For two months they had nursed it, but the pain, fever and weight loss I was experiencing told me it was a losing battle. The doctors agreed and on September 14 they removed the leg just below the knee.

Within a week, my condition began to improve amazingly. "When do I get fitted for a new right leg?" I pressed the doctor one day.

"You're in a hurry, aren't you?" he smiled. Soon both legs were ordered, but meanwhile several hospital corpsmen and I constructed two Rube Goldberg-looking leg devices made from rolled felt, plaster gauze, sponge rubber, a crutch tip and a strap. I expected to put them on, pick up the crutches and walk, but my muscles were so weak I could barely stand.

Soon I was allowed to go home. There, Mother and Chris played "catchers" for their new walker. The pain was excruciating, but as my body strengthened, the aching decreased. I knew if I was ever to fly again I would need to dramatize my case, prove my physical prowess. My progress diary tells the story:

November 1—Home from hospital; getting used to right artificial leg.

November 12—Drove standard shift car (tough to get small

crutch tip of left pylon on the clutch).

November 19—Back to work at Squadron office (a half day is all my back would take).

December 10—Worked a full day.

December 19—Merry Christmas. I received my left leg and discarded the makeshift pylon (walked without crutches or cane. A big day!).

January 10, 1963—Took the Navy aviators' water survival test, and passed it. (This includes underwater cockpit evacuation, life-saving and a 20-foot tower dive, parachute drag, etc. . . .)

January 26—Played touch football with the children.

March 15—Flew C-47 cross-country on ferry mission (taxiing requires different technique, but no problem).

April 16—Negotiated Frogman's underwater demolition obstacle course. Net climb, wall scaling, rope climb, etc. . . . (Legs fine, but arms—wow!)

May 11—Water-skied (no problems but my back is still weak).

May 19—Made parachute jump with San Diego Sky Divers. (On landing, twisted the right foot 45°. The unknowing spectators looked on in amazement when I sat down on the grass, straightened my foot out, got up and walked away.)

With all these physical tests, I had proved to myself that I could fly as well as ever, but convincing others was a different story. Extensive testing, evaluation, reevaluation still left the issue clouded. I was amazed that so many presuppositions existed about "handicaps." Mountains of paper work accompanied my request to be returned to unrestricted flight status.

Doctors, fellow officers, superiors all testified to my competence. My hospital doctor wrote, "Our board recommends that he be returned to full duty." My squadron flight surgeon reported, "Lt. Ellis has a handicap in words only."

Still the reports, which traveled all the way to the top, were met by one question, over and over: can a double amputee really fly as well as these reports say?

I was offered retirement with permanent disability pay. This only stirred me to make several trips to Washington, carrying my campaign to the Secretary of the Navy.

Finally, after 14 months of effort, word came from the Secretary of the Navy on September 18, 1963, that I had been returned to temporary flight status pending the aeronautical evaluation. Further testing in Pensacola, Florida, supported the ruling. I passed in every plane they put me in, but when the recommendation came in it read:

"The board recommends that Lt. Frank Ellis be returned to flight status in Service Group III (flying dual controlled aircraft only in company of a qualified co-pilot)."

I was stunned, but more determined than ever to prove myself. And so a new campaign began, one that I'm still waging. For the past two and a half years, I've been working on my master's degree in aeronautical engineering, receiving training which I will be able to use when the day comes that I can participate in our space program. And I am confident that day will come.

Meanwhile, I have strong feelings about mankind's view of handicapped people, particularly the patronizing sympathy which is often extended—and accepted. The most serious handicap is to be bound to an idea which is not necessarily true.

Since the accident, I have spoken to many civic and church groups around the country, and the response to these talks has convinced me how much handicapped people need to be encouraged in their battle for human dignity.

A note from a 13-year-old Brooklyn boy who lost both legs from electrical burns said, "You have convinced me I can do most anything I set my heart to. I bet I'll be able to walk all over the place as soon as they finish building my legs." Later, I heard that he was doing just that.

When I spoke at my home church recently, I concluded by saying: "I have been given a lot of praise and credit for what I have accomplished since the accident. It should all go to God.

He provided me with a keen sense of balance so that I can perform the normal daily ambulatory functions on a pair of artificial legs. He is the One who placed the numerous nerve endings in my remaining portions of leg so that I can tell precisely how hard I am pressing on the brake pedal of a car or the rudder pedal of an airplane. He is the One who deserves the praise. He has given us life. We can only reciprocate with faith."

It is through faith that I walk today, for this I know: whether one takes steps with limbs made of flesh or plastic like mine, nobody in the whole wide world walks alone.

Prayer of One in Pain

O God, I'm weak and weary
I do not understand.
There are some times when I can do
All things—at Your command.
And then there are these other times
And why? I cannot see
When anything that I would do
Is much too much for me.
You know the weariness that fills
This pain-wracked frame of mine.
Be merciful to me, O God,
And grant the strength that's Thine.
I know the privilege that's mine
To care for those I love.
Grant me, O God, for this one day
Thine own strength from above.

Helen Miller

Blind and alone, she had no expectation of ever seeing again in this life. Then, she met a man who asked her to believe ...

Some Day, Dorothy

by DOROTHY HARBAUGH DAVIDSON

SOME day you will see, Dorothy," Mother told me when I was a young girl. "When you get to heaven you will see."

Though Mother was a frail person, prone to much sickness, there was nothing weak about her faith. She was an eternal optimist. We always were poor, still Mother never complained. "God knows what is best for the Harbaughs," she would counsel.

I wasn't sure, then. To a young girl surrounded by continual darkness, Mother's hopes seemed a thousand miles beyond never-never land. I didn't want to see in heaven. I just wanted to see *now*.

My sight had been damaged by polio. When I entered the first grade tests showed that I had only one-tenth vision in one eye and even less in the other. Fitted with the very strongest glasses, I struggled through school until I was 11. Then it was decided that my sight was too poor to continue. This ended my formal education, but not my learning. Mother took over the teaching chores, and together we studied.

Then, at 18 I lost the only glimmer of sight I had left. I had been able to differentiate between dark and light, but at 18— a great nothingness.

By this time, I had come to depend on Mother completely. She was my constant companion. Together, we shopped, did the housework, attended church. She taught me to crochet, hook rugs and make artificial flowers. Then came a shock for which I was unprepared: Mother died. Her death followed

Dad's by three years. Now my biggest problem was loneliness. I yearned more and more for a companion and prayed that God would send me someone. I was thinking of an older woman, but God had different plans.

Four years after Mother's death I met Loyal Davidson. My cousin invited me to take a Sunday afternoon automobile ride with her and some friends; Loyal was in the group. He seemed so gay and friendly that I liked him immediately. He was quite surprised when one of the others in the car told him I was blind.

"How did you know what time it was a little while ago?" he questioned. Then I held up my Braille watch and everyone laughed.

Loyal and I saw each other again and he told me that he was a recent widower. I learned later that he had been praying for a companion too.

On January 24, 1958, we were married. It was the happiest day of my life. In Loyal I found the companionship I was seeking. I could imagine no greater happiness since I had long before resigned myself to a lifetime without sight. But Loyal said from the start, "Dorothy, some day you're going to see."

"You're right, Honey, when I get to heaven I shall see," I laughed, remembering Mother's words.

Then one day Loyal took me to the Cleveland Clinic for an examination. He felt that corneal transplants might restore my sight. The doctors reported that my optic nerves were severed. They gave us no hope. This seemed final enough for me, but Loyal persisted that I would see.

The first three years of our marriage passed quickly. Traveling was our hobby and we visited 48 states in all. Loyal was my eyes. At Niagara Falls, he described the rushing water and I felt the spray on my face; at the Grand Canyon, just his grasp for words convinced me of its vastness; and in Florida, he used "eerie and ghostly" to describe the Spanish moss, which I held in my hands.

The only joy in our lives greater than traveling was working in our church. Shortly after we were married we began attending Wednesday night services in Akron's old Calvary Temple Church. Akron is about 60 miles north of our home in Dover.

One Wednesday evening—January 17, 1962 to be exact—we attended a revival service being conducted at Akron's Cathedral of Tomorrow, a sanctuary which seats 7,500 people. That evening the Reverend Clifton Erickson's message was one of the most inspiring sermons on faith I ever have heard. I was deeply moved.

When he finished, he issued a call for people with special need to come to the platform for prayer. Loyal suggested I go forward. I agreed, more for him, I think, than myself. It was not that I doubted God's ability to heal me if He saw fit, but I questioned His desire to do it.

The prayer line seemed long, and I could feel the presence of many people in front and behind me. When it came my turn, Mr. Erickson inquired about the history of my blindness before he laid his hands on my head and prayed:

"Remove the affliction of blindness from this woman, in the name of Jesus."

Instantaneously, I saw light! A great pain shot through my head and a burning sensation stabbed at the back of my eyes. There was so much light that I tried to shield the glare with my hand. Great rejoicing was taking place all about me. Loyal wept aloud. Jesus was so close—so very close.

Though light was all I could see, none the less Loyal and I went home that night, walking on clouds.

By Saturday, three days later, I distinguished the form of a person.

Sunday I was able to tell colors of buildings.

Monday I saw the most beautiful thing ever: a full moon.

Wednesday—our fourth wedding anniversary—I made out the face of Loyal for the first time. Imagine seeing your husband for the first time after four years of marriage! (He is even more handsome than I had guessed.)

From that time on my sight has improved. I can now read and write, though I must bring the paper close to my eyes. The miracle is still a dream, but it is wonderfully real.

Why did God choose to heal me? I don't know, but I somehow feel that it is a reward for not allowing my heart to harden against Him despite years of blindness. Though there is no way to repay God for such a blessing, I feel that He wants me to share my story with others.

Now when Loyal and I travel about the country and we visit different churches, I am often called upon to speak.

Since the return of my sight, Loyal has been taking me back to the places we traveled to before. Already we have been in 20 of the 48 states visited previously. What a thrill to view the fabulous Niagara first hand; to stare across that great gorge, the Grand Canyon; and to see Spanish moss. (It's not ghostly, it's beautiful.)

But the really exciting things are just outside our back door. There I can see a blooming daffodil, a budding tree, a robin building a nest. It is difficult to explain how much these things mean.

"Yes, Dorothy, some day you will see heaven," I say to myself. And I feel that God has already given me a part of it here on earth.

This entertainer has known much pain in his lifetime, yet it has not changed his bright outlook—or has it lessened his gratefulness to God.

The Fire or the Scrap Heap?

by ARTHUR GODFREY

O N the walls of my office in New York hang a number of wise sayings I have had lettered and framed. Most of them are well-known but one is not.

It reads:

The fire, Lord, not the scrap heap.

I hung it there to remind me of a story. There was once a blacksmith who had great faith in God in spite of a lot of sickness in his life. An unbeliever asked him one day how he could go on trusting in a God who let him suffer.

"When I make a tool," the blacksmith answered, "I take a piece of iron and put it into the fire. Then I strike it on the anvil to see if it will take temper. If it does, I can make a useful article out of it. If not, I toss it on the scrap heap and sell it two pounds to the penny. Maybe God tests us like this. When suffering has come my way, I know that I've come out the better for it, so much so that I can honestly say, 'Put me in the fire, Lord, if that's what it takes, just don't throw me on the scrap heap.'"

I like this story because it suggests a creative way of looking at things that seem to be pure disaster. It tells me something about this stubborn hunk of iron and the fires through which I personally have passed.

My first fire came when I was 28 years old. I had a radio announcing job in Washington, D. C., then, and I liked to take the night shift so that during the day I could drive out to the old Congressional Airport and fly a Franklin glider.

131

I was headed there one bright September morning in 1931, driving a 1926 Chrysler on narrow Riggs Road, when suddenly a truck coming the other way crossed the center line and hit me, head-on. It happened so quickly there wasn't time to touch the brakes or turn the wheel. I remember the sound of crashing glass, the sight of a hot engine on the seat beside me and then nothing more for a full week.

The two guys in the truck came away with scratches, but when the police found me in the ditch beside the road they thought I was dead. At the hospital a team of surgeons put back the pieces: four broken ribs, a hole in one lung, two smashed knee caps, dislocated right hip, fractures of the right hip socket, left femur driven through its socket, 27 fractures in the pelvis, and other odds and ends of lesser consequence.

As I said, I was out about a week. When I came to one night I thought I was lying in my casket at my own funeral. There were flowers all over the place (sent in by radio listeners) and somewhere I could hear someone praying. Then I listened to the words and knew I was alive because the voice—a girl's —was asking God not to let me die. Later I wondered if the voice and the prayer weren't a dream, but the doctor told me that the same student nurse prayed over me every night during the time I was unconscious.

Anyway, when I became fully conscious, I discovered a cast from my collarbone to my feet. And there I stayed while the weeks stretched into months. Worse than the pain was the idleness: nothing to do all day and all night but listen to the radio beside my bed until 3 a.m. when the last West Coast stations signed off for the night.

And it was there, chained to the receiving end of the box that I'd only worked behind up till then, that I learned something which was to change my life. Something I might never have had an ear to hear if it hadn't been for that period of captive listening.

One day one of those "hello-out-there-you-in-radio-land" announcers read a commercial as if he were reciting Shake-

speare through a megaphone to a full house at Yankee Sta-
dium. "Heck, Buddy," I thought, "you don't have to shout.
It's only me."

And suddenly I wondered if it weren't always "only me."
Weren't radio announcers (me included) making a mistake
in imagining we were addressing great numbers of people?
In the aggregate, perhaps, but that was an abstraction that
had no existence in reality. Wasn't the reality always one person listening to another one: the invalid in his bed, the salesman in his automobile, the housewife at her ironing board? I
resolved that when I returned to radio I would in the future
address myself to one person alone, as if I were actually standing right next to him.

The discovery I made in a Washington hospital bed transformed my career. I left the hospital four months after the
accident, crippled, on crutches, but a tool sharpened a little
better to do the work that lay ahead.

There have been other fires in my life, of course, and in
every case it has seemed at the time that no conceivable good
could come of it. This last time the name of the fire was cancer. In 1959 a pain sent me scurrying for an X-ray which revealed the presence of a tumor, not in the solar plexus where
the pain was, but seven or eight inches above and a little to the
left of center. Tests proved malignant.

Fear has an antidote: hope—and this is what came to me
now in cards and letters from every corner of the country. "I
pray for you every day." "Keep it up, Arthur, we're all pulling
for you."

A competent, courageous surgeon removed the cancerous
lobe, and here I am as good as ever. Not exactly as good as
ever: a little better. For in the fire, subtle changes took place.

During my first 58 years I think I took the gift of life a little
lightly. Now I resolved to use my time better. I became a student again: art, music, literature, French. I've tried to do
something about my hostilities and prejudices. I try to contribute something every day to the betterment of mankind.

That reads kinda tritely stupid, but that's the general idea. It could be, y'know, that the "Man Upstairs" had a little something in mind. What if He wanted me to tell the millions who follow TV and radio that cancer is not necessarily a sentence of death? What if, through me, He wanted to put this list of cancer danger signals in your hands?

Why then, I can look back at my bout with cancer and agree with the blacksmith: the fires we pass through are not to burn us up, but just to make us worth keeping on this good earth a little longer.

SEVEN DANGER SIGNS OF

CANCER

1. Unusual bleeding or discharge.
2. A lump or thickening in the breast or elsewhere.
3. A sore that does not heal.
4. Change in bowel or bladder habits.
5. Hoarseness or cough.
6. Indigestion or difficulty in swallowing.
7. Change in a wart or mole.

As a vice president of a large southern bank, this executive had everything any man could want—until an alcohol problem cost him his job.

Could I Come Back?

by J. ARCH AVARY, JR.

THE other day a man came into my office to seek a loan. He put up quite a front, but I could see he was under terrific pressure. Soon his hands were shaking and his face was wet with perspiration.

"Let's be frank with one another, Mr. Harris," I said to the man. "You have a problem which you are trying to cover up. As an alcoholic who has been sober now for six years, I can sympathize with you and perhaps help you. But I don't think a loan is the real answer."

Then I told him briefly the story I relate here. At the age of 48 I had been an executive in another Atlanta bank, with a promising future. But I depended too much on the bottle I kept in my desk drawer. The bank finally let me go.

It wasn't long until I hit bottom. My wife filed for divorce and I couldn't blame her. Somehow I had enough sense to see my minister, who persuaded me to commit myself to Briarcliff Clinic, the Georgia state institution for alcoholics.

At Briarcliff, nothing much seemed to happen. There was almost no real work. We had little to do except attend therapy classes, where we worked with leather or learned to weave cloth. We took turns washing dishes in one-week stints, and we could rake leaves if we wished. I strongly disapproved of all the free time we had. I wanted work that would keep me from thinking.

I disliked the minister there. When I told him my problems he offered me far less sympathy than I thought I deserved, and brusquely informed me that a law court and a divorce lawyer could help me far better than he could.

But I considered a certain trained nurse in that institution to be even worse than the minister. One day when I finished my week's dishwashing chores, she called out over the public address system for me to report back to the kitchen.

There she gave me a tongue lashing before a dozen people.

"Though you once were a big banker, Arch Avary," she said, "you're just an ordinary drunk now, like everybody else in this place. I want you to get your hands back in that dishwater and really get those dishes clean!"

Meekly I obeyed.

Despite those humbling events, Briarcliff remained a pleasant place. I might have stayed there indefinitely had it not been for a conversation another inmate and I had one day while raking leaves together.

He was a professional hobo who fascinated me with tales of the years he had hopped freights between one shabby destination and another, with cheap whiskey for a traveling partner. And I knew something about trains also. I had been a director of a major southern railroad at one time.

But that day the hobo and I had plenty in common beyond a mutual love of railroad lore. We wore identical khaki work clothes and each of us clutched a leaf rake. I was telling him something of my past as a leader in Atlanta's largest Methodist church. I related how I had served for years as a steward, taught a Sunday school class and helped our church drive.

Then he asked me a blunt question. "I don't know much about religion, but tell me, what kind of religion made you wind up in a place like this?"

I was tormented by that question for days. It tried to blame my failure on the society I lived in; on the hypocrisy of our time, hypocrisy that permeated everything. "My church let me down," I said to myself in the mirror, but the image that it returned couldn't buy that lie. No, it was my selfish philosophy which felled the house of cards. I'd worn my religion like all the other ornaments of a well-ordered life—the right country clubs, stylish friends, even my banker's gray suits. My "religion" had been a sham, too frail to bear the weight of my weaknesses.

And so at last I faced myself honestly. I had turned from God and not the other way around. It was to blame—and no one else.

I went for a walk. Under an aged elm, I sat down and reopened negotiations with God.

"I'm afraid I've overdrawn on my account, God," I began. "I'm about as poor a credit risk as You've ever had, but from what I've heard about You in the past I know You are always open for business. Well, I need a manager to help me run my life since I'm obviously in no condition to make a comeback by myself. Maybe it's too late but if You'll help me I'll try."

When I was finished, I walked back to the house and made arrangements to leave Briarcliff. I knew what I had to do.

For the next six months I stayed with my aging parents. At this point, with no money, few friends and my wife divorcing me, I clung to this new closeness to God. For these months I went nowhere except to the church next door and for long walks. Silence surrounded me, except for occasional train whistles which reminded me of my old hobo friend and his penetrating question.

Off in the woods I would go with two companions: a Bible and my old barlow knife. I would read for a while, then I would whittle. Yes, whittle. It was the perfect rhythm by which to meditate upon God's word. I would pick up a dirty old stick and whittle off the bark until I was down to clean white wood. It reminded me of my condition. Slowly that black outer bark of my life fell away.

During those months I felt no desire to drink, but I suffered a constant, terrible case of jitters. Then one day a Bible verse spoke to me: "Be still and know that I am God." Over and over I repeated it. Gradually my nervousness ceased and left me forever.

Still I had absolutely no self-confidence. I longed to re-establish myself, professionally and as a man, but I lacked courage to begin. One day another verse exploded in my consciousness: "If God be for you, who can be against you?"

I promised God I would live my life for others if He would give me another chance in His vineyard. Then things began to happen.

My wife returned to help me. Next, I got a job with a Miami Beach bank. I stayed sober. Step by step I advanced up the ladder again, climaxed by the big day when an offer came from an Atlanta bank, which I now serve as executive vice-president.

So I have a story to tell to men like Mr. Harris—that no problem is too difficult to solve, no obstacle too great to overcome—with God's help.

EDITOR'S NOTE: There is a P.S. to this story, which is as impressive as Mr. Avary's remarkable comeback. In 1963 he underwent a cancer operation which necessitated a colostomy. Here was a great test of his new faith. Mr. Avary fought his way back from this operation and today, in addition to his career, finds time to speak far and wide on the subject of early cancer detection—evidence that Arch Avary is keeping his promise to serve God in His vineyard.

This Florida housewife cannot explain what happened to her. All she knows is that this incredible spiritual revelation made her a new person.

Three Months in His Presence

by VIRGINIA LIVELY

WHEN friends ask how I first discovered that my hands have been given a ministry of healing, I'm sure they don't expect to hear the kind of story which I am about to set down. Apparently the fact that I am a suburban housewife who saves grocery stamps and has to watch here weight seems a poor beginning to a story of divine intervention.

It started the year my father entered the tuberculosis sanitarium in Tampa. We had long since given up hope. He was too old for an operation and we had seen the X-rays. The last thing on earth that would have occurred to any of us— Mother or my sister or me—was to ask God to step in and change medical facts.

And yet my husband Ed and I were active church members. As a banker, Ed was head of fund-raising, our two children went to Sunday school and I belonged to all the groups. We were, in short, typical, civic-minded churchgoers. That is why the tears, when they began, caused Ed and me so much embarrassment.

It was in October, driving home from a PTA meeting, that I suddenly began to cry. I was in charge of the Halloween Carnival that year, and at the meeting there'd been some criticism of the plans. When I was still crying at bedtime, Ed put his arms around me and said:

"Honey, all the carnivals in the world aren't that important."

But it wasn't the carnival. Even as I cried I knew that these tears were for something far bigger. I cried myself to sleep and in the morning as soon as I opened my eyes the tears started again. I choked them back while I fixed breakfast. But as soon as Ed and the children left, the tears burst out again.

This incredible state of affairs lasted four days. I took to wearing dark glasses even in the house so that the family would not guess how constantly I was crying. I was sure I was having a nervous breakdown.

It was on the morning of the fourth day, after Ed and the children had left, that a curious change took place. I saw nothing. I heard nothing. Yet, all at once there was power in the air around me. The atmosphere itself seemed to hum and crackle as though I stood in the center of a vast electric storm. As I try to put it into words it sounds fantastic, but at the time there was no sense that something beyond the possible was taking place.

I had sunk into the high-backed chair in the living room when suddenly through the window I saw the eastern horizon. Trees and houses stood between me and it, but I seemed to see right beyond to the place where earth and sky came together. And there, where they met, was a ball of light.

This light was moving, traveling toward me with incredible speed. It appeared white, yet from it poured all the colors I had ever seen.

And then it was beside me. Although it seemed impossible that anything with such energy could hold still, it took a position at my right shoulder and there it stayed. And as I stared, I started to smile. I smiled because He was smiling at me. For I now saw that it was not light, but a face.

How can I put into words the most beautiful countenance I have ever seen? "He is perfect" was the first thought that came. His forehead was high, His eyes exceptionally large. But I could never fix the color of His eyes any more than I could the color of the sea.

More, much more, than individual features was the overwhelming impression of life—unhampered life, life so brimming over with power and freedom that all living things I had seen till that moment seemed lumps of clay by comparison.

Not for a moment did I hesitate to call this Life at my side "Jesus." And two things about Him struck me most. The first was His humor. I was astonished to see Him often break into outright laughter. And the second was His utter lack of condemnation. That He knew me down to my very marrow—knew all the stupid, cruel, silly things I had ever done—I realized at once. But I also saw that none of these things, or anything I would ever do, could alter the absolute caring, the unconditional love, that I saw in those eyes.

I could not grasp it. It was too immense a fact. I felt that if I gazed at Him for a thousand years I could not realize it all.

I did not have a thousand years; I had three months. For as long as that, the face of Jesus stayed before me, never fading, never withdrawing. Many times I tried to tell someone else what I saw but the words would never come. And meanwhile I carried on with my tasks—meals and shopping and the PTA with its carnival—but effortlessly, scarcely knowing I was doing them, so fixed were my thoughts on Him.

At the same time, I had never seemed so aware of other people. My husband, especially. How this was possible when my mind was full of Him alone I don't know, but it was true. Far from feeling that a third person had entered our marriage, I felt that Christ *was* the marriage, as though all along He had been the force drawing us together.

And the Bible! All at once I couldn't read enough of it. It was like tearing open a letter from someone who had known this Presence as a flesh and blood person, full of just the kind of specific details I longed to hear. Certain passages in particular had a strange effect on me: when the Bible described Jesus' healing someone, the actual print on the page seemed to burn. The hand that touched it would tingle as if I had touched an electric current.

And then one afternoon before the children got home, I was sitting, just looking at Him, when all of a sudden in a patch of sunlight on the wall appeared the X-ray of my father's chest. It was all scar tissue and cavities. Then as I watched, a white mist moved slowly up the wall. When it passed the diseased tissue, there appeared on my wall a picture of a healthy lung.

"Then Dad's well!" I said aloud, and at that the Person at my side burst into peal after peal of joyous laughter which said that wholeness was always God's way.

I thought my heart would burst as I waited for next Wednesday's X-ray. I enjoyed the scene in my mind again and again, imagining the ring of the telephone and Mother's voice stammering with excitement, "Darling . . . the most amazing . . . the most glorious . . . ."

But when Mother called, her voice was flat. "The most annoying thing, Virginia. They got the slides mixed up! Poor Dad's got to go back for X-rays tomorrow. Why, they sent down pictures of someone who never even had TB . . . !"

But, of course, the X-rays next day showed no sign of disease either; Dad was healed and lived out his long life in thanksgiving to God.

And it was Dad's healing that convinced me I must try to describe the indescribable that had happened to me. I went to an elderly pastor whom I had known a long time. To my astonishment he understood me at once. He gave me some books which described fairly similar things.

Then he said the words I have wished unsaid so many times.

"Don't be surprised, Virginia, if the vision fades after a time. They usually do, you know."

"Fade!" I thought, as I drove home with that joyous Presence beside me. Oh, it can't, it mustn't! For the first time in the whole incredible experience my attention veered from Him to myself. And in that instant the vision was diminished, actually disappeared for a second or two, though right away the radiant face was beside me again.

But the damage was done. The seed of self-concern was sown. The bright Presence would sometimes be missing for an hour or more. The more worried I got, the more self-centered

I grew. What have I done? What will I do without Him? When He did return there would be no accusation in His eyes, just a tremendous compassion as though He realized how difficult it had become for me to see Him at all.

At last all that was left of this experience was the strange tingling in my hands as I read the Bible stories of healing. One day I was visiting a friend in the hospital. She was hemorrhaging and in pain. On an impulse I reached out and touched her. My hand began to burn just as it did during the Bible reading. My friend gave a little sigh of comfort and fell asleep. When the doctor examined her, he found no hemorrhaging.

Over the next eight years there were dozens, scores of experiences of this kind, all as inexplicable as the first. And yet for me they were still years of emptiness and waiting. "I will always be with you," He had told me when I last saw Him.

"But how will I know if I can't see you?" I called to Him, for He had seemed so far away.

"You will see Me," He said, and then He was gone.

But the years went by and the vision had not come back. And then one day, while speaking to a church group, I saw those love-lit eyes smiling once again into mine. I looked again. The eyes belonged to a lady in the second row. Suddenly the room was full of Him; He was in the eyes of everyone in the room. "You will see Me. . . ."

I used to wonder what would have happened if the old pastor had never spoken of the vision fading. Might I have had it forever? I think not. I think that the days when Jesus was real to my eyes were the days of the "childhood" of my faith, the joyous, effortless time of discovery. But I do not think He lets it stay that way for long.

He didn't for His first disciples, He doesn't for us today. He gives us a glimpse only. Perhaps He let me look so long because I am slow to learn. But, finally, He takes away all sensory clues. He is bigger than our eyes and ears can make Him, so He gives us instead the eyes of faith, and all mankind in which to discover His face.

An automobile accident left filmdom's "man of a thousand voices" near death. "The chief thing that saved me was prayer—other people's prayer," he says.

The Most Important Voice of All

by MEL BLANC

IN Hollywood, they tell me, I'm known as "the man of a thousand voices." Like most Hollywood labels, this is an exaggeration, but where voices are concerned I do have quite a few. When you hear Barney Rubble's gravelly tones in *The Flintstones* on television, that's me. Such cartoon characters as Bugs Bunny, Daffy Duck, Woody Woodpecker, Porky Pig, Sylvester Cat and Tweety are all close friends of mine for the very good reason that they have to borrow my vocal chords before they can say anything. It's one of those slightly zany jobs that are good fun, pay well and bring other people innocent pleasure, and I wouldn't change it for the world.

But a few years back the man of a thousand voices found himself listening to one small voice that he had never paid much attention to before. The voice was inside him. I believe this same small voice is inside every one of us, but we're too busy or preoccupied or self-satisfied to listen. Sometimes it takes a terrific jolt, and the silence that follows that kind of jolt, before the voice can make itself heard.

In my case, the jolt was nearly fatal. One night as I was hugging a curve in my little sports car, an automobile coming the other way went out of control. There was a head-on collision at a combined speed of about 90 miles per hour. When they pried what was left of me out of the wreckage and rushed me to the hospital, they found that the only bone in my body that *wasn't* broken was my left arm.

When I finally came out of the fog of anesthesia, back to a

144

world of pain, the first thing I saw was Jack Benny sitting by my bed, looking miserable. I had worked with Jack for years; we were close friends. I summoned all my strength and whispered, "I'm going to make it, Jack." He said, "You'll have to make it, because I can't do my show without you." I was too weak even to try to reply, but he saw the glitter of tears in my eyes, and knew that I understood.

In the weeks that followed, I think I survived chiefly on the power of prayer—other people's prayers. I had never realized how much goodwill my cartoon characters had built up for me. Hundreds of letters came from all over the world with prayers for my recovery. They came from Catholics, Protestants, Jews—even from Buddhists and Mohammedans. Children sent cards and coins and their favorite toys. It was like being supported and sustained by a great flood tide of affection, of concern, of love. I'm convinced that it helped my shattered body begin to slowly heal itself. I also think it enveloped me in a kind of serenity that made it possible for me to hear a small, quiet, inner voice.

This voice did not speak to me in words; it was more like a sudden awareness of truths that had been around me all the time, truths that I had been too impatient and too self-centered to see. For example, I had always taken my talent for voice characterizations pretty much for granted. After all, I had been using it for fun ever since grammar school, and professionally since 1938 when I signed a contract with Warner Brothers to do multiple voices on "Bugs Bunny" cartoons. But now I began to realize that talent is a gift, a gift that can be withdrawn at any time, an unmerited gift that can be repaid only by a sense of constant, humble gratitude to the Giver.

Another awareness was of a quiet but mighty undercurrent of justice that runs through human affairs. I began to see that the universe really is an echo chamber, where sooner or later the thoughts you have and the deeds you do are reflected back to you.

For example, some years before my accident, a friend of

mine named Harry Lange had a heart attack while playing the part of Pancho in "The Cisco Kid." I offered to fill in for him for quite a long time—26 weeks, I think it was—and so during this period the studio was able to keep on sending his pay check to his wife.

Now, suddenly, the tables were turned; I was the one who was incapacitated. But like an echo, out of the past came an offer from Shep Menkin, a talented friend of mine, "Let me do your voices while you're laid up; I'll make sure that your family gets the money."

As it turned out, I didn't have to take Shep up on his offer. For a whole year I remained immobilized in a full cast, but thanks to the devotion of my family, and the ingenuity of my wife who turned our home into a combined sanitarium and recording studio, I was able to make the sound tracks that kept 125 people at Warner's working full-time.

I learned, too, during the long, slow period of recovery that pain is a solvent for all sorts of negative things. Antagonisms, for example.

There was one associate of mine whom I'd never liked. I thought him arrogant and conceited, and I'm afraid I showed my dislike rather plainly. But when I met him again during my convalescence, my inner voice whispered to me that the main thing wrong with this man was that he was reacting to the hostility in me. So I told him frankly that I had misjudged him, that I was sorry, and that I hoped we could be friends. His first reaction was one of amazement. His next reaction was one of warmth and self-accusation. Thus I learned that it is really quite easy to turn an enemy into a friend.

But the most valuable single thing that my inner voice taught me was the importance of expressing affection. I don't think that before my accident I was any more remiss than most people in this regard. But lying there in my cast, I recalled how my efforts in the past to tell people that I was grateful for their friendship, or to thank them for caring about me, seemed hopelessly inadequate.

And so I began to make a deliberate effort to set this right. To Jack Benny I said, "I want you to know how much I admire and appreciate and love you. I want you to know how much your friendship means to me. I'm grateful that my life has been spared so that I can tell you these things."

I expressed such feelings to other people too. Maybe they were a little startled, or even momentarily embarrassed. But every time, I'd feel a surge of warmth and closeness that strengthened the bond between us.

Today I walk with a cane, but that's a minor matter to a man who has spent a year in a cast. I go on participating, invisibly, in a lot of activity designed to bring joy and happiness to youngsters and young-oldsters. Sometimes I'm the chirp of the pet dinosaur in the "Flintstone Family," sometimes I'm the hiccough of a Disney cat. But believe me, I'm a happy hiccough and a cheerful chirp, because I've discovered that the more you express affection, the more you have to express, and the more comes back to you.

You don't have to wait until you're at death's door to learn this, you know. Anyone can be a man or a woman of a thousand voices too. Because there are at least a thousand ways to say, "I love you" . . . and all of them are good.

A Prayer For One Who Is Ill

Lord, Thou hast suffered, Thou dost know
The thrust of pain, the piercing dart,
How wearily the wind can blow
Upon the tired heart.

He whom Thou lovest, Lord, is ill.
O come, Thou mighty Vanquisher
Of wind and wave, say, Peace, be still,
Eternal Comforter.

Amy Carmichael

The doctors gave the little girl practically no hope.
Yet, the Sisters had a faith stronger than reason.

An Angel Named Maria

by ELIZABETH SHERRILL

"THERE was a baby born here two weeks ago that no one knows what to do with," the doctor said into the telephone.

He went on to explain that the infant was a vegetable: a hydrocephalic without sight or hearing or any human potential. The mother had disappeared from the hospital after seeing it and the state had no provision for handicapped children under the age of six.

"It will never live that long," the doctor's voice continued hastily. "At the outside it might live six months. Meanwhile there is the problem of care. . . ."

"Bring us the baby," answered the voice at the other end of the line. It belonged to Sister Marie Patrice, the nun in charge of the day-nursery which the Sisters of Mercy ran for working mothers in the Charlotte, North Carolina, area.

Sister Patrice was at the cottage door when a car pulled into the driveway that afternoon. The doctor carried a bundle in, then pulled aside the hospital blanket for the nun to see. For a moment she could make no sense of the two shapes before her. Then she realized that one was an enormous head; the other, where a back should have been, a tumor the size of the head. Stumps hung where there should have been legs and feet: only the little arms and hands were properly formed.

Sister Patrice stretched out her arms. "Give her to us," she said.

And so another baby joined the nursery—a baby for whom nobody called when day was over. A "vegetable" was the last thing she made the Sisters think of, for she cried constantly as though in pain. Whenever they picked her up, however, the crying stopped. So the Sisters began carrying her about with them while they looked after the other babies and while they ate and went to chapel and even while they slept.

Six months came and went. The baby they had baptized "Maria" grew so heavy that the nuns had to pass her more often from one pair of arms to another. But she would not startle at a noise, nor blink when a hand was passed before her eyes. Never once in all those months had she given a hint of awareness.

And then one day as Sister Patrice rocked her in the nursery playroom, the unbelievable happened.

"She smiled!" the Sister cried. "Maria smiled at me!"

Sister Patrice was the only one that day to see the smile. But a few days later another nun saw it, and then another, until the whole convent glowed with Maria's smile.

After that, the weeks and months sped by as the Sisters discovered first one talent, then another, in the baby that had no potential. They plunked the nursery piano and discovered that Maria had hearing. They placed her hands on the light switch just inside the cottage door and discovered that she had the muscle control to turn it on and off herself.

She was playing this favorite game one winter afternoon when she was almost two, making the room bright and then dark again while one of the Sisters held her up to the switch, when suddenly she turned to stare at the bulb burning in the ceiling. Her lips parted.

"Light!" said Maria.

As a first word it could not have been better chosen. For it seemed to the Sisters that with it came light from God about this child, that the next step to be taken in faith was removal of the tumor that dwarfed the little body on which it grew.

The surgeon they consulted was dubious. Without the tumor, he reasoned, all the excess fluid might settle in the head, distending it still further and hastening the inevitable death.

But the Sisters had glimpsed the hope that is stronger than

reason. The tumor was removed and the very reverse of the doctor's fear occurred. Instead of gaining fluid, the head began to drain. Over a period of two years it shrank nine inches until, as Maria herself grew, it looked very nearly normal. They were wonderful years. The Sisters bought a tiny wheelchair that Maria herself could roll with her strong arms and hands. They made a swing for her and a play table and a special seat in the chapel.

Most important, to Maria, they bought her shoes. As other children dream of being ballerinas, Maria dreamed of wearing shoes. She would never walk, but the Sisters understood that shoes are for more than mere transportation. And so they took her back to the surgeon, and he shaped a place on the unformed legs for shoes to go.

But meanwhile great changes had come to the little cottage on the convent grounds. As word got around that the Sisters were sheltering a defective child, another such infant was brought to them. Then another, and another. These children took more time than normal babies. Some, like Maria, had to be held constantly. Others went into spasms when touched. Some had to be tube fed, some needed oxygen.

The Sisters worked around the clock and still the babies kept coming, from all over the state and far beyond: the mongoloid, the microcephalic, the palsied. And to the Sisters, God's light had grown blindingly clear. There were other nurseries around Charlotte for normal children. For these injured ones, there was nowhere else.

I went to visit Holy Angels Nursery wondering how a home that held only deformed babies would affect me. A curly-haired little girl met me at the door, the ruffles of her starched blue dress concealing the arms of a wheelchair. "I'm very pleased to meet you," she said politely, "do you like my shoes?"

Of course it was Maria. Her shoes were white, with little bells on them and lace around the top, and I told her truthfully that they were gorgeous. Maria and Sister Patrice led me through the sunny new home built with gifts from Protestants, Jews and Catholics all over the country. And as we walked from room to room, misgiving gave way to a feeling I could not name. Baby blue cribs with new toys in them lined walls hung with Mother Goose scenes. Every baby girl wore a pretty dress, every boy a crisp romper, no two alike. Volunteers from a nearby girls' school crooned to babies in rocking chairs around the room. It was like stepping into the private nursery of a treasured only child—multiplied by dozens.

I believe they were each an only child to Sister Patrice as she recounted the life and death struggle waged over each crib. "We were so worried about Johnny last week, but penicillin is helping." "I did 80 miles an hour getting Ellen to the hospital Thursday. The police gave me two motorcycles, and the convulsion was halted in time." "The doctors don't give George another month. But—" squeezing the tiny hand, "we're going to fool them, aren't we, George?"

On we went, crib after crib—67 of them—and in each one, Sister's favorite child. I saw Jewish babies, Protestants, Catholics, Negroes and whites, children of architects and mill hands, doctors and migrant workers. The only thing I didn't see was a secondhand toy or a threadbare blanket. "Most of them can't see, you know," said the Sister. "That's why it's up to us to be sure they have only pretty things."

We reached the last room and I realized what it was I had been feeling. In each crib Sister Patrice had made me see a person, an individual unique in all creation, a human soul of infinite worth. When I told her so she beamed.

"Oh, yes!" she said. "And do you know what the greatest moment of all is? When this person leaps free at last from his poor, hurt body!"

She had been at the cribside each time a baby died, she said. "God tells me when He is taking one of them. And then this little person stands suddenly free, whole and straight, more beautiful than you dreamed. It's only an instant, you know, for these babies fly straight to the heart of God."

I stared at the Sister, at the bottles of blood plasma behind her, the oxygen tents, the rows of drugs. I hardly knew how to phrase the question that was in my mind.

"Why struggle then to keep them here as long as we can?" she asked for me. She ran her hand through the gold-brown curls that make a halo of Maria's head.

"God has all the bright angels of heaven for His joy," she said gently. "We struggling servants of His here below—we need angels too."

When Your Well Runs Dry

Pain and suffering leave deep scars on our minds and bodies, yet there are methods to renew our strength, says Dr. Theodore P. Ferris, distinguished minister.

● You have nursed someone through a serious illness: husband, son, close friend. They recover; the strain is over. But you find yourself in a terrible slump.

● You have done your best to help someone who means a great deal to you. Your efforts, however, are misunderstood and disharmony results. You are exhausted.

● You have worked hard meeting a series of business crises. With the worst over and things going all right again, you suddenly feel terribly depressed.

Or perhaps the reason for your slump is not so obvious. It can be hidden in the secret mysteries of the body's chemistry or in the delicate adjustment of the nervous system. It can come from wrong-doing. But when it happens—as it does to all of us—the fact is that our well has gone dry. The power has drained from our life. In such a state we are vulnerable to illness, temptation, discouragement—in fact, all the evils that befall us.

Tiredness may be traced to a physical ailment so a doctor's examination is the first logical step. But in 90 per cent of such cases your physician will not find anything organically wrong. He may not describe it this way, but what you have is *malnutrition of the spirit*.

How do you replenish the water of life? How is the spirit fed? The following Spiritual Workshop is based on the writings of Dr. Theodore P. Ferris, Rector of Trinity Church, Boston.

Step 1—Admit Your Helplessness

Accept the fact that your fatigue, depression, slump is a normal occurrence. We all go through it at various intervals. So sit down in a comfortable chair and admit your inability at this point to run your own life efficiently. At this low ebb you can't do things well, so don't put large demands on yourself. If you can't pray, don't try to. If you can't believe, don't try to. If you can't perform as well as you would like to, don't expect top performance of yourself.

John Keats, a poet and a wise man, used to call this process "diligent indolence—the power of passive existence." For the very yielding process begins to change the chemical imbalance inside you. At this point the well will begin to fill very slowly from the bottom, the way a wound heals from the bottom.

Step 2—Resume Your Normal Routine

Meanwhile, of course, the routines of life go on. The next meal must be prepared, an assignment done, an errand performed, a deadline met. So you get up and do what you have to do even though you still feel physically and emotionally spent.

Keats had his own method for resuming work. "Whenever I feel *vaporish* (the word our grandfathers used for this condition), I rouse myself, wash, put on a clean shirt, brush my hair and clothes, tie my shoestrings neatly—all as though I were going out—then all clean and comfortable I sit down to write."

It is a proven fact of life that the way you feel does not necessarily determine what you can do. At the time of very bad health and a great emotional upset in his life, Beethoven, who was deaf, wrote some of his greatest music. Robert Louis Stevenson had severe hemorrhaging spells and chronic lung trouble while he was writing his greatest works.

You will find that you can do what you have to do; and sometimes when you feel least like doing it, you will do it better than you realize.

Step 3—Seek Out Another

After years of experience, Dr. Ferris became aware that numerous people were coming to him simply because they were at low ebb. They would open the conversation something like this, "Normally I can handle things like this myself, but I have come to the point where I need to talk to somebody." Pastor Ferris learned to listen with receptive warmth and not try to play God. A prayer together, the recommendation of a Scripture passage to read, possibly a book suggestion—nothing too detailed. Yet he learned that while a person may go away with only a cup of water, it often was all that was needed to prime the pump.

A visit with a courageous shut-in or a trip through a hospital ward often will work a quick therapy. Bringing comfort to someone in worse straits than you can bring on a surge of gratitude and begin the inner filling-up process.

Sometimes you can get help from a person you meet between the covers of a book. Dr. Ferris recalls a time when his well was dry. He got up in the middle of the night and began to read Dietrich Bonhoeffer's *Letters From Prison.* He read on and on into the early morning. "If this man can show this kind of strength, under such conditions," he thought to himself, "I can certainly do any of the things I have to do under circumstances that are so much easier." Suddenly Dr. Ferris realized his well was beginning to fill because he was in the company of one whose well was not dry.

Step 4—Find Water for the Soul

There are times, of course, when you need more than just a person. Perhaps people depress you. So you go away for some rest, but the deadness is still there. This kind of weariness lies not in the mind or body, but in the soul. When the soul is sick, the body and mind soon register the defect.

To restore the soul, you must have new heart for life. And the secret of a fresh interest in life does not lie on the surface.

It lies in the recovery of God's purpose for you. *He restoreth my soul.* * This is the Spring that never fails.

Ernest Mehl, Sports Editor of the Kansas City Star, described vividly his method of handling malnutrition of the spirit. "I seek out the Person of Jesus Christ. I read everything I can find about Him. I pour over the Gospels. I seek Him through the communion table. In every possible way I get as close to Him as I can until I feel His Spirit flowing through me."

The sacraments of the church will replenish the spirit. The act of confession, taking communion bread, prayer, the singing of hymns—all can help you make connection with the extraordinary vitality of Christ. And if you continue to reach out for spiritual nourishment you will some day come to know what Jesus meant when He said, *Whoever drinks of the water that I shall give him will never thirst; the water that I shall give him will become in him a spring of water welling up to eternal life.* * *

Suggested Prayer

When our energies recede and our vitality is inadequate to meet the needs of the day, help us, O Lord, to learn to sit still, to do nothing; and then to give us the will to rise up to do the things we have to do, and go to those who can fill our empty wells, even unto Christ whose well is never empty. Amen.

* Psalm 23:3
* * John 4:14, RSV

LORD,
GIVE ME CONCERN
FOR OTHERS

LORD, give me concern for others" is a prayer each of us should pray every day of our lives. Unfortunately, too many of us—wrapped up in our own anxieties and desires—stop with the first three words, "Lord, give me. . . ."

Though it is human to want for ourselves and to prayerfully express those longings, such "me" oriented petitions are indicative of spiritual immaturity. True, Christ said, "Love your neighbor as yourself," but notice who comes first in the clause.

One of the most beautiful examples of this principle comes in Christ's prayer on the cross. In self agony His thoughts still were turned to others, "Father, forgive them for they know not what they do." Every time we can say, "Father, forgive him. . . Father, forgive her. . . ." we glorify God and take a giant step forward in our personal spiritual growth.

The stories in this chapter have been especially selected to demonstrate the power unleashed by intercessory prayer. Study them and consider trying the experiment recommended in the Spiritual Workshop at the close of this section.

4

Two questions raced through Father's mind: could the horses survive the frightful cold and would the ice hold?

Papa and the Bank Robber

by Louise DeGroot

I WONDER sometimes if we really know what it means to be a good neighbor today. Every time I get irritated at what a family does down the street, I scold myself and think back through the years to that incredible experience when my father risked his life to save a neighbor—who was a thief.

We then lived in Red Wing, Minnesota, and my father was a lawyer. I recall so vividly his iron-gray hair, deep blue eyes, wide square shoulders—and the way he always kissed me when saying hello or good-bye. He was strong, loved people and his favorite saying was, "A man's most priceless possession is his good reputation." He fought for this principle in court many times—often for no fee.

Across the street from us lived the Edwardses in a house somewhat nicer than ours. They had three children, as our parents did, and Mrs. Edwards dressed them beautifully.

Mr. Edwards traveled a lot and worked hard and people said the family lived beyond its means, something that was frowned on in those days. But our parents, who neither gossiped nor permitted us to listen to gossip, called the Edwardses "nice people who do the best they can."

Then late one winter day the unbelievable happened.

Papa was looking out the window of his law office at the snow and ice that had blanketed the town. Then, down the street, he saw Mr. Edwards suddenly dart from the bank and break into a run. Papa, curious, closed his office and joined the crowd that had begun milling around the bank.

160

Don Edwards had robbed the bank. Armed and desperate, he'd escaped with thousands of dollars before anyone could stop him.

The crowd began to mutter. Edwards had stolen the town's money. Bank deposits were not insured then, and for many the robbery could spell ruin if the bank failed.

But Papa wasn't concerned about the stolen money. His heart reached out instead to Don Edwards, who in one foolish moment was ruining his life. Sick to his soul, Papa walked as fast as he could the snowy mile to our kitchen door.

Mama couldn't believe the news about Mr. Edwards—nor could she believe what Papa proposed to do next. "Go after him?" she gasped. "Philamon Ballou Green, you'll do no such thing. The man has lost his reason and he has a gun. Besides, you'll never find him."

Papa's voice sounded calm and natural, but his blue eyes glowed when he turned to Mama. "Poor Edwards has made a terrible mistake," he said. "I must try to help him."

Then he patted Mama, kissed me and went to the barn to hitch up the sleigh. With a crack of the whip he was off.

It was quite obvious to Papa that Edwards had fled by horsedrawn sleigh in but one direction—across the frozen river. You'd have to see the great Mississippi River locked in its northern cold to imagine what Papa faced. As he started out across the ice floor, cruel, cutting winds whipped at Papa and the horses. For just an instant, Papa must have asked himself, "Why am I doing this?"

As the sleigh cut across the ice, however, he needed all his strength and determination. For he wasn't sure that strong ice covered *all* the river's width. And what about the tiny islands, with their growth of stubby trees and bushes? Frozen roots might trip a horse, and stiff branches could impale a man. Even barring encounters with obstacles, or a plunge into icy waters, how long could the horses survive the frightful cold?

As he did all his life, Papa put aside his fears and trusted in his God.

"Only three miles," Papa repeated half to himself, half to God. "Only three miles across the river, Lord, or maybe four. Protect the horses, Lord, and lead us to Don Edwards."

Directly across the broad part of the river was a small town. There was a hotel there. Papa reasoned that Edwards would head for the hotel that night, then resume his flight later.

Papa reasoned right, but Don Edwards never reached the town. After what must have seemed like hours, Papa's horses suddenly stopped in their tracks. The light of the moon shone on the figure of a man directly ahead. He was standing upright near the river bank, exhausted, unable to climb over the brink. His sleigh was nowhere to be seen.

Papa never told me what happened at this point, but from a fact here and a word there it isn't hard to figure it out. My father drove up to Edwards and looked into the face of a man in wild despair. "We're going home, Edwards," he said quietly.

"No, no," the nearly frozen man mumbled. He fumbled for his gun with desperate, pawing hands.

Papa took him firmly by the arm and propelled him into the sleigh. Then my father swung himself in beside Edwards, cracked the whip and headed the horses home.

While the horses stumbled onward, feeling their own way, Papa threw an arm around the fugitive who was huddled beside him, now trembling with terror and cold. Perhaps it was Papa's body heat, perhaps the ardor of his continuous spoken prayers, which revived and calmed Edwards. Miraculously, men and horses arrived home safely.

Our town greeted news of Papa's journey with wildest adulation.

But Papa wasn't interested in playing the hero role. He was concerned only about the human beings involved: Edwards, his wife and three children. First, the stolen money was returned. Then Edwards faced court action and was sentenced to a two-year jail term.

When his neighbor had served his time, Papa helped him get a job so that he could pay off his debts. The family stayed together and eventually regained a respected place in the community. No one ever dared look down on Edwards—at least not with Papa around. And I'm sure Edwards would have given his life for my father, he was so grateful.

As a lawyer, Papa saw much of the seamy side of life. But up to the day of his death in 1941, he never stopped looking for God in every single person he met.

You Prayed for Me

You did not know my need,
Or that my heart was sore, indeed.
And that I had a fear I could not quell
And so you prayed for me.
And as your prayer did soar
God did, in love, on me a blessing pour
They day you prayed for me,
              Rosina Stallman
              Garwood, Texas

It was an all-out battle between Claire and Meg. Both were unyielding. Then, a third party was brought into the clash.

Discord in the Choir Loft

by Evelyn G. Carter

I WAS drawn into the bizarre battle of the choir robes against my will. In a sense I should not be telling about it, for it is an intimate look at an inter-church squabble which, on the surface, seems silly and trivial. Yet these splits are common and hurt God's work. Also, the lessons we learned in this case are very much worth sharing.

Claire is the organist and choir director of the Presbyterian church in a fast growing Texas community where I teach school. A Juilliard graduate, Claire had been music director of a church in Philadelphia. But when her father's health failed, Claire resigned and came to Texas to be with him.

Claire's friends were sharps and flats. Every free minute she was at the church, practicing her organ, running through an anthem, rehearsing a soloist. Over the years she built up an excellent choir, and with it the respect of our thriving church. She even had a budget of her own. Part of the money was for her salary, but as chairman of the Choir Guild I knew that Claire seldom took her salary home. She spent it on her music. Musical excellence was the one thing she cared for and she got it at any cost.

And it was this characteristic that caused all the trouble.

As soon as Meg joined the choir I knew that one day there would be a clash between her and Claire. Meg was the new owner of the local grain-and-feed store. She was proportioned like one of her own sacks of grain and was called "Big Meg." I'll never forget the Saturday she appeared to audition for the choir. Out of the mouth of that enormous lady came a soprano such as we had never heard. Timbre and range and expression all belonged to Big Meg as a gift from God. We were surprised and we were delighted.

But then it came time for Meg to try on a choir robe. Claire got out her largest robes and held them up. None of them fit.

"Thank the Lord, honey," said Meg in a loud voice. "I wouldn't want to wear them anyhow. They stink!"

Claire looked stricken, mumbled something and turned our attention to the anthem, but we all knew the subject had not been dropped. If Big Meg had been with us for years she could not have chosen a more fiery subject because Claire would never spend any money on those choir robes. Vestments weren't "music" and Claire was interested in sound, not in sight. The long black robes had become soiled and threadbare. And they did have a certain perfume. Over the years we had tried every way we knew, short of actually firing Claire, to get them cleaned and repaired. Nothing worked.

When Big Meg entered the contest a change came into our struggles with Claire. For one thing, Meg did not just bellow, she offered to work. She asked Claire if she could take charge of the vestments and Claire refused. She sneaked a few of the robes to the cleaner, and Claire blew up over this interference. After that, Meg and Claire traded insults regularly and became the leaders of two opposing factions.

"Can't you see that Meg is right," said one camp. "We can't spend *all* our money on art . . . we've also got to keep clean."

"Claire's right," said the other faction. "We've got to defend the values of the heart against these apron menders."

You wonder how grown people could get so worked up over such a silly matter. The minister, distressed and perplexed, asked me one day to come into his office to discuss the problem.

"Evelyn," Mr. Dixon said, "this Mary-and-Martha situation has got way out of hand. I wonder if you'd try an experiment with me?"

Mr. Dixon hardly waited for my nod. He picked up his Bible. "Let me read something to you from the Gospel of John: *Whatsoever you ask in My Name I will do it.*"

Mr. Dixon paused as if expecting me to comment. Hesitantly I said that it sounded too easy, as if all we had to do was ask and our problem would be solved for us.

"Well, it isn't that easy," said Mr. Dixon, "because the key to why this works is in the words 'in my name.' Do you know what that means, Evelyn—to do something in Christ's name? It means 'in His love, in accord with His nature.' That's not easy. But once we do agree as to what His name would call for, we have Christ's promise that our prayers will be answered."

And so began our experiment. For weeks Mr. Dixon and I met every Saturday before choir rehearsals and struggled to find Christ's viewpoint for Claire and Meg. And in the end we saw that our thinking had been much too narrow. In His name we need not squirm and maneuver and compromise. In His name we could ask for a total victory for both Claire and Meg. Claire would then feel free to spend all of her energy on her music. And Meg would be free to use her talents to keep the robes cleaned and repaired.

We kept praying for His victory. And then we began to notice a change . . . first, in ourselves. For instance, one day in town I met Big Meg, arms loaded with pads of paper, pencils, chalk. "You going into teaching too?" I asked.

"No, I'm just getting supplies for the Sunday school."

I helped Meg carry her load down to the church and on the way I found myself saying, and meaning, "Isn't it wonderful that we can have someone in our church who will take an interest in *things!*"

And a week later I learned that Mr. Dixon—who had never expressed any particular interest in music—was making arrangements with Claire for an organ recital. These were not planned strategy moves. They just happened. The change in our approach had an effect on others. The shift was not dramatic, just a smile here and a word of appreciation there, but they were smiles between people on opposite sides of the battle-line.

And then, after many weeks of trying to imagine Christ's kind of victory for our church, Mr. Dixon and I prayed one day that Meg and Claire might each be creative in her own individual way. What happened next, I still cannot grasp except in terms of the passage *Whatsoever you ask in my name I will do it.*

It started by my making two luncheon dates. The first was with Claire and the second, an hour later, in a different part of town, with Big Meg. I went to these dates knowing that Mr. Dixon had closed his door and taken his phone off the hook and that he was in prayer with me while I met with Claire and Meg.

Claire was waiting for me when I arrived at the luncheonette. For most of the meal we just chatted. Then Claire said, "Well, I've made up my mind about those robes. They've always been a headache." And then wonderfully, incredibly, Claire added, "You know, Big Meg once offered to take charge of those robes. Do you think she'd mind . . . ?"

I closed my eyes. In my heart I was saying over and over again, "Thank You, Lord. Thank You."

Half an hour later I was seated with Big Meg on her wisteria-covered porch where I struggled through a second lunch. Big Meg listened with interest when I told her how Claire spent her own salary on music and extra organ repairs whenever the budget couldn't cover these expenses.

"Well," Meg said, "I've got to admire that. That takes strength." Meg paused. "But I still don't see why she bothers with patches and buttons. Too bad she can't turn the whole thing over to someone else who likes to work with her hands."

"Like you?"

"She'd never do it."

"Meg," I said, "Claire has already made the suggestion."

Just a few moments later I burst into the pastor's study to

tell Mr. Dixon what had finally happened when we brought Christ's creative love into a fight. But I didn't need to. The pastor was sitting by his window, smiling.

"I know," he said. "I know."

The "Hold-Up" Prayer

Some time ago a minister's wife wrote that she has been using her "hold-up" prayer for me—"just holding you silently in God's presence for a while."

Here's how she explains the prayer, "On numerous occasions in my life I have felt a certain lifting of spirit that meant just one thing: someone was praying for me. This knowledge sends me to my knees to pray for someone else. I don't try to tell God what that other person needs: He knows. My aim is simply to hold that person up before God for a while, in love and wordless concern."

Someone has been unkind; hold that person up in God's presence. A child has been difficult; hold him up for God to embrace. Friend, enemy, husband, wife, neighbor, minister, world leader—hold each up to receive our Lord's love. Who can tell what prayer power would result if enough people did this every day of their lives!

Lorraine Juliana

If you really believe prayer changes things, here is a challenge worth trying.

How Do You Pray About A World Situation?

by NORMAN VINCENT PEALE

NOT long ago at a formal dinner, someone offered a rather lofty invocation which ended this way: ". . . and Lord, we ask that Thou will bring peace again to our troubled and unhappy world."

As I sat down I realized that this prayer for peace, tacked on in that routine, colorless way, had made me uneasy. Certainly today we have no greater need in our world than peace. Why did the prayer seem like such a limp effort?

For some time now a vague restlessness has been building up inside me about the way so many of us approach praying for peace. Some people, strong believers in the power of prayer in other areas, don't even bother to petition God about the world's major problem. "It's too big a subject," I heard one acquaintance of mine say. "It's like trying to flood a desert with an eyedropper."

A graphic analogy all right, but what would happen if a hundred million people began squirting water on the sands with those eyedroppers!

There are people I know who pray for peace by rote. Awed and intimidated by the immensity of the task, they make vague little petitions which sound all right, but chiefly because a lot of other people have used and re-used the same familiar, now lifeless, words. Or if they do offer an original prayer, it is because a son, or a brother, or a husband is in Vietnam, and the prayer is not so much for a peaceful world as it is for "Danny to come home safely."

169

I believe that people who want their prayers for peace to count should *make them more specific.* The man at the formal dinner had asked God "to bring peace to our troubled and unhappy world." But what kind of peace? Did he mean at any price? Even at the cost of freedom? How many would want to pray for that kind of peace? It may be an old joke, but the most peaceful place in any community is still the graveyard.

No, it is clear that we need a sharper definition of terms. Peace is too general a word. Prayers from a thousand people for an undefined "peace" might mean a thousand different things—and thus such prayers would literally go nowhere.

What specific ways of praying are there? Single out the world leaders—regardless of which side—and pray that their hearts and minds will open to the power and love of God. Pray that our President will be given more wisdom in handling world matters. In your mind actually *see* the President burdened by problems and turning to God for help.

Using the same technique, picture in your mind an Arab and an Israeli shaking hands, see a white man apologizing to a Negro for some act of prejudice—and vice versa. The world needs millions of acts of forgiveness and repentance to flush out hate, resentment, bitterness. *See* this happening in your prayer. *See* God's love at work in men's hearts. Pray that we be shown His will.

A second suggestion for making our prayers for peace count is to *put more energy into them.* Put more of ourselves into them.

I remember a conversation I had with the great Negro singer Roland Hayes many years ago. We were on a train in New England watching the swirling snow whip around the end of the Pullman car. Somehow we got on to the subject of how prayer can push through all the forces of nature to reach the Almighty. That is, we agreed, *some* prayers do.

"My grandfather had very little education, but he was a wise man in spiritual matters," Mr. Hayes said. "He used to say that the trouble with most prayers is 'they ain't got no suction.'"

Quite a descriptive phrase—and another way of saying, of course, that prayers need force, drive, energy behind them.

Jesus was never casual when He talked to His Father. Jesus approached prayer as a major undertaking. He would go off by Himself and pray all night—or for days. Once He prayed and fasted for 40 days and nights. Christ would return from these sessions drained of energy, bathed in perspiration, sometimes tears still in His eyes.

There's a housewife in southern Florida, who prays the kind of prayers I'm talking about. At a conference weekend she stated recently that she seldom finishes a prayer without receiving some kind of guidance. Occasionally this is a feeling that there is something, some one thing, she is supposed to do. Usually it is something rather simple, like inviting a group of underprivileged children to her home for a cookout, or like buying some baseball equipment for a neighborhood boy who had a personality problem. But the important thing about this woman's prayers, I believe, is their intensity.

During a crisis in the Middle East, she felt a deep, inner calling to prayer. And she did pray. She prayed for two or three hours every day, getting up from each session as exhausted as if she had been doing hard physical work—yet with a sense of prayer-work completed. In reporting her experience, the woman described this kind of prayer as the total giving of self to Jesus Christ. "His mind and my mind became almost one," she says, "I feel that He wants all of me, all of my attention, all of my heart, all of my effort."

Prayer, plus action is my third suggestion for those who are anxious to make their prayers help offset the many hateful acts in our world. Too many people feel that one person can do nothing. My experience tells me just the opposite—that one idea expressed at a meeting, one letter sent to a senator, one person's stand for principle, can make a big difference, especially when such acts are the result of prayer.

In World War II we were asked by our government to buy war stamps to help the cause. My son John collected stamps at every opportunity and began filling a book with them. I remember vividly John putting these war stamps in a book. As he stuck each stamp on the page he pounded it with his fist, saying, "I'm winning the war."

Boyish naïveté, you might say, but the repetition of that phrase had an impact on me. John felt that his small action was helping win the war and, multiplied by thousands of others, his certainly was. The small actions of individuals are important.

If you want your prayers for the world to count, be specific. Put your whole body, mind and soul into them. Seek God's guidance as to how, after your prayers, you can put your love to work. And don't say that "prayer can change the world" unless you are ready to do your part.

A Prayer For Steadfastness

O God, our Father, Thou searcher of men's hearts,
help us to draw nearer to Thee in sincerity and truth . . .
Make us to choose the harder right instead of the easier
*   wrong,*
and never to be content with a half truth when the
*   whole can be won.*
Endow us with courage that is born of loyalty to all
*   that is noble*
and worthy, that scorns to compromise with vice and
*   injustice,*
and knows no fear when truth and right are in
*   jeopardy . . .*
Kindle our hearts in fellowship with those of a cheerful
*   countenance,*
and soften our hearts with sympathy for those who
*   sorrow and suffer . . .*
Help us, in our work and in our play, to keep ourselves
*   physically strong,*
mentally awake and morally straight, that we may
*   better serve Thee and our Country.*
An *excerpt from the* West Point Cadet's Prayer

"Does God hear every prayer? If so, why is it that mine isn't answered?" This is an oft-posed question and here is one person's response.

When Your Prayers Seem Unanswered

by CONSTANCE FOSTER

WHAT are we to conclude when we have prayed for a long time and nothing seems to be any different from before? Is God whimsical, given to listening to one person but turning a deaf ear on another, or hearing us on some occasions and ignoring us on others? Many people ask themselves these questions. When they pray and things remain much the same or even grow worse, they may come to the conclusion that prayer is at best uncertain and at worst futile.

I became so much interested in this subject of apparently unanswered prayer that for several years now I have been gathering records of such instances.

Carol W. was a young college student when she first came to my attention. In spite of hard work and great ambition, Carol was failing to make passing grades in certain subjects and had been warned that unless she did well on her term examinations, she would be dropped at the end of the year. Carol was praying sincerely for success in her exams. But a month later she phoned me and her first words were, "Well, I prayed but nothing happened."

Carol had flunked two courses and the college dropped her. Certainly surface appearances here would seem to justify her conclusion that "nothing happened" as the result of prayer. But wait! And never forget that God knows more than we do about what is for our highest good.

A few weeks after she returned home, Carol consulted a

173

psychologist who was an expert at determining in what areas an individual's best talents lay. He gave her a battery of aptitude tests that revealed she was extremely gifted in spatial perception and mechanical ability. They also showed that she was not naturally a good student where abstract subjects, such as she had taken at college, were concerned.

Carol took a course at a technical school in X-ray therapy and medical techniques. Today she is head of a large hospital laboratory with a dozen assistants under her direction, making a good salary and happy in her work. Did nothing happen when she prayed? Graduation from a liberal arts college was not the right answer to her needs and abilities. Carol didn't know it. But God did.

Now let us turn to another example of apparently unanswered prayer. It concerns an elderly widow whose husband's death had left her almost destitute and in danger of losing her large home. She could no longer meet the heavy expense of maintaining it. Mrs. Horton wrote me for prayers that she might be able by some miracle to keep it, together with all her cherished possessions. A few months later another letter from her reached me. "We both prayed," she wrote, "but nothing happened." The house was to be sold at auction the following week. Mrs. Horton was heartbroken.

During the next few days Mrs. Horton went through her house with tear-stained eyes, sorting and discarding the accumulation of long years of living in it. In the attic she ran across an old stamp collection that had been in her husband's family for years. She almost threw it in the pile of rubbish. Of what use were a lot of old stamps? But something made her put it aside to save.

A year went by before she thought of it again. The house had been sold. "Nothing had happened." She was bitter. Her prayer had not been answered. Then one day she happened to see an advertisement in a large city newspaper, listing the value of certain rare stamps. Mrs. Horton made a special trip to see the dealer, carrying the old collection with her. When she left his office she was dazed and unbelieving, for in her purse she had his check for nearly $11,000!

The big old house had been much too large for one woman to care for comfortably. She did not need all that space. Today she realizes it. What she required was smaller living quarters together with enough money in the bank for her expenses. That is exactly what God gave her in answer to her supposedly "unanswered" prayer.

Then there was the businessman who had been praying for an increase in salary. Instead his company reshuffled its personnel and he was placed in a different department with a pay *decrease*. They told him he could leave if he was not satisfied to stay on at the lower figure.

He phoned me about the new development and his voice was bitter, "What good is prayer?" he demanded. This is just another variation on the "But nothing happened" theme. Where was God in all this, he wanted to know. Where indeed? Right where He always is, of course, busy making all things work together for good in our individual lives. Had nothing happened?

It seems that my friend had never before been engaged in selling but the new job gave him a chance to try his hand at it and he proved to have a genius for it. Today, three years later, he is sales manager for his firm at a salary five times larger than the one he was receiving when he first prayed for an increase. More important still, he is doing work that is productive and rewarding. Had he not been "demoted," the promotion could never have happened.

My final story concerns a very dear neighbor whose retarded child could not seem to learn. Betty came to me in great distress one day. "It's the last straw," she burst. "As if I didn't already have enough grief and trouble with poor little Karen, now I have to take in my husband's father. He's practically senile. Oh please pray as you never prayed before that we can get some other relative to take care of him."

But there was no other relative able to take in the old man.

The day Grandpa arrived my neighbor echoed the same old sad refrain. "We prayed, but nothing happened. I'm stuck." Nothing happened? It looked that way, didn't it? But God had something wonderful in store for that mother. He had the highest welfare of her retarded child at heart. For tiny Karen began to blossom in Grandpa's company. They seemed to understand each other and soon they were inseparable. Grandpa was not critical of her failings and never pushed her beyond her capacity. He accepted and loved her as she was and for herself alone.

For hours on end Karen sat in Grandpa's lap while he rocked and sang to her. She began to talk and laugh and play. Today she is a practically normal child and although the old man now is no longer living, the family is eternally grateful that God brought him to stay with them and love Karen into overcoming her handicap.

Make no mistake, there is no such thing as an unanswered prayer. God hears every whisper of our hearts but He loves us too much always to answer in the precise terms that we ask. He often has a better answer.

So never say "but nothing happened" when your prayers are not immediately fulfilled as you think they should be. Something always happens. A spiritual force has been set in motion that never stops vibrating in the universal atmosphere. A great chain reaction takes place which may not bring you exactly what you asked for, perhaps, but something infinitely better for your eternal advantage. In short, it is impossible for you to pray and then be able to say truthfully, "But nothing happened."

This Florida insurance executive was exhausted and as he boarded the plane he had only one thought in mind: sleep. But God had another flight plan for him.

The Vacant Seat

by DON MOTT

GOOD morning, sir, it is 4:30 a.m.," the cheery voice of the hotel operator broke into my dreams. As I stumbled to my feet I think I had never been so sleepy: this speaking tour meant a different town each day, long distances between.

At the airport I was the first person aboard the plane. As I dropped into a seat next to the window I repeated almost mechanically the prayer I always say when traveling, "Lord, if there is anybody on this plane You want me to talk to, let him take the seat beside me."

The other window seats filled up rapidly, then the aisle seats. The one next to me remained empty. At last the plane door was closed, the steps rolled away and we were bumping over the ground to the runway. With a sigh of gratitude I let my seat back as far as it would go, fastened my seat belt, and shut my eyes.

"Lord," I said, "I'm going to sleep from here to Chicago." But God had another flight plan.

It was at that moment that I felt someone sit down beside me. I opened my eyes. It was the stewardess, buckling into a belt for take-off. I was about to close my eyes again when I saw that she looked quite upset.

"What's the matter?" I whispered.

She gave me a startled look. "My goodness, does it show?"

Reluctantly I let my seat straighten up. "I'm afraid it does," I said.

The young woman didn't speak again until we were air-

177

borne. At last she said, "The man I was going with has dropped me. I think he ran off with another woman."

"Well," I said, "why don't you thank the Lord and get yourself a good man?"

For the first time she looked straight at me. "I want to talk to you," she said. "But first I have to get the tea and coffee orders."

When she sat down again after serving us, she had apparently looked up my name because she said, "Mr. Mott, what does a girl do when she's going to become a mother and she's unmarried?"

"You tell me," I said.

"I had an operation." Her voice was very small. "But I know now it was wrong. I feel like a murderer and have considered killing myself. That's why I'm going to a psychiatrist."

I was trying to choose words to say to her when all at once I realized that they had already been chosen for me.

"Here in my briefcase I have a copy of a prayer that a man prayed who was guilty of the same two sins that are haunting you," I told her. "This man had committed adultery and he had committed murder. And yet as a result of this prayer, God forgave him. He cleaned him inside and out and made him as innocent as the day he was born."

She said, "I sure would like to read that prayer."

I opened my briefcase, took out my Bible and for the rest of the flight she and I studied the 51st Psalm, David's prayer. I explained to her that if she would confess her sins to God, hiding nothing, but just surrendering everything, He would give her in place of her old life, the life of His Son Jesus Christ.

At last she asked me, "When will all this happen?"

"Before we get to Chicago if you ask Him."

"I don't know how to ask," she said. "Will you help me?"

And there, before the plane descended over Chicago, we bowed our heads and she prayed, repeating after me words that I believe she meant from her heart.

"Oh God, I have sinned. I confess my sin. I pray that You

will forgive me. Thank You that Jesus died on the cross for sinners like me. I now accept Him as my Saviour. Come into my heart, Lord Jesus, and make me a new creature."

There were tears of joy glistening in her eyes as she stood up. I followed her with my eyes as she walked back to her hostess station. And as I did I noticed every seat on that entire plane—with the single exception of the one beside me—was occupied.

The plane came to a stop. The aisle filled with people and coats and briefcases, but I sat still. I was remembering that I had been the very first one aboard, that every one of these people had had to decide against taking this seat.

I was reflecting what a serious transaction prayer is, even such a sleepy, half-grudging prayer as mine had been this morning. I was thinking that when we ask God to use us, we mustn't afterwards be surprised when He does.

For One Who Is Tired

Dear child, God does not say today, "Be strong,"
He knows your strength is spent, He knows how long
The road has been, how weary you have grown,
For He who walked the earthly roads along
Each boggy lowland and each rugged hill,
Can understand, and so He says "Be still,
And know that I am God." *The hour is late*
And you must rest awhile, and you must wait
Until life's empty reservoirs fill up,
As slow rain fills an empty upturned cup.
Hold up your cup, dear child, for God to fill;
He only asks today that you be still.

Grace Noll Crowell

A former actress turned minister's wife, this mother found she had lots to learn about life's priorities.

My Family Comes First

by COLLEEN TOWNSEND EVANS

JAMIE had wakened and cried during the night. I had comforted him, fed, and cuddled him and then tucked him back into his crib. Then I'd just gotten back to sleep when Tim had fallen out of bed, so I'd had to dash to pick him up.

As I sought sleep once more I thought to myself that being the wife of a busy young minister, mother to four youngsters, cook, maid, chauffeur, as well as hostess to our entire church was altogether different from the life I had had as an actress.

Deliberately, happily I had given up my own career to marry Lou. Yet now sheer physical weariness, the sense of being burdened with more than one woman could handle was beginning to take away the glow.

I loved Lou dearly. I reached out a finger now to touch him for reassurance. He needed that sleep. Day by day he was giving all of himself to other people in the name of Christ. I would not have exchanged my happiness with him and my children for any career in the world.

"No, Lord, a career outside my home is not what I want," I found myself praying. "It's just that I don't want the glow to go. I want to be able to handle this. But I'm desperate. I've too much work to do. Please show me how to do all that's expected and still keep my health and the right attitudes too."

Right then I discovered an important truth about prayer: it has to be honest—or it isn't even prayer. Yes, even if we have to let resentment spill out. God honors honest anger and then can dissolve it for us, but He can't honor bottled-up feelings and unreal piety.

I also discovered that though God heard my cry for help, He was not going to give me all my answers that first night nor ever in any simple, neat package. The answers were to come slowly, painfully, over a matter of weeks. Looking . . . seeing . . . asking . . . receiving. They were given to me in a variety of ways too: through insight; through Scripture; through a relationship, a living relationship with the Person of Jesus Christ. And because I think that many have the problem I did—that of feeling burdened with more than they can handle—I'd like to share some of the help that I received.

The first insight was that I was harassed because I did not know how to say No. One morning as I was reading a verse from Deuteronomy, it had leapt out at me from the page: *As thy days, so shall thy strength be.**

But then that inner voice, which I have gradually come to recognize as one of God's valid ways of speaking to us today, had added firmly, "But that is true only if you will let Me tell you when to say 'Yes' and when to say 'No'."

Experimenting with this, I soon found that some of my tasks were motivated by my ambition, my hunger for unnecessary praise, or my insistence on doing things my way. But the things that were really necessary to keep my family healthy and happy and spiritually whole, yes, for these I did have strength.

And I found God's directives fascinating. One day it might be that reading aloud to my children was more important than scrubbing the kitchen floor. Or that a cake from the bakery would do as well as a home-baked one, so that I could take the children to the beach. I began to realize that the children wanted *me* and my attention more than they wanted my cake. And out of a feeling of rightness about these times with them, new joy flooded into our reading-aloud times or our joyous romps on California's beautiful beaches.

I also had to learn to say "No" to some other people in order to say "Yes" to my family.

* Deuteronomy 33:25

For example, there was the time I was asked to be the speaker at a religious conference. It would have taken me away from my home and family for two weeks. The theme, ironically enough, was the role of the Christian wife and mother.

At first, I was puzzled about whether or not I should go. My conscience reminded me of the need to share Christian experience with other wives. "But what about leaving my family that long?" I reasoned. "They're my greatest opportunity to serve God. If I miss the mark with them, will anything else matter?" So I turned down the invitation.

Shortly after that I was reading Paul Tournier's book *Guilt and Grace,* and came across the passage, "False guilt comes from saying no to people. . . . The only true guilt comes from saying no to God."

This was it! False guilt had too often robbed me of energy and joy that rightfully belonged to our family. From then on, saying "No" became easier and one of the secrets of released time for me.

The second answer to my sense of being overburdened was the "how" of acquiring that inner quietness and poise without which our life flies to pieces in busyness. In the beginning of our marriage, a time of quiet meditation and prayer had been a part of my daily schedule.

But then had come the busy years. Ours was such a new church that for four years our home was the center for board meetings, Bible studies, Sunday school planning, prayer meetings. The house always had to be clean and often cookies baked.

Although all these activities brought a real sense of joy and love, I found it hard to adjust to all the pressure. But with four active pre-school children to be taken care of—and the doorbell and telephone to be answered over and over again—there were no quiet times. Gradually I came to feel spiritually famished.

Perhaps at that time I was feeling a bit sorry for myself because God's truth was jolting. . . . "You think you're too busy. Your real problem is that you have allowed Me to be pushed from the center of your life." My heart told me suddenly that this was so. My burning desire to spend some time alone with that living Presence had gradually cooled. So the real problem was not with my activity but with my affection for God.

And when I asked, "But *when* do I have a quiet time . . .?" His answer was, "You don't, not as you have understood a quiet time. For a few years, until the children are older, you're going to have to learn to pray on the run, in the car, in any odd place. Try this new way."

So I did, and found that it made no difference to God whether I was walking or driving or kneeling or sitting or lying down. The chinks of time—in a dentist's waiting room, before the PTA meeting, or while I was standing over the stove stirring a custard—could be blessed times of communion.

How real some of these times have been is shown by their fruits. For out of this "on the run" communion I have learned much about human relationships. And so many creative ideas have come—like the substitute for expensive toys for our children. Lou fills up the trunk of our car with scraps of all shapes from a woodworking shop. We keep them in the garage in large plastic tubs—bright red, yellow, blue. Then we turn the boys and their friends loose with hammer and nails to make whatever they can. The only requirement: tools back in place and garage cleaned up when they finish.

Or that idea for our vacation one year in the High Sierras . . . books were carefully selected ahead of time such as—*Cry, The Beloved Country* and *To Kill A Mockingbird*. As the children lay snugly in their warm sleeping bags, looking up at the stars, Lou and I would take turns reading to them. I think that all their lives our children will remember that summer, for never have we felt more closely knit as a family. And every so often, one of them will quote something from one of the books, "Remember the summer when. . . ."

*The President of Holiday Inns and one of America's
most successful builders tells why he finds nothing in-
consistent in asking God's favor and blessing on his
work.*

Why I Pray To Succeed

by WALLACE E. JOHNSON

I ONCE heard a religious philosopher say something to this
effect: "The man who asks God to help him in his business
is praying wrong. He is simply trying to use God for his own
profit."

If this is true, then I have been praying wrong for a long
time. For it is my practice to take everything to the Creator in
prayer—problems concerning health, family, friends, church
and the $4,000,000 loan I need to construct a new housing
development.

I admit quite openly that I am totally dependent on God
for help in everything I do. And if I kept Him out of my
business I honestly believe it would start to fall apart in a matter of months.

Now someone will say that it is all right to include my
business in my prayers; I just shouldn't pray for financial
success. Here again I find myself in disagreement. When I
surrendered my life to Jesus Christ some years ago, I turned
everything over to Him: money, possessions, goals, dreams,
business. Any success I have achieved since is His success. All
money earned is His money. How can I separate the different
areas of my life and pray for some and not the others?

I haven't always felt this way, however. The turning point
in my life came back in 1939 when I was a building supplies
salesman earning $37.50 a week. I was frustrated and dis-
couraged. Nothing seemed to go right.

Although I went to church and believed in God, I had somehow disassociated my job from my religion. One night I made my prayer more specific: "Lord, I've been trying to make a go of it as a salesman, but I'm not doing very well. What am I doing wrong? Show me, Lord, the direction I should go, the people I should see, the way I should use my time."

From the moment I stopped trying to accomplish everything with my own resources and prayed to God for guidance, things were different. Names of people to see, places to go, popped into my mind. Where did these suggestions come but from God? Ideas certainly hadn't flooded my mind *before* I asked Him for help.

One passage of Scripture so summed up this experience for me that I always keep it on a card in my billfold to refer to frequently:

*Ask, and it shall be given you; seek, and ye shall find; knock, and it shall be opened unto you: For every one that asketh receiveth, and he that seeketh findeth; and to him that knocketh, it shall be opened.**

These words from Matthew provide us with one of God's greatest promises. Yet it is a little one-sided. It provides us with a philosophy of receiving, but not of giving.

One day while my wife Alma and I were seeking God's guidance for a personal problem, I came across a verse that has ever since been a daily reminder to me of what my responsibility as a businessman is to God. The verse reads:

*Study to shew thyself approved unto God, a workman that needeth not to be ashamed, rightly dividing the word of truth.***

Again and again have I measured my actions against that one phrase: *a workman who has no need to be ashamed.* Like every Christian who gropes for the truth, I go off the track at times and get so involved with problems of loans, unions and

---

* Matthew 7:7-8
** II Timothy 2:15

balance sheets that I forget Him. Sometimes Alma wakes me up or occasionally He will get through to me, and then I face up to the demands of that verse in Timothy.

Not too long after my first prayer for guidance, I saw a way in 1940 to change from salesman to builder. By 1945 there was a great demand for housing. I firmly believe that the home is more than just a physical shelter; it is the spiritual center of our culture, almost more so than the church. I remember asking for guidance to construct 2,000 homes in 1945: it seemed like a fantastic goal! Where was the money to come from? There were endless difficulties.

I began making a daily list of items to ask God about. Sometimes on note paper, sometimes on the back of an envelope, I'd write down my concerns:

1) Legal advice on gas line. Where put?
2) Lumber delivery is late—why? Change supplier?
3) Another loan needed. Where do I go?

Even as I jotted down these items, I was praying for guidance. I believe the key to close communion with God is to begin with words, usually spoken aloud. In the case of a foreman some years ago who was quite a problem, the words went: "Lord, thank You for Your love and concern. I need help with Jerry. He can't get along with anyone; something may be wrong in his home life. Show me how to reach him."

After the spoken prayer to God, I conceive of the request going into my subconscious, where God can deal with it in His own time and way. Then I go ahead and do what I have to do in the hope that God will help by directing my steps.

We actually built 3,000 homes in 1945. And we have built an average of 1,000 homes every year since.

In 1952, our firm built the first Holiday Inn in Memphis, Tennessee. With so many people on the move in automobiles, we saw the need for clean, wholesome places to stay—a home away from home. Our effort was met with enthusiastic response and more hotels followed.

As the Lord helped us to prosper, He obviously had many

ideas of His own as to where the money was to go. The tithing of our time and money to churches and charities was a beginning.

Alma and I have done everything together from the day we were married. My wife is not only a brilliant executive secretary who knows as much about my business as I do, she is also a spiritual partner. Every day we read Scripture together and pray about our mutual concerns.

One day back in 1953 Alma received word that her father, Mr. Ernest McCool, was very ill and needed institutional care. The problem was that in all of Memphis, Tennessee, we did not then know of any acceptable institution that could give him the long-term care he needed. In desperation we placed him in a general hospital, although he did not require intensive treatment. Yet there was no alternative, and the last five years of his life this fine old gentleman lived in a hospital.

At that time, Alma and I said that if the Lord would guide us, we would build a convalescent center for others having ailments similar to those of Mr. McCool. We envisioned an attractive complex of buildings set off by trees and gardens. The facilities would feature ramps, comfortable furnishings, a recreation area and modern decor throughout. Inpatient care would be provided at moderate rates.

The first convalescent center was built in 1961 in Memphis, and 11 more have been opened in the past five years. These were the forerunners of Medicenters of America, Inc., which my partner Kemmons Wilson and I are developing.

How we wish Mr. McCool could have lived out his last years in one of these centers. But he certainly played his role as the instrument which God used to reach Alma and me.

Today, whether in Memphis or San Francisco or Rome, I still use a paper and pencil to write down special concerns for prayer. The list may be long, but Alma and I do not want to overlook anything. For we are grateful that God honors our prayers by reaching into our minds with His guidance and using us as instruments for His work.

"Kate felt estranged from God's love. I wondered if there were any way I could help her feel His concern."

The Misfit

by Lucille Campbell

YOU mean to tell me God loves every one of the 'undesirables' in this world?" Kate demanded in obvious disbelief. Our women's Sunday school class was studying a lesson stressing the imporance of the individual and God's love for him.

"Well, listen to me!" she snorted. "Nobody ever loved me! Not my parents, not the two husbands who deserted me. Why, even my children don't. And I guess God doesn't love me, either! What has He ever done to show me He loves me?"

She rose and stamped out of the class as we watched her, stunned.

Kate had first come to our church one hot morning. She would admit no special need.

"Just came to sit down because my feet hurt," she claimed.

I especially enjoyed having her the few Sundays she came back. She started our liveliest discussions by daring to voice aloud those problems we all ponder sometimes in the secret places of our hearts.

After her outburst, Kate didn't return. I couldn't forget her, though. Her angry words had been a call for help. I kept thinking, too, of her question: "What has God ever done to show He loves me?" And I thought of myself. Why was I so sure of God's love?

It came to me that I hadn't needed theological assurances of His love. His love had come to me through my parents' love, my husband's faithfulness, my friend's devotion. Their love was the transmission of God's. And this is what Kate had missed.

Could I do anything to show it to Kate, I wondered? Wondering and finding no answer, I prayed for an answer. As a result I was prodded to go to see Kate. I drove to her street. The sidewalks were heaved and split, a few dusty weeds sprouted in the cracks. Various odors, rotting, moldy, drifted from alleys.

Kate, surprised to see me, recovered her poise and invited me into the better of her two rooms. She jerked up a broken shade to give light, kicked a bottle quickly out of sight under the bed. A boy was building a tower of some scrap pieces of lumber on a chair. She brushed it off so I could sit down, gave him a sharp slap when he started to protest.

"Jimmy," she indicated him, "worthless like his father." Nodding to two big-eyed little girls crouching in the corner, she added: "Judy and Joyce, souvenirs of the second bum I married."

The resentment in her voice was frightening. It was as if she hated the heat, the dirt, the bleak poverty and blamed it all on those defenseless children.

I had come intending to have a little visit with Kate and to urge her back to church. Now I could see she needed more than talk. She needed understanding, a chance to respect herself, help to care for the children, person-to-person love.

From the first Kate didn't take graciously to being helped, and she was difficult to like, let alone love. One friend of mine took her a good assortment of used clothing, dishes, pans, some pieces of stout furniture. Kate looked them over carelessly.

"I do wish," she drawled, "that people who donate old things to me would have the good taste to buy decent stuff in the first place!"

She once expressed a wish to make her own living—she existed on a welfare check—but when several of us offered her housework and sewing, she plainly didn't appreciate it.

"No, thank you! Not me!" she sniffed. "Why should I break my back doing someone else's dirty work? The government won't let me starve."

Kate's darkest side was her treatment of the children. At times she struck them physically, but it seemed to me that her cruel words hit them hardest of all.

"You were born dumb!" she told Jimmy once, looking at his report card. "You'll never learn!"

"Always dirty, always noisy, always in the way!" she charged the little girls.

We felt a separation would benefit both Kate and her children, and so some of us often took the little girls to play in our homes with our children. They made friends readily, and blossomed like tightly closed buds opening to the sun. One neighbor hired Jimmy to work on his lawn and garden four hours a day.

Things grew better slowly. When she wasn't with them all the time, Kate was more patient with the children. Then she had to have an operation. We cared for the children, seven people from the church gave blood for her. When she returned home, I visited, taking a cake I'd baked.

"Food," she said bitterly, "but I don't have a dog to feed that cake to."

"Kate," I said firmly. "This is the best cake I bake. I bake it for all my family and friends at times like these. Eat it. I think you'll like it."

Tears were suddenly in her eyes.

"Oh, I don't mean to be hateful and say those things. I will like it. And thank you."

In the hospital, she'd become interested in the practical nurses working there. She wanted to be one, and the welfare office cut through red tape to finance the year's education and training. As she worked towards her goal, she gained a lot more self-control. She was kinder to the children.

Jimmy brought seeds and bulbs home from where he worked and made their yard bloom that summer. He cleaned up the trash and cut the weeds. The little girls picked great bouquets of flowers to put about the house in odd cans, glasses, a pickle jar.

"Crazy kids!" Kate laughed when she saw them bringing the gay handfuls to her. But you never saw more pride, anticipation, and fervent gladness on a face.

Soon she was attending church again. There one Sunday I had a message that a relative was dying. My husband must drive me to her.

"Now I'll look after the kids," Kate said immediately. "Don't you worry about them a minute."

My heart sank. That rough neighborhood! That miserable house! Yet I sensed she needed to do this, and she beamed when I chose her offer over those of relatives and older friends. The children had a fine time and excellent care.

When Kate finished her training, she took work in the hospital and went off relief. Two elderly ladies invited her to share their large home. They loved her children, and badly needed someone younger and stronger in their house. In this way they could remain independent, yet be safe with competent care at hand.

The last time I saw Kate, she invited me to sit down in the kitchen and chat while she served me coffee and cake. The little girls were laughing over a new game. Jimmy was frowning over homework.

"Pretty good for me, after I messed up everything for 30 years," she mused, her gaze taking in the neat apartment, the well-dressed children. "I have a lot to be thankful for."

She really did. And I was reminded of Kate's long-ago question: "What has God ever done to show me He loves me?"

God had answered that question by changing Kate from an angry, resentful misfit into a responsible, worthwhile person. We who shared Kate's rebirth learned—better than through any Sunday school discussion—that God's unfailing love and power awaits anyone who reaches for it and, more important, for anyone who shares it.

Motel-keeper Ellie Armstrong trusts God implicitly.
The result is He has given her a most unusual ministry
to travelers.

God's Work Is Where You Are

by CATHERINE MARSHALL

EVERY time I hear someone complain that he has "no
time" for God, I think about our friend Ellie Armstrong.
Ellie is in full-time religious work—running a motel.

It's a small but neat motel on U.S. Route 6 in the rolling hills
of western Pennsylvania. Ellie was behind the desk when my
husband, Len, and I stopped there one night recently. She's
in her early 30s and the eyes framed by the dark hair are very
blue. It's the eyes which invite you to linger and chat awhile
after you've signed the register.

The place, she said, had been named Port Motel—after the
nearby town of Port Alleghany—long before she borrowed the
money to buy it three years ago. "But isn't it the very name
you would choose if you were starting a motel new?" she
asked. "A name Jesus used about Himself!"

"He did?"

"Of course! *I am the door* (the portal): *if any man enter in,
he shall be saved . . . and have life . . . and have it more abun-
dantly.** Isn't that the point, with everyone we meet, to lead
them to that door? And a motel—well, it means a chance to
meet new people all the time!"

The blue eyes returned our startled looks with surprise of
their own. "That's why I wanted a motel, you know," she
said, as though wondering why else one would be in business.
"To meet people who might not have heard about Him."

* John 10:9, 10

192

Like, for example, the unsuspecting drug salesman who had stopped for a good night's sleep a few months back. As he registered at the desk, Ellie noticed a large growth on his left eye, almost forcing the lid shut.

"You don't have to have that growth on your eye," she told him.

The salesman stared at her. "What do you mean?"

"I mean Jesus can take it off. He doesn't want you to have it. He'll take it from you."

"Look, lady, I don't believe in magic. I don't even believe in God."

"But," she said gently, "that doesn't stop Him from believing in you." And with that Ellie showed him to Room Three, which she knows secretly as "the miracle room for unbelievers."

"The miracle room?" I broke in.

Well, Ellie said, in a way all the rooms were miracle rooms. Each of the 14 motel units had been dedicated to God for a specific purpose: a room for healing, a special room for honeymooners, one for alcoholics, another for the mending of broken relationships, the conviction room, the happiness room, and so on.

No outward sign set the rooms apart, she said, just a ceremony held on April 20, 1965, when she had formally offered the motel to God. Ministers and friends came to take part in the service. First came a dedication prayer, then the group walked from room to room claiming each for its special purpose.

"We even anointed the doors and the beds with oil, the way it says in Exodus: *And thou shalt take the anointing oil, and anoint . . . all that is therein, and shalt hallow it.** Oh, I know it sounds a little crazy," she added hastily, catching what must have been slightly quizzical looks from us, "and of course we don't know what God is going to do with the different people

* Exodus 40:9

who stay. We just asked Him to be present in each room, to meet each guest."

As in the case of the salesman. That night some members of Ellie's church were meeting for prayer in her living room. She invited the salesman to join them, but he declined. And so they prayed for him in his absence.

He left the next morning before anyone else was up. A few days later he was back. Even before he got to the desk Ellie could see that both eyes were perfectly normal—no growth.

"Shook me up," he blurted out. "I was driving down the road that morning when I happened to look in the rear view mirror, and that thing was gone! Simply wasn't there! Lady, I told you I don't believe in God, but maybe, if you introduced me. . . ."

If the salesman was surprised, Ellie was not. Answered prayer is a common experience here. In fact, keeping the motel open at all requires daily answer. To cut down expenses Ellie, her sister and her mother not only do all the maid work but also the painting, repairs and upkeep. Even so there are many debts, for in order to purchase the motel Ellie had to borrow not only the mortgage money but the down payment as well.

"I asked God then never to let me miss a payment, even by a day, to any of those people who had believed in the idea of the motel. And He never has."

He has, however, tested Ellie often and taught her much through this life of constant financial dependence. There was the time one mid-winter when a $300 mortgage payment was due in a few days. She had but $50. For five consecutive nights not a single car had stopped at the motel. And so, as she had done so often when money was lacking, Ellie began to pray. At last an inner voice seemed to tell her: "Send the $50 to Dave Wilkerson in New York for his work with young drug addicts."

Ellie was as startled as any of us would have been. Surely this was not the time to give away money! And then she remembered that Jesus had said, *Give and it shall be given unto you.** It took courage, but she mailed off the $50 that afternoon to Mr. Wilkerson. That same night nine cars came in, one right after the other, taking most of the rooms. The rest of the week the motel was filled to capacity. The mortgage money was paid on time.

Len and I sat silent a moment, digesting this idea. "And all these customers," Len said at last, "how did you know which rooms to put them in?" For some, like the salesman, it would be obvious, but most motorists stopping overnight simply pick up their room keys and say goodnight. How often, we asked her, do people stay to talk about their troubles?

Ellie's blue eyes smiled at us. "More often than you'd think," she said. "And when they don't, then I simply ask God about them."

One evening God seemed to tell her to put a certain man in the room where alcoholics had often been helped, although there was nothing in his appearance to suggest this problem. Only next morning did she learn what happened.

The guest was a "cured" alcoholic who had not had a drink for two years. But this night he was despondent because he had just lost his sister to cancer. Life was meaningless, he had decided. He tossed his suitcase on the bed and was turning to leave the room, intending to get drunk, when he saw on the night stand a book, *The Cross and the Switchblade*. Curiously, he picked it up. Three hours later he finished reading it. "I knelt down by the bed," he confided to Ellie next morning, "and once again rededicated my life to God." The man has been returning regularly for what he calls "refilling."

The literature in each room is part of the ministry, and it goes far beyond the usual Gideon Bible. In our room, besides several books, I spotted the latest *Upper Room* and *Guideposts*, and a pamphlet, "The Incomparable Christ."

But even more important than what travelers read, Ellie is finding, is what they say, when they know that someone

* Luke 6:38

is listening. She meets so many lonely people, crushed by problems or isolated in prisons of self, and she is often up half the night hearing their griefs. Indeed, the night we were there she sat up until two, talking and praying with a young couple who had just left their baby in a home for the retarded.

But there Ellie was, next morning, bright and early, a stack of clean towels in one hand, a can of scouring powder in the other.

"Isn't it too bad," I said, "that someone else can't do these routine jobs, when God has given you so much work to do for Him?"

"For Him?" Ellie looked puzzled. "Oh, but this is the best time I spend with Him! This is when I go into each room and thank Him for His presence there."

As she sweeps, she said, she asks God to sweep away also the fears, angers or doubts that have been left behind. Washing windows, she prays that His light may shine into the room. And making beds—

"I've always had a bad back and making so many beds each day used to be a problem. Then I discovered that if I made beds kneeling, I wouldn't have to stoop over, and now it's the best prayer time I have!"

Stop doing God's work to wash and sweep and clean? Ellie can't. For as she sees it, floors and beds and motel windows are as much His as church pews and stained glass. In fact, there is no work that cannot be done for Him.

"God, if there is a God, save that boy," the coach had prayed. Later, the boy asked the coach to pray again—for himself.

The Prank that Changed My Life

by C. A. ROBERTS

AS I remember it, Charlie was the one who suggested we go over to Coach Morris's house and roll some rocks off his roof. It sounded like fun to the rest of the group, so off into the night the five of us trooped.

We were all freshmen or sophomores in high school and Mr. Morris was our basketball coach. He was a heavy drinker, and for entertainment we used to play pranks on him. The rocks-on-the-roof bit always threw him into a rage.

This night we got more than we bargained for. Coach Morris had been drinking as usual, maybe more than usual. We bounced a half dozen stones off the roof when out into the backyard he staggered. "You——. I'll get you!" There was a loud bang.

He had fired a shotgun at us figuring to scare us off, but his aim was too good. Three of us were hit—me seriously.

They rushed me to St. Joseph's Hospital in Fort Worth and prepared me for surgery. The pain was so intense I don't remember much, but I shall never forget what I overheard Dr. Hall tell my mother when she and Dad arrived at the hospital.

"Your boy is not going to live, Mrs. Roberts. He is bleeding internally and is in a state of shock. We will do our best, but I'm afraid time will run out before we get very far. We can only hope and pray."

Dad leaned down and kissed me on the cheek. "Don't worry, Son. Everything will be all right. Just trust the Lord."

Thoughts whirled through my mind: "Trust the Lord . . .

197

he won't live . . . everything's all right . . . he won't live . . .
trust. . . ."

As the nurse wheeled me into the operating room, I prayed
as I never had before. I really expected to die and I pleaded
God to forgive me, especially for what I'd done.

Miraculously, I made it through the operation and slowly
recovered. I lived, but my basketball coach died; at least it
was a kind of death.

Though charges against him were dismissed, he lost his
job, his wife left him and he hit the bottle—even more heavily.
Eventually, he just drifted away, a broken man.

On the other hand, the shooting incident and my recovery
gave my life a new zest. I believed that God had spared me for
a reason and I decided I could serve Him best as a preacher.
Whereas church had been a perfunctory sidelight before, now
it became one of the two main focal points in my life. The
other was basketball.

I practiced most of the time, often giving the game prece-
dence over eating and sleeping. In my senior year I made the
first string and earned a scholarship to Baylor. That fall I
went off to college to play basketball and to study in preparation for seminary, but my plans went awry in a hurry.

The problem was poor eyesight. Though I couldn't see well
enough to walk down a flight of steps or read a textbook without my glasses, I tried to play basketball without them. My
eyes began to feel the strain and I started getting headaches
that wouldn't quit. Finally, I went to a doctor and he told me
to do two things: wear prescription sunglasses all the time and
stop playing basketball. I was inconsolable.

The news so shook me that I considered quitting school.
However, I remembered the shooting and my scrape with
death. "If You want me to go ahead into the ministry, Lord,"
I prayed, "give me some sign." It did not come quickly. In
fact I had grave doubts if God really could use me in the ministry. Finally, the semester ended and I went home for the
summer.

I had no more than unpacked when the phone rang. My minister told me of a city-wide youth revival that was to take place in one of the city parks. He explained that they wanted a hometown boy to lead one service. "You're planning on a career in the ministry. This would be good experience. Will you speak?" I hesitated, but he persisted and I finally agreed.

Then came the big night and I stood up before a throng that looked to me like 60,000 instead of 6,000. After a nervous start I grew more confident and soon I was telling the story of our prank on the basketball coach four years before and how it had led to near tragedy. I mentioned that I didn't know where my ex-coach was. I said I was sure God had forgiven me but I wished I could ask Coach Morris to forgive me.

The next day I received a call from a woman who had been at the meeting. She said she thought the man I had described was living next door to her, and, if so, he needed help badly. I went to the address she gave me, rang the bell and waited. Finally, a bleary-eyed man came to the door. There was no mistaking Coach Morris—broad frame, steel gray hair and flushed complexion.

"Coach, remember me?—C. A. Roberts?" I began nervously. "I just wanted to come by and tell you that I'm sorry for what happened that night four years ago."

He stood there so silently that I thought he didn't recognize me. Then I saw his eyes fill with tears. He reached forward clumsily to shake my hand.

"What are you doing, Boy?" he asked. I told him I was in college, thinking of becoming a minister.

"I'm not a religious man, but every day you were in the hospital I prayed the same prayer: 'Dear God, if there is a God, save that boy!'"

"Coach," I said, God answered your prayer. In fact, I believe God used you to bring me to Him. Now I believe He wants to use me to bring you to Him. Would you like to pray about it?" He nodded yes.

Together, we knelt on the porch as naturally as if he were

giving me coaching instructions in a huddle. He began by asking God to help him find himself and become useful again. He said, "I can't do it myself, and I wouldn't blame You if You don't want me, but I'm asking You anyway." A simpler, more beautiful prayer, I have never heard.

Then we went into the house. It smelled like a barroom. I asked him where his wife was and he told me. I called her apartment and told her what had happened. "Will you come over?"

She said she would be there as quickly as possible.

A few minutes later, she knocked at the door and there in the doorway they embraced. Tears of happiness streamed down their faces.

I slipped out of the house and paused on the walk. The air was never purer and I had never felt cleaner. And I never again asked God if He wanted me to be a minister. The open doors He has provided have answered the question.

Teach Us, Dear God

Teach us, dear God, to have compassion enough to realize that all men are created equal in Thine image. Help us to understand that man's ultimate happiness depends upon his desire to seek greater wisdom for living so that he may share it with all mankind.

Marian Anderson

Persecution forced early Christians to worship secretly —often underground, in small cells. Today, also in small units, Christians are rediscovering that same first-century power and spiritual vitality.

From a Small Group, a Big Answer

by FLORENCE PERT

MY neighbor and friend, Ev Kaiser, was on the phone. "Florence," she asked, "could you and George come over for a while after dinner? Something has happened and Bob and I would like to talk to somebody."

During dinner George and I speculated over this "something." A problem in their marriage? The Kaisers, however, had impressed us as being one of the happiest and in love couples in our suburban community of Scotch Plains, New Jersey. Bob, a Phi Beta Kappa at Dartmouth, a champion golfer and a decorated veteran of World War II, was now president of a small business. Ev was a sparkling social leader in the community—and a devoted mother of their four children.

Bob's face was drawn and tense when he greeted us. He came quickly to the point. "Our company has been merged with another. I'm out of a job."

George and Bob went into the living room to talk while Ev and I cleared off the dishes and sat at the kitchen table. "It's been quite a blow to Bob," she said. "He's had to dismiss a number of his old employees too. But I don't think losing the job is quite as bad as the loss of his self-confidence. He is terribly depressed."

On several occasions Ev and I had *talked* about prayer and *talked* about religion. The time had come to stop talking and begin praying. And so, sitting on kitchen stools, we prayed for Bob's physical and mental health in this crisis.

Meanwhile, in the living room, George and Bob were taking a somewhat different route. In his quiet way, George began suggesting to Bob that perhaps he was trying too hard to run his own life, that he might do better if he sought God's guidance and direction. We spent several evenings with the Kaisers, trying to be helpful. One night Bob came to a conclusion. "What you're telling me, George, is that there's a big difference between being the nominal Christian I've been for so long and really offering my life to Jesus Christ."

That same evening Bob took what he called the gamble of an outright transferal of his life and will to God. As George and I were leaving, Bob said, "I think we'd be interested in that fellowship group you mentioned to us one time."

George and I were delighted. Meeting regularly with a small group of concerned Christians had meant spiritual lifeblood to both of us for many years, both before we were married and after. Furthermore, many of our ideas of what a marriage could really become resulted from spiritual fellowship with other married couples.

So it was that the negative fact of Bob's losing his job had a positive result—the formation of a small fellowship group in Scotch Plains. Being new in the community, George and I could not have brought this about without people like the Kaisers to spark it. The timing was perfect, for it was through this group that Bob learned how to receive God's guidance.

The first meeting was held in the Kaisers' living room. On hand were five married couples and one elderly widower.

Since George and I had already experienced 16 years of leading small groups, we had learned certain pitfalls to avoid. George's opening statement went something like this:

"We're here tonight as a group of friends who want to grow spiritually. Many of us have felt a sense of vagueness about our religion; here I hope we can get down to the nuts and bolts of trying to live out our Christian faith every day. We expect to learn from the experiences of one another, from the Bible and through prayer."

It was agreed that we would meet every Wednesday night in a different home. We decided to open each session by reading a chapter from the Gospel of Mark, then explore how that particular Scripture related to our personal lives. Our prayer period would be silent or vocal, as the Holy Spirit moved us.

At the first meeting Bob told about his effort to redirect his life. "All of you know what has happened to me and how I completely lost confidence in myself," he said. "There is no question in my mind that the decision to put my life in God's hands has already kept me from a serious breakdown. I still don't have a job, nor do I know what the future holds for me and my family. But I'm not as fearful as I was. I am seeking God's help and I would appreciate your prayers."

This kind of open request for God's guidance made before members of a group always seems to produce a chain-reaction effect. After the prayer petition—and a quiet-time to listen for answers—one person asked if Bob were sure he was in the right field. Another thought of a company which was looking for an executive director. In the days ahead, interviews and contacts multiplied. Bob was kept busy day and night seeing people.

He soon came to one conclusion about the quest for direction from God. It would be wrong to sit around waiting for it to explode in his face. He was to follow up every possibility. He was to be active.

Several weeks later Bob reported to the group as follows: "These interviews have given me a chance to re-think everything about my life. Perhaps God really is trying to tell me that I belong in a different field, as was suggested in our first meeting. I've enjoyed my job in industry, but deep down I've often wondered if my real talent might not be in the field of education."

Weeks passed. Meanwhile, things were happening to other members of the group. One housewife healed a bad relationship with her neighbor. One of the men who had aimlessly stuck to a job he didn't like came to the clear decision to make a change—and did so. His wife became more reconciled to the loss of a loved one that had long kept her deeply depressed.

Meanwhile, Bob and Ev had the sudden impulse one day that they should visit his sister in Hanover, New Hampshire, where Dartmouth is located. While making arrangements on the phone, Bob's brother-in-law, also a Dartmouth graduate, jokingly asked, "Why not work for the College?" Bob took it seriously, however, and before they hung up, his brother-in-law had agreed to arrange an interview with Dartmouth's Vice-president of Alumni Affairs.

During this interview, and several more with other college officials, it turned out that a man holding an important job in the Development Office was retiring. It seemed that Bob had just the combination of qualities and experience Dartmouth was looking for in his replacement. Was he interested? He certainly was.

With excitement in his voice, Bob later told the group about the chain of events that had led to the New Hampshire trip. "You just have to believe that there is something to this matter of God's timing," he concluded.

But I noticed that Ev did not share Bob's enthusiasm for the Dartmouth job. She was silent at the meeting, unusual for her. Several days later I found Ev alone in her kitchen. She had been crying. We talked about recipes for a while, but finally she opened up her heart.

"It's no use trying to hold back my feelings," she said. "Hanover is a fine place, but I can't bear to leave our lovely home and the wonderful friends I have here in New Jersey. I've been so upset I didn't even want to go to that last group meeting; I don't want to pray; I don't even want to talk about these things to you, Florence."

She smiled ruefully. "I'm off base and I know it. I've tried to keep my feelings from Bob, but he knows something is wrong."

"You've been honest with me. Why don't you talk to God in the same way," I suggested.

So she did.

We learned something together that afternoon. So often when we ask God for help with a problem or in making a decision, we don't really want His guidance, we simply want His confirmation of a plan we already have worked out ourselves. Or we want God's help in a limited way. "Give me Your guidance, Lord, just as long as I don't have to do this—or that." God can't help us with these restrictions, for His Plan for our lives is often so much bigger and better than we could work out for ourselves.

Ev went through a period of agonizing struggle before she could say this prayer: "Lord, I want what You want for our family. I'll move anywhere. I may not like it, but I'll trust in You that it will be best for us."

Bob's job offer from Dartmouth came several weeks later, and he took it.

Seeing such good friends move was sad for all of us. Yet there was a sense of jubilation at the way it had come about. A few weeks later we heard from the Kaisers. They were settled in a large, roomy house, had made new friends, loved the community. Bob was finding the job a great challenge and delighted in the fact that it combined two factors: use of the business experience he had accumulated over the years and work with young people in education, which he had always yearned to do.

"When we look back over the past months," wrote Ev, "it amazes us how God's hand was in everything—our first call to you for help, the starting of the group, the leads and contacts which changed Bob's thinking and steered him to Dartmouth, and even the way my attitude changed. I know you'll also be interested in learning that we have started a fellowship group here in Hanover that is meeting new needs. How great God is!"

Creative Prayer for Others

You don't have to quit what you are doing to say a prayer, says Frank Laubach, one of the great spiritual teachers of our time.

DO your prayers for other people seem rather feeble? "Nine out of 10 people pray weakly, ineffectively, somewhat like a low-grade broadcasting station," says Frank Laubach, world-famous author and teacher. "By persistent training, however, we can make our prayer-life a radiant, creative force."

Dr. Laubach then goes on to describe in his book on prayer* how any person can do this through a sense of imagination and discipline. The purpose of this month's Spiritual Workshop is to challenge you to try some prayer experiments along the line of Dr. Laubach's suggestions. This prayer will not concern self, but the well-being of others.

GET OUT OF YOUR PRAYER RUT

First, be willing to discard or change old habits of prayer. For example, Dr. Laubach makes it clear that *the position of your body during prayer does not matter.* "It is not essential to close or raise your eyes, to kneel or stand, to fold hands or lower head," he states. "Some positions are valuable if they relax your mind and body."

USE THOSE FRAGMENTS OF IDLE TIME

During the day every person wastes dozens of small time segments: in the bath, dressing, walking down stairs, riding

* *Prayer—The Mightiest Force in the World* by Frank Laubach. A Fleming Revell Inspirational Classic.

or walking to a destination, in an elevator. Such moments can be filled with a prayer 10 seconds to a minute long. Dr. Laubach calls these "flash prayers."

When you climb into your automobile and remember that a friend is soon going into surgery, the thought may come, "Lord, be with Janet and guide the doctor's hand." Dr. Laubach describes how he sits in a bus and looks around at the other riders. He picks a face that seems discouraged and aims prayer at the person, saying to himself several times, "Jesus will help you."

"Flashing hard and straight prayers at people in a bus while repeating, 'Jesus . . . Jesus . . . Jesus . . .' will sometimes make those near you act as if they had been spoken to," says Dr. Laubach. "When I do this, it seems to me that I am pushing these prayers from my breast and fingers, as well as from my brain—from my whole nervous system. After a while the bus, or car, or room, seems gently 'excited' like the magnetic field around a magnet."

To skeptics who consider such prayer pointless, Dr. Laubach states that if it raises the spirits of a few people on a bus, lifts the atmosphere in a roomful of tense people, or simply changes one person's thinking from negative to positive, then it is *real prayer at work.* And if enough people did it in and about our tense city areas, it might change the whole climate in a neighborhood.

PRAY WITH PENCIL AND PAPER AT HAND

Find some time each day for meditation. When God sends a thought, write it down and keep it visible until it can be carried into action. Pray for individuals by name. The clearest thoughts are often written so tersely they snap like a whip. Be sure to record any results of your prayers. A notebook is recommended for this.

PRAY WHILE YOU READ

When reading a newspaper, pause for a second over the name of a world leader, or a man suffering hardship, and whisper, "Lord, this man may be hungry for Thee." If it becomes a habit you soon will be spreading thousands of secret blessings over the world.

PRAY WHILE LISTENING TO MUSIC

While sitting quietly listening to music, try this prayer, "What do You have to say to me now, Lord? Think Your thoughts in my mind. Use me as Your channel to reach the person that needs You now." Believe then that He is using you to reach a son, a daughter, mother, father, a friend, a mate, or an enemy.

PRAY WHILE WALKING

Walking and exercise can be a very definite aid to prayer. As you walk, talk to Him in the rhythm or cadence of your steps. Dr. Laubach finds it exhilarating to stride into a crowd and "waft prayer" in all directions. "This will help strengthen your soul, just as victims of paralysis strengthen their weak muscles by physical exercise," he states.

PRAY WHEN FALLING ASLEEP

When people have trouble sleeping at night, they waste endless hours. Try putting these sleepless hours to use. You can do this by simply turning those fragments of thought into prayers for the people who come to mind. For example, "Lord, help the President to realize his need for You . . ." "Lord, be with Jim. . . ."

One man discovered that his nightly prayers for friends and relatives were more effective when he had their photographs all about his room. In the darkness, he would single out one person and shine a flashlight on the picture as he prayed. To his astonishment he received several letters from these close friends, written, he learned later, a few moments after his prayer for them.

PRAY WHILE YOU WORK

Alta Vail of Emporia, Kansas, wrote in *Sunshine Magazine* that she found a new way to pray one day while ironing. She got to thinking about how many lines there were—bus lines, telephone lines, clothes lines, fishing lines. Why not a prayer line? Result: she strung a short rope across one corner of her kitchen and hung cards on it with names of shut-ins, of the sick and the bereaved. As she irons, she prays for these people by name. When friends heard about this, she began to get regular calls, "Hang me on your prayer line, please."

A powerful story of intercessory prayer was told by an alcoholic who was taken to a hospital for pscyhopathics in San Diego a few years ago. He was placed in a room with three other patients who did nothing but scream. When night came, he prayed to be able to sleep, but the screams continued.

Then suddenly he began to pray for his three roommates "May God give you peace," he said quietly over and over. The screams stopped. "Not only that," the alcoholic reported later, "it was as if something broke in me. Praying for them released my own tension. I was free."

As it happened, at the next examination the doctor smiled and pronounced him well enough to go home. He was truly a free man.

When you have a sense of creative spontaneity in your love for God and people, you will find that your prayers not only become a kind of adventure but also increase tenfold in power.

THE UNLIMITED POWER OF PRAYER LORD, FILL ME WITH GRATEFULNESS

Count your many blessings, count them one by one,
Count your many blessings, see what God has done.

SO goes the old hymn. The question we might pose here is: how long has it been since you have taken inventory of God's goodness to you and how long has it been since you thanked Him for His benevolence?

No matter how few your possessions, how scanty your material wealth, how fragile your health, there is one blessing everyone reading these words has in common—it is the blessing of life. Life with all its possibilities and opportunities. But few of our assets stop there: most of us have some work to do, or we should have. Most of us have a place in which to live, food to eat, friends and loved ones interested in our well being. We also—each one of us—have problems with which to deal. These, too, can be a blessing if we learn how to accept them as a fact of human existence.

The people who speak in this chapter come from all walks of life. Many of them have known adversity, but they have not been shackled by it. They have learned to thank God not only with their prayers, but with their lives which witness daily to His great love.

"If you can increase your sense of gratitude," says this distinguished American," you will become a happier person."

The Two Magic Words

by JAMES FARLEY

NOT long ago in my mail I received a request from a college student in Pennsylvania, a young man who said he was writing a thesis on government. He knew of my background in politics, and asked me to fill out a questionnaire.

There were at least 40 questions, and some of them called for detailed and complex answers. I was quite busy but, believing that any interest in government should be encouraged, I sat down with my secretary and dictated a long reply. It took most of one afternoon, but I finally sent it off with the little glow of satisfaction that comes from completing an arduous and voluntary task.

I looked forward to receiving from this young man some acknowledgment as to whether I had helped him or not. But I have yet to hear from him to this day.

I told myself that it was a matter of no great consequence and to put it out of my mind, forget it. But obviously, since I am writing about it now, I didn't forget it. I didn't forget it because I was disappointed.

The truth is, ingratitude hurts everyone. It also hurts the person who fails to show appreciation because he may make an enemy where he could have kept a friend.

Simply feeling gratitude isn't enough; it has to be demonstrated, one way or another. Perhaps the boy in Pennsylvania *was* appreciative but if so his appreciation is wasted because he never told me. Two words—*thank you*—could have made all the difference.

Furthermore, the incident made me examine myself. When someone's performance hurts or displeases you, it is a good idea to ask yourself whether traces of those unpleasant characteristics may not exist in *you*. So I asked myself, how much do most of us appreciate the countless little daily acts of courtesy or kindness on the part of other people that make our lives smoother and more comfortable? How grateful are we, really, for the privilege of living in a country where it is possible for most of us to take freedom and justice and security for granted? How much thankfulness do most of us feel for the marvelous gift of life itself, and how adequately do we express this to the Giver?

The honest answer to each of these questions was painfully clear. Not enough. Not nearly enough.

And so I have decided to make a New Year's resolution to try to change my attitude from a passive to a more active one where gratitude is concerned.

. . .To thank the people who make my world run smoothly —waitresses, elevator operators, taxi drivers, barbers, anyone —not just with a casual word or an impersonal tip, but with some expression of genuine interest in them as fellow human beings.

. . .To make myself more aware of the miraculous privileges involved in simply being an American, and to show my thankfulness by working without thought of reward (yes, even answering unsolicited questionnaires!) to make the best country in the world even better.

. . .To remind myself every day of the infinitely precious value of every minute of existence, and to show my gratitude to God not only with prayers of thanksgiving but by living as close as possible to the way He wants me to live.

A basic rule in showing appreciation, I have found, is this: *do it now*. Do it while your sense of gratitude is fresh and strong. If you put it off, it becomes all too easy to forget it. When Christ healed the ten lepers, only one came back to thank Him, and He commented a bit sadly on this frailty of human nature.* If you feel a flash of thankfulness, act on it before the impulse dies away.

If you do train yourself to act, you will discover that gratitude is by no means a simple thing. I believe, myself, that there are several stages or degrees. The first—and most familiar—is the spontaneous feeling of thankfulness for benefits received.

Children have this strong sense of gratitude. A few years ago, out in Iowa, a teacher asked her fourth grade pupils to write a prayer of thanks "for the small blessings which make your life happy and good." The 29 papers that were handed in gave thanks for such things as "the sound of laughter—erasers that make mistakes disappear—the smell of chocolate cake in the oven—colored leaves that swirl and fall in the autumn—big, red, garden tomatoes—my sister's smile on Christmas morning—and for God's care."

A second stage of gratitude is thankfulness, not just for the pleasures and benefits of life, but for its hazards and hardships as well. It takes some insight and maturity to realize that troubles and difficulties have values, but they do. All of us have heard of handicapped people who struggled so fiercely to overcome their handicap that ultimately they became champions. The Pilgrims thanked God for their first harvest, but they might well have thanked Him also for the difficulties that they met and overcame, because it was on this anvil of pain and suffering that they forged the character of a new nation.

The third stage of gratitude is what the poet E. A. Robinson had in mind when he wrote that there are two kinds of thankfulness, "the sudden kind we feel for what we take, the larger kind we feel for what we give." When you begin to feel gratitude for the opportunity to be of service, to help others, to make the world a better place, then you are getting close to the self-forgetfulness that the Bible tells us is the secret of true happiness.

If you can increase your sense of gratitude and your willing-

* Luke 17:12-19

ness to express it throughout the coming year, you will make the people around you happier, and you will become a happier person yourself. There is a great magic in those two words —*thank you*.

It is impossible to be grateful and embittered at the same time for gratitude must have an object, and if one is grateful for life, then one must be grateful to the Giver of life, the Giver of all things.

"Gratitude," says an old quotation, "is the fairest blossom which springs from the soul; and the heart knoweth none more fragrant." This I will remember as I try to keep my resolution this year and in all the years God gives me.

A Prayer of Thanksgiving

Because I have been given much,
I, too, must give:
Because of Thy great bounty, Lord,
Each day I live
I shall divide my gifts from Thee
With every brother that I see
Who has the need of help from me.
Because I have been sheltered, fed,
By Thy good care,
I cannot see another's lack
And I not share
My glowing fire, my loaf of bread,
My roof's safe shelter overhead,
That he, too, may be comforted.
Because love has been lavished so
Upon me, Lord,
A wealth I know that was not meant
For me to hoard,
I shall give love to those in need,
Shall show that love by word and deed,
Thus shall my thanks be thanks indeed.
                    Grace Noll Crowell

The Way of Acceptance

by Arthur Gordon

A FEW years ago some friends of ours were given the heart-breaking news that their teen-age son was going blind, that nothing could be done. Everyone was torn with pity for them, but they remained calm and uncomplaining. One night as we left their house, deeply moved by their fortitude, I tried to express my admiration.

I remember how the boy's father looked up at the stars. "Well," he said, "it seems to me that we have three choices. We can curse life for doing this to us and look for some way to express our grief and rage. Or we can grit our teeth and endure it. Or we can accept it. The first alternative is useless. The second is sterile and exhausting. The third is the only way."

The way of acceptance . . . how often that path is rejected by people who refuse to admit limitations, hide behind denials and excuses, try to shift the blame for failures, react to trouble with resentment and bitterness. And how often, conversely, when someone makes the first painful move toward repairing a damaged relationship or even a broken life, that move involves acceptance of some reality, that has to be faced before the rebuilding can begin.

It's a law that seems to run like a shining thread through the whole vast tapestry of living. Take alcoholism, for instance, that grim and mysterious disease: where does recovery begin? It begins with acceptance of the unacceptable, with the uncompromising four words with which members of Alcoholics Anonymous introduce themselves at meetings: "I am an alcoholic." Or take a failing marriage: Any marriage counselor will

216

tell you that no reconciliation succeeds unless it involves acceptance of the other partner, faults and all—and acceptance, too, of the fact that the blame for the trouble must be shared.

Difficult? It's hideously difficult! But in terms of courage and cheerfulness and ultimate happiness the rewards can be beyond measure. I knew a man once, an Episcopal minister, who through some hereditary affliction was very deaf and almost blind. He went right on preaching, visiting the sick, listening to people with his hearing-aid, laughing uproariously at jokes and having a marvelous time.

I remember going with him at Christmas time to buy some trifle in a crowded drugstore. On the back of the entrance door was a mirror, so placed that as we turned to leave my friend's reflection came forward to meet him. Thinking that someone else was approaching, he stepped aside. So did the image. He moved forward and once more met himself. Again he retreated.

By now an uneasy hush had fallen on the spectators. No one quite knew what to say or do. But the third time my companion realized he was facing a mirror. "Why," he cried, "it's only me!" He made a grand bow. "Good to see you, old boy! Merry Christmas!" The whole store exploded in delighted laughter, and I heard someone murmur: "That man really has what it takes." But what "it" was, surely, was the gift of acceptance, acceptance of limitations that in turn brought the power to transcend them.

Is there any way to be receptive to this gift or grace, to learn to rebound from the inevitable slings and arrows that wound the ego and try the soul? One way is to face your difficulty, your problem, your loss, look at it unflinchingly, and then add two unconquerable words: *and yet*. This is the situation, you have to say to yourself, and yet . . . All this has happened to me, and yet . . . The words are unconquerable because they shift the focus from what has been lost to what remains and what can still be gained.

Some people confuse acceptance with apathy, but there's all

the difference in the world. Apathy fails to distinguish between what can and what cannot be helped; acceptance makes that distinction. Apathy paralyzes the will-to-action; acceptance frees it by relieving it of impossible burdens. Former President Eisenhower's mother was a deeply religious woman. When he was a boy, she would say to him, "Ike, the Lord deals the cards; the way you play them is up to you." There's acceptance in that philosophy, and without a hint of apathy. There was no apathy, either, in the acceptance of our friends whose boy lost his sight. They helped him learn Braille. They convinced him that a life could be useful and happy even though it had to be lived in darkness. He's halfway through college, now, doing splendidly, and his attitude seems to be cheerful: "My handicap's blindness; what's yours?"

What acceptance really does in such cases is liberate people by breaking the chains of self-pity. Once you accept the blow, the disappointment, then you're free . . . free to go on to new endeavors that may turn out magnificently.

I remember being given a glimpse of this truth quite early in life. It was during my first year at college. Home for a brief visit, I was faced with the unpleasant necessity of telling my parents that my brave plans for working my way through college were not succeeding—at all.

The field I had chosen involved selling. Students ran the campus concessions for such things as dry cleaning and laundry, and freshmen could compete for positions in these organizations by selling service contracts. I waited until my last night at home. Then I told my parents that I had done my best, but that I was not going to be among the successful candidates. My father asked why.

Nothing is so indelible as the memory of failure. I remember how the coal fire muttered in the grate and the tawny light flickered on the shadowy bookcases. "Because," I said slowly, "I'm a terrible salesman, that's why. I get self-conscious. I get discouraged. Other people do the job much better. I'm in the wrong pew, that's all."

On the mantel, the old clock ticked. I waited for the remonstrance, the exhortation, the you-can-do-it-if-you-really-try lecture. But there was just silence. Finally my father laughed gently. "Well," he said, "that's fine. It's just as important to learn what you can't do as what you can. Now let's forget about that and talk about getting you into the right pew!"

Accept . . . forget . . . move on: some great Americans have ordered their lives along those lines. Abraham Lincoln once told a visitor that in the fiery crucible of the Civil War he did the best he could, regardless of criticism, and would do it to the end. "If the end brings me out all right," he added, "what is said against me won't amount to anything. If the end brings me out wrong, ten angels swearing I was right would make no difference." Acceptance . . . acceptance of the iron rule that results matter more than intentions. On President Truman's desk was a wry little sign: "The buck stops here." Again acceptance . . . acceptance of the frightful responsibility, the awful loneliness of the presidency.

Just as acceptance has its rewards, so non-acceptance has its penalties. We knew a couple once who had three children. The oldest was a girl, sweet-tempered, but very slow. It was clear that there was a degree of mental retardation, but the parents could not bring themselves to accept this. They tried to pretend that the child could do anything a normal child could do. They put her in schools where she could not keep up. They begged for performance that she could not give. They tried to rearrange the whole world to fit her limitations, meanwhile neglecting the emotional needs of their other children. They meant well; they thought they were doing right. But their lack of acceptance made life a burden for all of them.

Perhaps in the long run the beginning of wisdom lies here, in the simple admission that things are not always the way we would like them to be, that we ourselves are not so good or so kind or so hard-working or so unselfish as we would like to believe. And yet, we can say . . . *and yet* . . . with each sun that

rises there is a new day, a new challenge, a new opportunity
for doing better.

"O Lord," goes one variation of the old prayer, "grant me
the strength to change things that need changing, the courage
to accept things that cannot be changed, and the wisdom to
know the difference."

People have called it the prayer of acceptance. They are
right.

A wise housewife tells how to double the pleasure of giving.

The Second Thank You

by PHYLLIS AMY WOHLFARTH

FOR my birthday last year I fixed a celebration dinner and after dessert my children brought forth their presents. All were wrapped in a sun-burst of mis-matched colors.

My husband Fred's gift was a gold lapel pin, but other than a quick, small thank you to him, I didn't have a chance to tell him how lovely it was.

The children were anxious for me to open their gifts and their voices buffeted me from all sides of the table. "Open this one, Mama," John shouted. "No, I'm the oldest," Janet announced, "she's going to open mine first."

So, putting aside the small pin box, I quickly gathered the children's gifts in front of me, shut my eyes and chose the first box to open. Slightly mollified, the children quieted down as I quickly slipped the wrapping from first one and then another, assuring each that his was a gift that I truly needed.

I'm ashamed to say it wasn't until the next Sunday that I thought to thank Fred again for his pretty pin. Dressing for church, I fastened it to the shoulder of my suit. It looked lovely against the smooth Italian knit. I smiled at Fred, "Thank you, Darling. It was very thoughtful."

His face had a sudden wistful look. "I'm sure glad! I didn't think you really liked it. . . ." Then, hesitatingly, he added, "My grandmother used to wear it to church. I've always admired it. I remember so clearly watching her pin it on, when we kids lived with her. I found it recently in a box of old things of hers in the attic. I thought of you at once."

As I rushed across the room to hug him, tears filled my eyes.

I'd never have known how important the little gold pin was or how deeply Fred cared if I hadn't said that second thank you.

The first thank you on receipt of a gift is often perfunctory, but it is the second one, rendered after the gift has been savored, appreciated and put to use, that is the deeper expression of gratitude. I hope never to forget this second thank you.

A Housewife's Prayer

Let me delight in the little things
 In the morning dew
 In the thrush that sings
 In the green pine tree
 In the dainty violet nodding to me.

Let me speak simply of common things
 Of a clean, starched shirt
 Of twin wedding rings
 Of a child asleep in his own small bed
 Of a fluffy cloud floating overhead.

Let me be grateful for everyday things
 For the food at my table
 For the joy music brings
 For a star at my window winking at me
 For a cooling swim in a salty sea.

When I cry aloud from the world's harsh stings
 Let me think of my treasures of little things.

Let my spirit soar; let my heart take wings.
 Joy and peace fill my storehouse of everyday things.
       Phyllis Weichenthal

"In our family we've rediscovered a pathway to God so direct and simple that it's almost as natural as breathing. It's the old custom of expressing gratitude at mealtime for the wonders and blessings of life."

The Glow of Grace

by John H. McCombe *

FOR a long time, saying grace in our family was a pretty cut-and-dried affair; bowed head, quick mumble, scrape of chairs, what's-for-supper? But the time came when the dizzy pace of modern living began to weaken the bonds that held us together. When we asked ourselves what we might do to regain our lost companionship, the Latin derivation of that word *com* (with) and *panis* (bread) suggested an answer. If we could become better companions at mealtime, the rest of the day might take care of itself.

Looking for a way to make a fresh start, we remembered a prayer I learned from my Irish father:

Back of the loaf is the snowy flour,
And back of the flour is the mill,
And back of the mill is the wheat and the shower,
And the sun and the Father's will.

We started saying this in unison before every meal. Soon, with the chains of habit broken, we found ourselves trying all sorts of innovations. One is to go around the table asking each person to name the thing for which he feels particularly thankful. A child may be grateful for a pet turtle or a passing grade on a school test. A guest may express appreciation for the privilege of living in America. The *cause* of the gratitude isn't the important thing, we've found; it's the expression of it that counts.

* Mr. McCombe is Vice-President of the American Bible Society.

Another change of pace is what we call a blessing "in the round." One person starts with a brief phrase, the next adds his, and so on around the table. Sometimes we find ourselves laughing at our efforts. But after all, why shouldn't a grace have a smile in it, like any other joyous thing?

Some of the smiles come from our attempts to add music. We stumbled on our singing approach one day when Kathy, then about five, came to the table humming loudly, "Mary Had a Little Lamb." She kept humming, much to the annoyance of her seven-year-old brother, Scott, whose turn it was to say grace. "All right," said Scott finally, "let's *sing* the thing!" He began using the words of "God is Great," and we all joined in:

> *God is great and God is good,*
> *God is good, God is good.*
> *God is great and God is good,*
> *We thank Him for our food.*

When we were visiting friends some months ago, they called upon their 11-year-old son to ask the blessing. He prayed:

> *Thanks be to Thee for love that's shared.*
> *Thanks be to Thee for food prepared.*
> *Bless Thou the cup; bless Thou the bread;*
> *Thy blessing rest upon each head.*

Putting this one to music was quite a challenge. Later, around our own table, we tried to fit it to several tunes and finally came up with "How Dry I Am." Hearing us sing it, one amused guest recalled that the early church often used popular ditties to spread its message.

One sure way to enhance a sense of closeness, we've found, is to join hands around the table while grace is being said. Psychologists tell us that touch is one of the deepest and most basic forms of communication. Certainly it's almost impossible to feel antagonism for someone whose hand is linked with yours.

One Christmas when several relatives were visiting us, a polite sort of cold war threatened to break out because there

were just too many people in our small house. But, at the dinner table, when we joined hands, I could literally feel the
tension vanishing. The little things that were pushing us apart
gave way to the big things pulling us together, and our Christmas was saved—by grace.

Saying grace can also forge a chain that links you to the
past—and the future. The other night on the train I was talking
about this with a fellow commuter. "When I was a child," he
said, "we youngsters spent the summers with our grandpar-
ents on a Wisconsin farm. There were 18 of us cousins. Before
every meal we had grace. Now our family uses the same grace,
and the families of my 17 cousins use it with their children.
Whenever we visit one another we say it and the years fade
away, and we're all together again, not just physically but
spiritually and emotionally, with warm, wonderful memories."

A sense of gratitude is a contagious thing. It can start with
just a glimmer in one person and then cast its spell over a
whole group. One evening last summer, just before supper-
time, a magnificent double rainbow appeared in the eastern
sky. One of the children called us to the porch to see it. It
blazed so brilliantly against the dark backdrop of thunder-
heads that the mighty phrase from Genesis leaped into my
mind: "I set my bow in the cloud, and it shall be a sign of the
covenant between me and the earth."* So I went and got the
Bible and read that passage aloud, and the one that tells of
God's great promise: "While the earth remains, seedtime and
harvest, cold and heat, summer and winter, day and night,
shall not cease."**

When I finished, a guest quietly added a quotation from
the Apocrypha: "Look upon the rainbow, and praise him that
made it; very beautiful it is in the brightness thereof. It com-
passeth the heaven about with a glorious circle, and the hand
of the Most High hath bended it."†

* Genesis 9:13 RSV
** Genesis 8:22 RSV
† Ecclesiasticus 43:12, 13 Douay

We all stood there, spellbound, while the "glorious circle" faded. At last we went in to supper. But that evening I felt that we truly brought grace to the table with us.

Sometimes I think it's possible to bring grace to the table without even knowing it. The other day I was with a family who has no formal ritual. But as we all sat down, the father said to the mother, "How nice the table looks, my dear." And as he unfolded his napkin he said cheerily to the eight-year-old, "Well, it's raining again, but you didn't leave your bike out—smart fellow!"

Not prayers of thankfulness, exactly, and yet there was a glow all through that meal because even a simple compliment is a note in the symphony of living. I remember too the night at our house when there was tension in the kitchen and Mother wasn't far from tears. But when the soggy biscuits and charred roast were placed on the table, our Karen rose to the crisis and literally offered a word of grace: "Oh, Lord, tonight we had trouble with the stove, but we're all here together—and that's what we thank You for tonight."

A tradition that I think might be ignored now and then is the one that automatically assigns the saying of grace to any clergyman who happens to be present. Ministers, priests and rabbis are well equipped to offer thanks, of course, but several have told me that it's heartening and rewarding for them if some layman offers the blessing. We forget sometimes that ministers need to hear other people pray.

More and more, as the years pass, we're finding that giving thanks at mealtime overflows from the dining room into all aspects of life. No doubt there are many other ways to show appreciation, to feel grace, but these quiet moments of reverence have become absolutely indispensable to us. In our headlong rush through life, in our clamorous hunger for more and more, for better and better, for thrills and excitement, for recognition and success, we desperately need these little islands of serenity where we can pause and, at peace with ourselves, realize how incredibly blessed we are.

An unforgettable man, with a contagious philosophy.

It's a Beautiful Day for It!

by Wilbur Cross, III

IN the summertime, when school was out and we were
spending our vaction in New Hampshire, my brother and
I always were up and dressed and downstairs at dawn. Our
alarm clock was the sound of our grandfather tossing birch
and maple logs into the old wood stove and rattling the dented
kettles as he warmed water with which to shave.

Part of the attraction was breakfast. We never knew just
what kind of concoction Grandpa would make. But in the eyes
of two boys, eight and 12 years old, you could be sure that it
would be something startling. One of his favorites was a bowl
of shredded wheat, garnished with slices of banana, sprinkled
with blueberries he had picked himself, amply basted with
thick New Hampshire cream and topped with crumbles of
bacon and a steaming hot poached egg.

Looking back, perhaps the ingredients of Grandpa's "Sunrise Sundae" were not as surprising as was the realization that
this 67-year-old, rumple-topped apparition in baggy work
pants and scuffed shoes, was a former Yale University dean,
Wilbur Lucius Cross, then serving the first of what were to
be four terms as a distinguished Governor of Connecticut.

"Well . . . " he would say to us as we burst into the kitchen,
"it's a beautiful day for it, isn't it?"

"Yes, Grandpa," we would agree, glancing expectantly at
each other. It *was* a beautiful day for it. Now all we had to do
was wait and see what "it" happened to be.

I recall one cold, drizzly August morning when Grandpa
came out on the porch to greet a caller. "Beautiful day for it,"
he said. The caller looked puzzled, wiping the rain off his fore-

head. What he had come for was to call off the proposed outing for that afternoon. He was afraid "the old gentleman"
would catch pneumonia. At Grandpa's reaction to the weather
he changed his mind. The outing was a big success.

On another occasion, this time in the middle of winter, he
greeted a boy my age and his mother with "Beautiful day,"
apparently oblivious to the fact that a wet snowfall was freezing into ice. The mother merely gave a nervous laugh, but
the boy responded eagerly, "You bet, Dr. Cross. My buddy and
I are going up the hill with cardboard boxes and have an ice
slide!"

Much of Grandpa's optimism sprang from the Bible. He had
memorized long passages of it, as well as poetry from many
sources. His "beautiul day" outlook may well have originated
with Browning's familiar *Pippa Passes*, which he quoted again
and again, especially the ending, "God's in His heaven—all's
right with the world."

It was two years after his retirement as Dean of the Yale
Graduate School that he ran for Governor of Connecticut and
was—to the great surprise of everyone, including his Demo-
cratic party, which had not had a governor in 35 years—elected
by a slim margin. When asked why, at the age of 67, he had
committed himself to the rough and tumble of political life,
he would reply, "Men and women of faith have a responsibility to enter politics."

Many felt that even his optimistic "beautiful day" outlook
would never be able to weather the bitterness and the personal
attacks that any man in public office must face. Yet when he
finally left office—eight years and four terms later—he was as
vigorous and optimistic as ever.

If it were sunny, he might head for the yard, to scythe the
tall grass. If rainy, he would usually stoke up the old pot-
bellied stove in the dining room, then settle down with books
and pads and enjoy a truly beautiful day—beautiful for reflecting and writing.

How many days were wasted, he used to caution us, because

the weather would not cooperate with what people had planned.

Grandpa is gone now, but never forgotten. I always remember him somehow when rain or snow has interfered with plans we have made for our children. I like to wonder what my grandfather would have devised for the occasion. No time for a picnic, perhaps, but certainly a beautiful day—for *something*.

A Prayer For Joy

Lord, I am a fool. I sought joy and fulfillment in worldly things and have become increasingly empty. I see now that all along You have been waiting to give more joy, yet I have been unwilling to receive it from You. So now I make this act of holding out empty hands, a waiting heart, an unfilled life for You to fill. May the power of Your love and gladness drive gloom and drabness from me. And help me become the kind of person who can radiate Your joy to others. Amen.

Catherine Marshall

*A world famous concert pianist recalls a desperate
time in her life when she could do nothing but trust
God.*

My Hands Were in His

by Lili Kraus

WE thought at first that it was my husband the Japanese
wanted. We had been in Java several months before
the Japanese invasion in February, 1942, and, as enemy aliens,
we prepared ourselves for trouble. In a few days, we learned
we were on the Japanese death list.

My husband, Otto Mandl, had officially renounced German
citizenship, and he was Jewish—perhaps reasons enough to
put him on the death list of Germany's ally. Also, he had trans-
lated into German the books of H. G. Wells, including *The
Shape of Things to Come,* which was severely critical of Hit-
ler, another mark against him.

During the first weeks of the occupation, the Japanese had
rounded up Europeans on the island, putting men and women
in separate camps. Because I was still free, I gave concerts at
the camps, and I secretly used these occasions to deliver letters for the separated husbands and wives. I also brought them
a great deal of money, as much as I could hide on myself, with
which to buy food. But I couldn't believe this was enough to
put me on the death list.

The waiting was torment. At last, late in March, I was com-
manded to appear at the Japanese headquarters, and my husband went with me. The commandant said: "We are not interested in your husband, Mrs. Mandl. We want you. You are
under arrest."

"For what?" I asked.

He said, "I cannot tell you now."

I was allowed a moment alone with my husband.

Then my shoes were taken away from me and I was led to an underground jail where there were three small cells, 4 by 4 by 12, like kennels, two for men, one for women. Fifteen women were in the cell when I was ordered to crawl into it.

One woman I knew. She was Christine von Starkitenborgh, an American who, because her father was with the State Department, had been raised in embassies around the world, and thus she had met and married the man who was then the Governor General of Java. "Christine," I asked, "why are we here?"

"I suppose I'm here since I'm the Governor's wife," she said, "but I don't know why you're here, my dear."

I tried to figure it out. I had been born in Hungary and began my music studies there. At 17, I entered the Vienna Acadamie; at 20, I was a professor there. I met Otto Mandl in Vienna. The fact that he was 20 years older than I bothered some of our friends, but not us; the fact that he was Jewish and I was Catholic bothered our families, but not us. Each of us practiced as much of the other's religion as our own allowed.

When the Germans occupied Austria in 1938, Otto and I agreed that we did not want to raise our children in a Nazi country. We moved first to France, then to England. Some months later, the Netherlands invited me to make another tour of the Dutch East Indies, but we had become a family without a country, without travel documents.

When H. G. Wells learned this, he arranged to get us British papers.

We were aboard ship, approaching Java, when we learned by radio that Germany had invaded the Netherlands. At Java, we were advised to remain there because ocean travel was now far too dangerous. We rented a small house; Otto lectured at the university and tutored our two children; I practiced and taught.

And then the Japanese came.

Unless the Japanese greatly exaggerated the importance of

the letters and money I had smuggled to the imprisoned husbands and wives, I could find nothing in my life that should
put me on a death list. Days dragged by in the crowded cell.

Finally, after two weeks, I was taken to the commandant
and I learned the charge against me. Someone, perhaps to save
his own life, had told the Japanese that Christine and I had
been smuggling weapons to men in prison to encourage them
to start a resistance movement against the invaders. I could
not convince the commandant that this was a lie.

I was sent to a camp high in the mountains where there were
already 800 women prisoners. A few I knew slightly, and the
sight of them tore at my heart. In so short a time they had
given up. Unsure of their future, they had already lost hope,
dignity, self-respect. It was in their face, in their voice, in their
stance, in their crude treatment of each other. . . .

But I wondered how long I could bear prison life. I knew I
had to make a choice. Either I would deteriorate or I could
make this experience the treasure fund of my life by falling
back wholly on whatever I had within myself. I chose to cling
to God.

I remembered when, at eight, I had read the passage in St.
John's Gospel where Jesus is described as "the Light," and it is
written that those who receive Him also receive the light and
become children of God. In my child's mind, I pictured Jesus,
aglow, in a great crowd. I saw myself there and, scattered
through the crowd, my family and friends; all of us, I knew,
believers, and we were all aglow, and somehow there was a
marvelous unity among us.

As my faith matured, I came to believe that those who are
united in God are never separated, even by death. In prison,
though apart from my family, this belief kept us uniquely together. And just as I unconditionally accepted my imprison-
ment as God's will, so did I accept His will for whatever lay
ahead, for an actual reunion with my family in this world or
the next. I prayed the reunion would be here, but I realized
the chances were utterly remote.

Like all prisoners, I was assigned to hard labor. One job I did regularly was to clean a concrete gutter with a rag and soapy water. My nails broke; my fingers split. Another chore was to draw water in a bucket attached to a metal chain from a deep well. My palms were blisters that broke but never festered, although the rest of my body was a mass of festering wounds.

As a pianist, my hands were vital to my career, but I had made up my mind that if being a prisoner was the state of life in which God had placed me I would not shirk its burdens, nor resent them. One day Christine was sympathizing with me about my hands, and I said, "If God wants me to play again, He will take care of my hands."

Time and again I was summoned by the camp commander and questioned about the smuggling of weapons, and time and again I could only deny the accusation. Each such experience left me weakened, frustrated and afraid, and I grew to dread them, praying that my word would be enough to save my life.

One day the commander led me into his private office, and what I saw made my heart stop. I didn't know how or when it got there, but there was a piano. It looked like an altar to me, and my yearning must have shown in my eyes. The commander said I could play if I wished. I went to the piano without a word. My last loneliness drained out of me.

After half an hour, the commander stopped me, and said: "If you wish to play again, you must tell me the truth about the weapons."

I just shook my head.

Since music has always been a spiritual experience that half hour had filled me with the joy of having spent the time at prayer. As I left the building, I saw that scores of women had stopped at their work. Others had come out of their cells. The guards had lowered their rifles. They had been listening. I hoped I had given them the same peace I had received.

That night and for the next few days, an unusual quiet settled upon the camp. There was less dissension among the women. The guards were less brutal, less threatening. The work went easier. The next time the commander summoned me, he said: "You will play an hour one afternoon a week." He did not mention the weapons.

My ordinary life continued. I still had to clean the gutter and draw the water and work in the fields. I still had to sustain myself on two meals a day of the same food—a cup of rice and a bitter herb as vegetable. I still was questioned regularly about the weapons. And yet I was happy.

We had no chapel; there were no organized religious services, but for one hour a week I was alone at the piano speaking to God in the best way I knew. I somehow felt that, with me, everyone else—captors and captured—were all at prayer.

One day after a year, I was put on a truck and, without explanation, driven toward the city. I refused to think of what awaited me; I begged God to give me the strength to accept His will. In the suburbs, we reached a residential section that had been enclosed by a high, wire fence. We went through the gate and stopped at a garage beside a house. Otto was standing there. So were our children. What a glorious reunion!

For the next two years, the garage was our home in what was called a "privileged" camp. But there were few privileges. Everyone worked just as hard as in the mountains, and the accommodations were just as severe.

But for me, I knew, the worst was over, and yet I also knew that what had just ended were the best years of my life. In the worst circumstances of my life, I had thrown myself entirely upon God, and He had sustained me entirely. I had not known He could be so close, that He was so ready to uncap physical and emotional resources in me when I needed them most. I had learned that only by complete trust in God could I be enabled to have any hope for myself.

A famous actor gratefully remembers his father's gift of listening.

A Time for Silence

by LORNE GREENE

IN 1956, three years before I was given the part of the father in *Bonanza,* my father died. But in another sense he lives every time Ben Cartwright walks before the TV cameras. The way the role was originally conceived, for example, Cartwright was an aloof, unfriendly sort of person who greeted strangers with a rifle. I remember one early line I had to speak.

"We don't care for strangers around here, Mister. Git off the Ponderosa—and don't come back!"

Well, I said it, but my heart wasn't in it, and gradually I began to play Ben Cartwright more like the father I knew best. His way of greeting strangers was to invite them home to dinner. There were only three of us in our family, Dad, Mother and me, but our house in Ottawa, Canada, always seemed to be full of people. My most typical childhood memory is of creeping halfway down the stairs after my bedtime to listen to the company talking in the living room—and wondering in the morning who had found me asleep and carried me back to bed.

The people Dad, who made his living as a shoemaker, invited home most often were actors, artists, musicians, anyone connected with the world of beauty and make-believe that had been closed to him as a child and young man. Dad's family had been poor. He'd gone to work early, apprenticed to a leather worker at 15, and Dad's friends filled in a part of life he'd missed.

Dad was a huge man. He wasn't unusually tall, but he was tremendously broad across the chest and shoulders. And like so many big men, he was exceptionally gentle.

235

He had one special quality which I have come to think of as the essence of his fatherhood. It's such a simple thing, on the surface. He knew that there is a time for silence.

I remember the day I discovered this quality in my father. It was my eighth birthday, and Mother and Dad had given me a watch—a gift so far beyond my wildest dream that I had to keep taking it from my pocket to be sure it was real. At bedtime Dad warned me about winding it.

"It's wound tight now. Tomorrow, when it's run down some, I'll show you exactly how to do it."

Of course, I promised not to wind the watch and went to sleep in a fever of impatience for the morning.

Several times that night I woke up: would daylight never come? At last I drew the watch from safekeeping under my pillow, stared into its phosphorescent face and came to the incredulous conclusion that it was not yet three o'clock.

Surely it was later than that! My watch must be losing time! It was as though my dearest friend lay dying in my arms. Dad had said not to wind it, but wasn't it almost murder to let it run down?

And so after a regrettably brief struggle, I wound the watch. After every few twists I held it to my ear but the watch ran no faster. Desperate now, I wound and wound until finally I fell asleep. . . .

Early next morning Dad came into my room. "Well Lorne! What time is it?" Dad picked up the watch, his eyes still shining with the pleasure that giving the gift had brought him. Then he frowned. "Five minutes past three?" he said. He held it to his ear, then tried the stem. "Lorne, did you wind this watch?"

I must have felt much like Adam in the garden, with the taste of apple still in his mouth. "No, Dad, I didn't wind it."

I looked up at Dad and there in his eyes I saw some deep communion broken. For a full 10 seconds he watched me without speaking and then he left the room.

He didn't speak of the matter, then or ever, and he had the

broken mainspring on the watch repaired, but his silence demolished me. I sobbed for hours. I hated myself—whereas a lecture might have let me twist things around and hate him— and I never forgot it.

I was 15 before I tried deception on my father again—and this time I went in for it in a big way. It happened that Mother went to New York for two weeks to visit her sister, leaving Dad and me alone in the house. The more I thought about that house, standing empty and peaceful all through the day while Dad was at the shoeshop, the more delightfully it contrasted with the restraints of school. I took out a sheet of Mother's note paper, experimented with her signature until I was satisfied, then signed an illness excuse and began to enjoy a few days of leisure.

One morning I picked up my pile of books as usual, and left the house. Dad always left for his shop at 8:30, but I was taking no chances: I waited until 9:30 before going home. I let myself in, gloating at my own cleverness, and slammed the front door behind me.

"Who's there?" Dad's deep voice boomed through the hall.

He stepped out of the bathroom, a towel around his shoulders, and my cleverness deserted me. Staring into his eyes the only thing I could think of was:

"I—uh—came back for an umbrella."

Both of us instinctively glanced out the window. As luck would have it there was not a cloud in the sky. In the immense silence proceeding from my father I went through the wretched pantomime of taking an umbrella from the closet. I was halfway out the door when he spoke.

"Aren't you forgetting your rubbers?"

Miserably, I crept back for those, too.

"Lorne," Dad said, "let's you and me have lunch together today."

Now ordinarily this was a great treat, to meet him at a restaurant downtown during the school lunch hour, and I tried to sound hearty as I accepted.

I knew what that lunch date was for: it was a chance for me to tell him anything that might be on my mind. But somehow when I got there the words stuck in my throat. Dad didn't press me on the subject of my behavior; he maintained that powerful silence of his which said so much more than words. After the meal, he said simply, "I'll walk you back to school."

We walked up the high school steps, down the hall, into the principal's office, and there, of course, it all came out: the illegal absences, the forged note, everything. That principal bawled me out for half an hour. He threatened and harangued and banged the desk and said a great many things, all of which were probably very well put and doubtlessly true. And five minutes after we left his office I couldn't have told you one of them. All the while Dad said nothing at all. He simply sat looking at me. And whereas I cannot tell you a thing the one man said, the well-timed silence of the other has haunted me ever since.

I remember once during my first semester at college when I faced a decision about the future. I was enrolled in the chemical engineering course at Queen's University in Kingston, Ontario, about 100 miles from home. I'd been intrigued by chemistry for years, but I had another love, too, perhaps born on the hall stairs one night as Dad's guests talked in the living room. I wanted to be an actor. Not professionally, perhaps, but as a hobby. One reason I'd chosen Queen's University was because of the Drama Guild there.

But as soon as I started classes I made a jolting discovery: being a scientist was going to take all of my time! There were lectures in the morning, labs all afternoon, and written assignments for the evening. Only people in non-lab courses could go out for the Drama Guild.

Suddenly I wanted very much to be talking this all over with Dad. I put through a phone call and raced the three-minute limit to get it all said.

"Isn't this a coincidence!" Dad's voice interrupted me. "I'll be passing right through Kingston tomorrow on my way to

Toronto. Why don't I stop by the school and you can tell me more?"

Today, of course, I know he didn't have to go to Toronto any more than he had to go to the moon. He closed his shop and made that 100 mile trip because there was a boy with something on his mind who needed a good listener.

At the time I only knew that we sat all that September afternoon on the shore of Lake Ontario while I poured out my thoughts, my hopes, my dreams for the future, and that by the time I had finished I had chosen a lifetime in the theater.

What he thought about my plans, whether he would have been prouder of an engineer in the family than an actor, or whether he cherished completely different dreams for me, I never knew.

I was talking with a friend not long ago about Dad's gift of creative silence. My friend, Joe Reisman, is a song writer, and suddenly he picked up a piece of paper and started jotting down some of the things I'd said. Here's what he wrote:

> *You can talk to the man.*
> *He's got time. He'll understand*
> *He's got shoulders big enough to cry on.*
> *Tell all your troubles, and take your time.*
> *He's in no hurry. He doesn't mind.*
> *It matters not how bad you've been:*
> *You can talk to the man.*

Now I'd been talking about Dad. But by the time Joe had set the words to music and we'd made a record of them, the word "Man" had become capitalized, and the record was about God the Father of us all.

But that's a natural progression, when you come to think about it. Doesn't what we know of the Father in heaven start with a father here on earth? We believe in His love because we've known human love. We believe that He listens to our prayers because another father has listened to our words.

Being grateful to someone and expressing that grate-
fulness are two different things. The vehicle for this
man is writing "unnecessary letters."

Put a Halo on Someone's Day

by FRED BAUER

JUST a short time after I had finished college and had taken
a job with a weekly newspaper in Ohio, an editor of a
nearby metropolitan paper sent me what must rank as one
of the most pleasing letters I ever have received. The newspaperman wrote praising a column of mine.

The letter was a handwritten memo, no more than three or
four lines long. Yet the phrase "solid piece of writing" flashed
in front of my eyes like a neon sign. Strange that I cannot remember what the column was about, but I do recall showing
the note to my wife, Shirley. Trying to restrain my pride I
casually mentioned the letter as if I received such "fan mail"
every day. She saw through my facade—as usual.

Later, when I learned to know this newspaperman better I
found that he made a practice of sending—every day—dozens
of letters much like the one I received to people everywhere.
He called them his "unnecessary letters."

When I pressed him for a definition, he explained that these
were letters that no one expected to receive; correspondence
that he was in no way obligated to write.

Friends of mine have received his amiable missives too, and
always the tone is cordial, optimistic. One person described
his letters as "inviting as a fireplace on a cold, snowy night."

Over the years I have found great enjoyment out of imitat-
ing my friend's letter-writing habit often with gratifying response. Just last week, I received a *reply* to one of my *unnecessary* letters. What happened was this: in the newspaper,

a short article told of a friend's election to a state office in an organization she has served faithfully for years. I cut the news item out of the paper and pasted it to a sheet of stationery. Then I jotted a few words of congratulations alongside the clipping. That was my letter.

Her grateful response was most reassuring. "Your letter put a halo on my day," she wrote back.

Wouldn't it be wonderful if we all passed along a halo or two every day?

History has known a good many halo donors. For instance, Helen Keller has written some beautiful, *unnecessary* letters. I am particularly fond of one she mailed to the Reverend Phillips Brooks, composer of *O Little Town of Bethlehem*. Helen was 11 years old when she penned:

"My Dear Mr. Brooks: Helen sends you a loving greeting this bright May day. My teacher has just told me that you have been made a bishop, and that your friends everywhere are rejoicing because one whom they love has been greatly honored. I do not understand very well what a bishop's work is but I am sure it must be good and helpful. . . . It is very beautiful to think that you can tell so many people of the Heavenly Father's tender love for all His children, even when they are not gentle and noble as He wishes them to be. I hope the glad news which you will tell them will make their hearts beat fast with joy and love. I hope too, that Bishop Brooks' whole life will be as rich in happiness as the month of May is full of blossoms and singing birds."

Imagine Mr. Brooks' pleasure from such a letter. Young Miss Keller's charm is reflected in every sentence. Her sincerity and honesty make this a classic example of good letter writing.

One of the most famous *unnecessary* letters was written by Abraham Lincoln. After learning that a mother had lost five sons in battle, the President wrote her:

"I cannot refrain from tendering to you the consolation that may be found in the thanks of the Republic they died so to save. I pray that our Heavenly Father may assuage the anguish of your bereavement, and leave you only the cherished memory of the loved and lost, and the solemn pride that must be yours to have laid so costly a sacrifice upon the altar of freedom."

I am sure that at some sunrise in the future his message became a treasured memento of the family.

Even St. Paul, who is credited with writing 14 books in the New Testament, sent many letters which were not obligatory. His personal correspondence with such friends as Titus and Timothy and Philemon illustrate the Apostle's great Christian concern for others.

Take the letter he gave Onesimus, runaway slave of Philemon, to deliver to his master. In his persuasive letter, an imprisoned Paul wrote:

"I always thank God for you, Philemon . . . for I have heard how you love and trust both the Lord Jesus Himself and those who believe in Him. . . . I am appealing to that love of yours, a simple personal appeal, from Paul the old man in prison for Jesus Christ's sake. I am appealing for my child . . . Onesimus. O, I know you have found him pretty useless in the past but he is going to be useful now, to both of us. . . . It occurs to me that there has been a purpose in your losing him. You lost him, a slave, for a time; now you have him back for good, not merely a slave, but as a brother Christian . . . welcome him as you would welcome me. . . . I know you'll do what I ask—I believe, in fact, you'll do more. . . ."*

There is a tradition which says Philemon did do more than Paul asked. It is believed that Onesimus became a minister.

History is full of friendships that sprouted and blossomed as the result of *unnecessary* letters. Poet Robert Browning took time one day to write a note praising the poetry of a lonely invalid named Elizabeth Barrett. The couple's correspondence resulted in some of the most beautiful love sonnets of our time, and eventually marriage.

* J. B. Phillips

Robert Louis Stevenson, Benjamin Franklin, Charles Lamb, John Keats, George Bernard Shaw—all were writers of the *unnecessary* letter.

Though not in an abundance, we all have beloved acquaintances who willingly share themselves in such unobtrusive ways as making an *unnecessary* phone call to someone who needs friendship; paying an *unnecessary* visit to a shut-in who is lonely and depressed; or writing an *unnecessary* letter to someone who needs encouragement.

Each day they pass along "halos" which inspire defeated people to pick up the pieces of a shattered life and to try again. This concern for a fellow traveler shall not go unrewarded, for we are told *the King shall answer . . . Inasmuch as ye have done it unto one of the least of these my brethren, ye have done it unto Me.**

* Matthew 25:40

Prayer for Small Blessings

Lord, give me a heart that often sings,
And finds great joy in little things;
The song of a bird, the smell of a rose;
A gentle breeze that playfully blows;
A savory meal with loved ones dear;
The sound of a church bell sweet and clear;
A mother's love, a child's caress;
These are the things that truly bless.

Mildred Kirkland

*This talented comedian gets serious for a moment and
reveals a life-shaping incident.*

"Yes, Please"

by DENNIS DAY

RECENTLY I read an article about a woman whose secret
of happiness was to be found in two words which she
had printed in large letters and placed in a frame over her
sink. Those two words were "Yes, Lord."

I recognized immediately what those words meant to that
woman because out of my own life there are two similar words
that I'd do well to frame.

I came across them for the first time—in a meaningful way,
that is—in the 1930s, back in the heyday of radio. On one
memorable occasion I had the chance to audition for Jack
Benny's vastly popular Sunday night program. Kenny Baker
was leaving the show and they needed someone to replace
him.

At that particular time I was just out of college and was
about to enter law school in New York when a sudden ap-
pendix operation kept me idle for a term. I had done some
singing on radio in New York during school days and somehow or other a recording of me singing "I Never Knew Heaven
Could Speak" got to Jack Benny's wife, Mary Livingston. She
suggested that I be added to the long list of prospects.

There was great secrecy about the audition. When I went
into the office and saw Jack Benny sitting there, I nearly fell
through the floor. Eventually I was taken to a studio where I
sang over a microphone for Jack, who sat listening in another
studio. I sang for 20 minutes. I did a variety of songs and then
I heard the instruction through the intercom: "O.K. Take a
rest."

And so I did. I just sat there. The time passed. The silence in that studio was nerve-wracking. Then suddenly the intercom called out my name. I jumped up and quickly, without thinking at all, blurted out an innocent "Yes, please?"

I didn't know it at the time, but that remark had convulsed them in the listening room and when I later landed the job they wrote "Yes, please" into the weekly radio script.

The remark was accidental; yet, there is within it an attitude which reflects the type of upbringing I had as a child. Like "Yes, Lord," the idea of "Yes, please" suggests readiness to respond to requests. I think that this world is made up of yes-please people and no-thanks people, and, thank God, I was blessed by being born into a yes-please family.

My four brothers and one sister and I grew up in New York's Bronx where my father was a city engineer. We didn't have much money. But somehow or other we became imbued with the idea of grabbing hold of life as it was given to us and then wringing as much good from it as we could.

All of us kids worked hard—eventually all of us graduated from college—and we played hard and prayed hard. We Mc-Nultys (I was born Owen Patrick McNulty) were totally, unabashedly Irish. Mom and Dad both spoke with heavy brogues. There was lots of singing of Irish songs and frequent step-dancing to an Irish accordion. We were a houseful of yes-please optimists.

Even later, when we had grown up and gone away from home—but never really away from one another—I found examples again and again of how my family accepted life with joy and willingness. I think in particular of my brother John who suffered from cancer of the stomach for two years and nine months. John never complained.

At last John was forced to enter a hospital and there he stayed for six months. One night I was in Milwaukee playing *Brigadoon* and I telephoned long distance to see how he was. My sister answered and put him on the phone. He seemed as chipper as ever.

"Now don't forget," he said, "send me your reviews. I want to see how well you did."

Two days later John was dead. At the very moment I talked to him, they were saying the rosary for the dying.

Whenever I see people who accept life willingly, in good times or bad, I draw strength from them. Maybe this outlook on life is too simple for some people. Maybe "Yes, please" on a sign would be pointless to anyone but me. Nonetheless, I have found that when people say "No," or even "No thanks," they tend to look down. When they say "Yes, please," they look up. And I like to look up.

Our Prayer of Thanks

For the gladness here where the sun is shining at eve-
ning on the weeds at the river,

Our prayer of thanks.

For the laughter of children who tumble barefooted
and bareheaded in the summer grass,

*Our prayer of thanks.**

Carl Sandburg

As parents they could have been filled with bitterness
toward God. But they took a more positive stance.

Thank You for Chuck

by WALTER D. MATHENY

THE hour which my wife and I anticipated so happily for
so long was now turning into a nightmare. I was in the
delivery room with her, holding her hand as we both watched
the doctor try to slap life into our son. One minute passed,
three minutes, then five.

Both Marguerite and I had backgrounds in science (she
as a zoology teacher and I as an instructor in corrective physical education in the same high school in Hibbing, Minnesota),
and we both knew that the human mind could not survive
three minutes without oxygen without suffering some damage.

Ten minutes passed. Fifteen. I squeezed Marguerite's hand
and said, "He'll be all right." She said nothing.

The doctor glanced at us. "I'm awfully sorry," he said softly.
"Do you want me to keep this up?"

"Keep it up," I told him.

Thirty minutes after our son Chuck was born, he let loose
his first scream. That was all that mattered to us: he was alive,
he was going to live, we would have him to love.

With time, it became apparent that Chuck had cerebral
palsy, a neuro-muscular condition in which the control over
the motor nervous system is decreased in proportion to the
extent of the congenital brain damage. Mild cases can be almost imperceptible; severe cases usually involve sight, speech,
swallowing, a weakness of the extremities, and the ability to
learn may be impaired.

Nobody knows why cerebral palsy occurs. Those first few
months I wondered why it should happen to Chuck.

Chuck had a bad case. He could not stand until he was three and a half. To prevent any malformation of his pelvic region, Marguerite taught him to sit up in a corner, braced, putting proper pressure on his pelvis to assure correct bone development. And when at last he could stand, we helped him take his first steps in parallel bars made of a mop and a rake so that it would strike him as fun.

As time passed we observed that though Chuck had serious physical disabilities he also had a high degree of intelligence. This meant he could learn; he could be taught to take care of himself.

The more we discussed it the more the idea grew between Marguerite and me that we ourselves should teach Chuck, and not only Chuck but other children like him. We could open a school for cerebral-palsied children. We had the background for it, the personal involvement with it, and a deep concern for all such children.

We discussed the idea with Dr. Winthrop Phelps, a cerebral palsy specialist in Baltimore, who not only encouraged us but offered to give us special training when we were ready.

On December 1, 1946, with $3,000 I borrowed on a GI loan, we bought an old frame building near Burnt Mills, New Jersey, and opened our school. We had three pupils: Chuck, a Florida boy sent by Dr. Phelps, and a Massachusetts boy referred by a Boston doctor.

First I went to Dr. Phelps to study for three months, then Marguerite went. During her studies she came home on weekends to do last week's laundry and next week's baking to save on staff expenses. By the end of the year we had 23 students, and we had to plan our first move to a bigger house as we began to grow.

In these past 19 years Marguerite and I haven't *worked*. We've *lived*. If the hospital authorities are correct in rating our school as one of the best, it is because the generosity of our friends has enabled us to build our present facility and to gather together an outstanding staff. But equipment and skills alone could not have worked the wonders I've witnessed without a large portion of the vital tonic called love. This, at the school and more so at home, is what the handicapped child needs more than anything else.

The experience of having a handicapped child can bring out all the good in a husband and wife, and infuse them with more love for each other and the child than they ever imagined they had; but if there is the slightest contention between the parents, the experience may serve to worsen it.

Some parents feel guilty and they search their lives for some sin for which they think one or the other is being punished. That is sad and ridiculous. Science merely knows that there are seven children born with cerebral palsy for every 100,000 births; that, in fact, in one out of every 14 births the child is going to be different somehow. Nobody knows the reason. Guilt, self-pity, accusation or resentment smother love, and when there is no real love the child is lost.

Time and again I hear parents ask the same question I asked 25 years ago—"Why me?" I had no answer then, but I believe I have one now.

If our son Chuck hadn't been born with cerebral palsy, Marguerite and I never would have gone into this work, the school never would have been built, hundreds of children never would have been helped by the wonderful staff we have been able to assemble. We believe now that we have done with our lives exactly what God wanted when He allowed Chuck to be born as he was. We believe that loving God, loving each other and loving Chuck was the avenue over which God's guidance traveled, giving us the idea to start the school.

We believe, too, that when love is shut off by bitterness, God's will is thwarted and all the world is worse for it. We have learned, now, when tragedy strikes, not to ask, "*Why me?*", but rather, with Paul, to ask: "What is it you want me to do, Lord?" With time and with open hearts He lets us know, and what He wants serves to bring all men closer together and closer to Him.

For Marguerite and me, the rewards began at the beginning. Of our first three pupils, the Massachusetts boy proved untrainable and is now in a custodial home, but the Florida boy is a successful man in the citrus-fruit business.

Chuck, too, is a successful man. He is employed at our training school as gardener and general handyman, earning extra money by doing chores for the resident staff. He takes complete care of himself, he travels alone, he has his friends and hobbies, and he is his sister's idol. He could get a job anywhere but he prefers to work at the school where he is an example to others who are just starting out on his road.

We thank God for that.

Prayer of My Middle Years

Dear Lord, who made the face of me
Not all that I would have it be,
Not really homely, only plain,
But strong and patient in the main.
Coy youth would have its praises sung,
It is important to the young.
Yet one there was, a man apart,
Who found me fair and gave his heart.
Now Lord, that I have grown more sage
Since passing into middle age,
I only ask, as face grows lined,
A countenance described as kind;
That wrinkles by my eyes will show
A little humor as I go;
That I may view my humble scene
With glance of one content, serene,
Through grateful, shining eyes that see
The blessings You have given me.
                                   Ruth Perry

What Thanksgiving Can Do for You

A three-step program designed to heighten your appreciation of life.

IF we could extend the mood of thanksgiving to the entire year, would we be a happier, more out-going people? Better friends and neighbors? Would we develop a stronger faith? Grow closer to God? This month's Spiritual Workshop is presented in the belief that the answer to all the above questions is YES.

In the pages that follow are three specific suggestions as to *what you can do* to increase your flow of thanksgiving. We suggest that you undertake this workshop as an experiment and continue it to Thanksgiving Day. Then evaluate any difference it has made in your life.

Guideposts editors believe that the person who has developed a natural and instinctive thankfulness has made a crucial breakthrough in his search for a oneness with his fellowman and God.

(1) Every day, surprise someone with a "thank you."

Surprise is the key here and rules out the thanks anyone could expect from you in the conventional course of things. There is a children's book used in many nursery schools which shows a little boy visiting a farm to thank the cow for the milk he had for breakfast. Then he goes to the hen house to thank the chickens for his eggs; he thanks a sheep for his warm bathrobe and so forth. The idea, of course, is to help children become aware of the bigger world on which their small daily rounds depend.

Most adults would balk at thanking animals whose gifts are

unintentional, but all of us could use thanks as a door to awareness of much that we take for granted. We have various services delivered to our homes without ever considering a word
to show our appreciation. How long has it been since you
thanked the mailman, milkman, or newspaper boy for their
reliability or punctualness? Is there a certain radio program
or newspaper column that's always part of breakfast? These
people don't know unless you tell them the part they play in
your life. If you receive over-ripe fruit do you complain to your
grocer? Do you likewise tell him if it was especially delicious?

Opportunities to surprise people with thanks present themselves all day long. In his book *Try Giving Yourself Away*
David Dunn suggests "second thanks" as a way of adding surprise even to conventional thank you situations. Whenever,
for example, he receives a book, he thanks the giver at once.
Then when he finishes it—perhaps many months later—he
writes again, mentioning specific ways in which the book has
been helpful to him. He has found he can apply this technique
to any kind of gift.

Most of the time you will never know what effect your
thanks have on the recipient—though you can be sure that
occasionally they will be more important than you dream.

The story is told of a housewife who came across an old
geography book while cleaning in her attic. As she leafed
through its dusty pages, the woman remembered the spinster
teacher who had taught the course, telling stimulating stories
which painted indelible pictures of far away places in the
minds of her young students. The housewife, who loved to
visit new lands, loved to read about the people and customs of
other countries, realized that the seed had been planted by
this teacher. Taking the book to her desk, she wrote a note
thanking the teacher for "doing more than teaching geography." A short time later, an answer came to the housewife.
The teacher, since retired, wrote in scrawling letters, telltale
of her age, "You are the first student in all my years of teaching
who ever said thank you."

Though response to your efforts is unpredictable, the effect on your own life is certain. You will be training yourself day by day in seeking out the good and praiseworthy around you, rather than the more attention-catching evil and annoying things.

These results will not come about overnight, but they will come with persistence. The important thing is not to let a single day slip by without surprising someone with a thank-you.

(2) *Every day, thank God for something you have never until now thanked Him for.*

Thankfulness toward other people is, of course, both a preparation for and an indication of our thankfulness to God. It is probably easier to develop a sense of gratitude to other human beings just because their goodness to us is of necessity limited and specific. But from God "all blessings flow"—and in that "all" we run the risk of losing sight of the individual instances around which human emotion centers.

It is good to start any prayer of thanksgiving to God with some statement of overall indebtedness: as the Book of Common Prayer states it, "For our creation, preservation, and all the blessings of this life." But this month also try to add each day some different, perhaps very tiny blessing for which you are grateful.

The day will probably suggest its own specific. The gift of sight on an autumn morning, apples at cider time, warm clothes as days grow colder. The discipline of thanking God for a different blessing each day doubtless could be continued for a lifetime without repeating.

One family took turns around the dinner table, a different child returning thanks each evening. When the four-year-old's turn came his grace was, "Thank You, God, for wallpaper." The mother wrote Guideposts that she has enjoyed wallpaper more ever since.

Your thanks always will not be confined to little things, of course. There will be days when a Christian is overwhelmed by the magnitude of Christ's sacrifice for him and can thank God for nothing less.

One of the saddest stories in the Gospels is Christ's healing of the 10 lepers. On their way to the priests' house where Jesus had sent them, they discovered what had happened.

One of them, St. Luke records, *finding himself cured, turned back praising God aloud. He threw himself down at Jesus' feet and thanked him. . . .*

At this Jesus said: 'Were not all 10 cleansed? The other nine, where are they?' *

All 10 had been recipients of a miracle, but in only one was the thanksgiving faculty so developed that at the moment of great elation he knew both where credit was due and how to express it.

(3) *Every day, thank God for something about which you now are not happy.*

This is both the hardest exercise in thanksgiving and the one that comes closest to the heart of the spiritual life. To the oppressed Ephesians an imprisoned Paul wrote, *In the Name of our Lord Jesus Christ give thanks every day for everything to our God and Father.* **

Clearly, this kind of thanksgiving goes deeper than simple thanks rendered for good received. We commonly think of thanksgiving as following an action of God's. But what if it also works the other way? What if an attitude of thanksgiving for *everything* that comes to us is a first step in getting our hearts and minds in line with God's purposes and making us open to His goodness that flows through everything?

Someone has called thanking God for seemingly bad events and circumstances the first step of faith in *action.* If you can stand before a financial setback, a disappointment, even death itself, and thank God for what in His hands these circumstances will become, you are acting out your conviction that He can bring good when you yourself do not see it.

* St. Luke 17:12-19 New English Bible
** Romans 8:28 New English Bible

The story of Joseph is certainly one of the best illustrations of this. He could not understand his brothers selling him into slavery or why he should be cast into prison, but Joseph was faithful unto God and in retrospect he told his brothers, *You thought evil against me, but God meant it unto good.* What seemed to be a terrible injustice did, in fact, become a great blessing in Joseph's life. If *All things work together for good to them that love God,* we can in confidence give thanks for *all* things.

During this experiment between now and Thanksgiving keep a day-by-day record of the new ways you have discovered to show appreciation to both man and God. Review your experiences often. They might suggest follow-up actions.

In particular, record the unwelcome circumstances for which you have, in faith, given thanks. Leave space next to these for insights as they come. One month or one year, or even one lifetime may not be long enough to watch God bring to completion each event with which you have trusted Him, but the practice of thanksgiving will bring about increased faith.

LORD, TEACH ME TO DREAM BIG

IN Proverbs we are told: "Where there is no vision the people perish." Few men question the great wisdom in this simple statement, for it is our hopes and dreams which sustain us through the trials in life. A man without a dream is a rudderless ship, it has been said.

What is your dream? Is it some vague ambition or can you articulate it in specific terms? Have you shared your dream with God or is it of questionable merit, one which you feel He might disprove?

In this concluding section of The Unlimited Power of Prayer, you will read of the dramatic stories of people who learned to dream big. They are not big *day* dreamers, but big *night* dreamers and day workers who with God as their partner achieved some remarkable feats.

Following these articles is the final Spiritual Workshop, one of the most significant of the entire book. Read it carefully and hold it up against the dream you cherish for yourself. What you discover could affect the rest of your life.

6

A prize winner in Guideposts' annual writing contest for youth, this girl talks about the person who inspired her most.

The Teacher Who Taught Me to Dream

CHILDREN, please repeat after me, 'I am only one, but I *am* one. I can't do everything, but I can do *something*. What I *can* do, I *ought* to do; and what I ought to do, by the grace of God, I *will* do!'"

That was my introduction to my eighth-grade homeroom teacher—the one special person who did most to make my faith grow. She was to be my homeroom teacher for the next three years and my English teacher for the eighth and eleventh grades.

Mrs. Carolyn Long was the smallest person in the room, but she dominated it. She smiled and we all were glad we had chosen that school. She walked, talked, and even seemed to eat too fast. She seemed to feel that time would run out before she taught us anything and that if it did the fault would be hers.

Yet there was no lack of patience with us. Instead she made each of us feel that we were special people without bestowing special favor upon anyone. She always found time to give each of us "his five minute" as she called it. None was neglected.

I came to her thoroughly convinced that I was never meant to be anybody of importance. I had long ago decided that no one cared and nothing mattered, so I existed from day to day without any thought of tomorrow. The distant future was beyond my conception. Drab and unhappy circumstances had stunted my growth, killed my faith and left me floating on a directionless sea of time.

My home, I felt, was merely a place to go when school closed. I thought it a prison. My mother provided food and shelter for my body but really had little time for me. Separated from my father, she had full responsibility for my nine brothers and sisters. There just were too many other things which took her time. I never got my "five minute" with her as with Mrs. Long. We just never talked about the things I had on my mind.

I felt life was hopeless—and it was—until I met Mrs. Long, who kept nudging me with remarks like, "Use your mind, Linda, and free your body." "You can break out of the prison of your environment if you study hard and do your lessons everyday." Or she would say, "You can be somebody if you want to be."

The Lord knows I wanted to be somebody.

She continued to admonish us daily with that devotional chant, "You are only one, but you are one . . ."—meaning we ought to be proud of ourselves and if we weren't, we ought to have guts enough to do something about it. I tried not to listen, but I heard her. I tried to ignore what she meant, but I got the message, loud and clear. I told myself she was a fake, a too-good-to-be-true pretender, but she *sounded* so sincere. When I was on the verge of becoming a convert, I angrily denounced her for fussing all the time.

Then, one day she asked us to look out of the window and to write about whatever came into our minds as we looked. It was a dark, wintry day. I wrote a little poem about whispering leaves and the snow-kissed earth. She was ecstatic. One would have thought she had discovered another Shakespeare. I had never dared to show anyone my poetry before lest I be ridiculed. Her enthusiastic praise melted my sorrow and broke the dam of my resolution. I wrote all my themes in poetry that year.

She wouldn't accept dirty, incorrect work. We had to write it over until it was pretty and clean and errorless. Then basking in the glory of her smile we would pin it on the bulletin

board. "See! Everyone can create beauty," she'd say, pointing
to our themes, which, I must admit, did look beautiful. Sloppy
work, she swore, would develop sloppy characters in us and
that would blight our futures. Heaven forbid!

I could go on forever enumerating how this little, energetic,
enthusiastic lady rekindled my faith in myself and my ability
to fight against the odds; how she inspired me to a greater
faith in God; how she helped me to believe in the innate goodness of my fellowman.

Slowly, I believed and slowly, believing changed me. I
joined the Student Council. I accepted an invitation to appear
on an assembly program. She helped me, encouraged me and
was waiting to praise me when it was over; but sweeter than
that was the thundering applause of my schoolmates who
proved that she was right.

My sprouting wings continued to grow to full strength
through my high school years. It was not always easy, but Mrs.
Long was my radar, able to detect my wavering convictions,
always encouraging, urging and pointing the way.

"That's good, Linda, but you can do better," she would say
and I would do better. If I stumbled she'd say, "You can't stop
now, Linda," and I would try again.

With her help I have achieved confidence in my ability to
face the future. I understand myself and my potential. I also
understand the circumstances about my home.

My determination to find a way led me into business education and a trade. My dogged "do it well, if at all" training has
gotten me a part-time job in one of the school offices and the
confidence of my superiors. I dare to dream of a college degree, and I have the faith to believe that somehow, some way,
I shall achieve it. After all, I am only one but *I am* one. I can't
do everything, but I can do *something*. What I *can* do, I *ought*
to do; and what I ought to do, by the grace of God, *I will* do!
My most fervent prayer is that someday Mrs. Long will have
cause to be really proud of me and that I shall be able to wrap
the mantle of her faith around another child like myself.

One of the greatest players in the history of professional basketball reflects on his youthful battles with failure.

Last to be Picked

by Bob Pettit

AT the age of 12 I was thin and frail and had the coordination of a broomstick. I could not run fast, nor was I strong. Whenever they chose sides for any game, I was always the last boy picked.

During my youth we had no Little League in Baton Rouge, Louisiana. There was no community recreation set-up for boys. Nor was there any athletic program in grammar school. We simply played before school and during recess. I never had instruction of any kind in sports until I entered high school.

As a freshman I went out for football even though I was only 5-foot-7 and weighed but 118 pounds. I wasn't any good at all —but somehow I made third-string tackle. When I finally got into a game the other team ran a play over me that went for a 65-yard touchdown. After that my football career was over.

I went out for baseball and got to play second base one game. Then some guy hit a ball to me and it went right through my legs. That ended my baseball career.

In my sophomore year at high school I had begun to grow some so I decided to concentrate on basketball. I was one of 17 boys to try out, and it was Coach Kenner Day's job to pick 12. I gave it all I had, but when the coach posted the list on the bulletin board my name wasn't on it.

The only way I can describe my feeling at 14 when I wasn't good enough to make the team is that it seemed the end of the world. I was unwanted—a failure.

At first I just moped around the house. Then I started going down to my church—St. James Episcopal—where I sang in the choir, served as an altar boy and took the collection at Sunday services. The pastor—Mr. Philip Werlein—was friendly and very understanding.

He talked to me about the Person of Christ, who would help me when I was discouraged and who was always there to pick me up if I stumbled and fell. This kind of talk didn't seem too practical to a teen-age boy consumed with a desire to play basketball, but the words must have sunk into my subconscious because years later I used the very same words to try to help other boys overcome disappointment.

But Pastor Werlein did have one suggestion that appealed to me at the time. "Why don't some of you boys form a church team?" he asked.

The result was that we found enough boys who hadn't made the high school basketball squad to form a three-team church league. Now, for the first time, I was a member of a team—and somehow important.

I started practicing at home. I bent a wire coat hanger into a hoop, attached it over the garage door and shot tennis balls at it. My father, impressed by my determination, went out and bought me a regulation basketball and backboard.

Then began a routine of hour by hour practice which I followed for seven years. After school I shot baskets from 3:30 to 5:30. Then came dinner, homework and by 7:30 p.m. I was out shooting baskets again, by the light of several lamps placed on the windowsill facing the back yard.

Every trash and garbage can became a challenge to my basket-shooting form. At lunch I'd try an overhead shot to the corner wastebasket with my crumpled-up napkin. Apple cores, candy wrappers and scrap sheets of homework paper all became small basketballs for shooting purposes. Then, too, I would spend hours in front of the mirror checking my scoring form.

From a boy who couldn't hold a basketball properly I developed quickly through this practice and became the leading scorer on our pick-up church team. This period could really be called the pivotal point in my athletic career because from then on my goal was clear—if I were ever to excel in anything it would be basketball.

I lacked natural strength and so began daily exercises. Every night I would stand on the back steps, hold onto the screen door and do calf rises to build up my legs. Then I would go inside and grab window shade weights and do curls to build up my arms. During my sophomore year in high school I grew five inches in height and filled out quite a bit.

When I became a junior I could hardly wait for the basketball season to begin. During the first fall practices Coach Day was still with the football team. The assistant basketball coach, meanwhile, had installed me at center. When Coach Day arrived for his first practice he asked, "Who's that at center?"

"Bob Pettit."

"I can't believe it. He wasn't good enough to make the junior varsity last year."

But Coach Day kept me at center. Our team became state high school champions in my senior year. Then came more championship teams during my four years at Louisiana State University, and a professional career with the St. Louis Hawks, that covered 11 years.

Today I am retired from professional basketball and devote my energies to the business world. Yet my heart is very much in sports. I am a part of the Fellowship of Christian Athletes and speak at all kinds of sporting events. I try to get across these ideas to young people:

Find a worthwhile goal in life and persist toward it. . . . Remember that what you think about yourself is what you tend to become. . . . Learn self-discipline. . . . Never quit on yourself. . . . Don't work for awards and records—the one record with which you should be most concerned is your record as a person, a child of God.

Her dream and prayer was that God would send a child but after seven years there seemed little hope.

The Promise

by FRAN LARSEN

WHEN the doctor told Dick and me that we could never have a child, we didn't believe it. We went ahead and bought a house on a horseshoe-shaped street where cars didn't go too fast. We chose our yard for the big climbing-trees out back, and the neighborhood so that our children wouldn't have to walk far for friends.

But the years passed and no child came. I took to haunting the baby carriages in front of grocery stores and begging my friends to go out so I could baby-sit. Three babies in particular, through the years, I loved in a special way. They were all girls and every one of them had blonde hair and deep green eyes. When I held one of them my heart would start to thump and I'd have to blink back tears.

I couldn't understand it: neither in Dick's family nor mine was there yellow hair or green eyes. Yet, each time I picked up one of those babies I felt that she belonged to me.

And all this while, we prayed—not for a baby, just that His will be done. And yet whenever I pictured His will for us there was always a baby right in the center of it. I even got the room ready. It wasn't until afterwards that I realized I'd chosen green walls and yellow curtains.

One warm summer night in 1955, when we had waited seven years without a child, I woke up with a tremendous elation racing through me. I tried to get back to sleep but instead I grew wider awake every minute. At last, afraid that I would wake up Dick, I got up and went into the living room.

I switched on the lamp and sat down in our old brown armchair. On the table beside the chair was a book of Bible quotations. I picked it up but I felt too exhilarated to read. It slipped to my lap, falling open. At the top of the page where the book had opened, in letters that looked 10 feet tall, were the words:

"For with God nothing shall be impossible."

And then the whole living room filled with light. The lamp was on, it's true, but all of a sudden the room was *full* of light; the way sunlight sometimes shines on dust particles, causing one to see that the air all around is crowded and active instead of empty. In the same way I was suddenly aware that Christ occupied the whole room.

After a while the awareness passed, but not the certainty. I never doubted for a moment that Christ had shown me His all-powerful creativity to tell me that our prayers for a child had been answered.

In the morning I told Dick that we were going to have a baby. On the calendar in the kitchen I drew a big red circle around the night before. Then I phoned my mother and told her, and then I told my next-door neighbor. Soon there was scarcely anyone I hadn't told.

"Are you sure?" Mother asked. "Have you seen a doctor?"

But to me that would have been lack of faith. I had a promise from God! What did I want with a doctor?

But yet as the days passed, doubt arose in my mind too. And at last I didn't need a doctor to be crushingly, utterly certain that no baby was coming to us.

If I had fallen from a mountaintop I couldn't have dropped so far and so hard. I stopped answering the telephone. When my next-door neighbor rapped on the kitchen door I flattened myself against the wall until I heard her footsteps going away. I couldn't see anyone. I couldn't talk about it.

And yet, even at the worst moment of my disappointment, I couldn't get away from what I had seen and felt that night. Something had happened. But what? And how could I have misread it so completely?

That October, more to take my mind off myself than anything else, Dick suggested that we make the rounds of adoption agencies again. We'd been doing this for several years but the waiting lists were so long that we'd never even gotten our names down. This time, however, one place in New York City was more encouraging. Yes, they would take our application. Yes, we would be hearing from them.

It was in April, the following spring, when a phone call came. "Mrs. Larsen," the case worker's voice said, "your little girl is here."

Dick rushed from his office and met me at the adoption agency. We scarcely dared to look at each other. Then the caseworker brought in a small bundle wrapped in a pink blanket. "Here she is," she said.

But I could have picked her out of a thousand babies! There was the little wisp of fair hair, and the green, green eyes.

When Claudia was three weeks old we brought her back to the green-and-yellow room that had waited for her for so long, back to the house that she had suddenly made a home. With her came a very, very brief sheet of facts: parents' blood types, length of pregnancy, weight at birth, first formula. . . .

All during those busy first weeks I kept trying to put that sheet of paper away, but something wouldn't let me. Like a fly buzzing around my head, something about it wouldn't let me alone. I'd brush it away; a few days later it would be back. The paper. Look at the paper.

At last, to quiet the buzzing once and for all, I picked it up from the kitchen table where it had lain and began to read. My eyes stopped at the space for the months and weeks before the date of birth. It was very precise, down to the number of days. Slowly I took down the calendar from the wall and, getting last year's calendar from a drawer, I began counting back.

I knew the answer before I ever got to the month with the triumphant red circle. But I finished the count. And with the last number my finger rested on the very day and night when our house had been filled with the promise.

We were indeed to have a baby, that much I had grasped. That another was to bring her into the world, I had not guessed. Nor did I know what confusion and grief were the other part of the story, nor how in His love Christ was reaching out at that moment to the boy and girl who were the parents. I only know that in His mercy He reached out to us, too, and that the new little life so marvelously beginning was ours from the very moment of conception.

"Flesh of my flesh and bone of my bone" are lovely words, the loveliest—I used to think—that a mother could say. But I know more beautiful ones still, the words I say to my daughter: "Hope of my hope, longing of my heart, the promise of my Lord."

The Greatest of These

Reason faces up to life,
And sees things as they are;
Hope sees things as they ought to be,
And wishes on a star;
Faith dreams of miracles to come
That only God can do;
Love goes to work with patient hands
To make those dreams come true.
Helen Lowrie Marshall

This young African nursed an "impossible" dream all the way to reality by making an incredible 2,000-mile walk across his continent.

Barefoot to America

by LEGSON KAYIRA

MY mother did not know where America was. I said to her, "Mother, I want to go to America to go to college. Will you give me your permission?"

"Very well," she said. "You may go. When will you leave?"

I did not want to give her time to discover from others in our village how far away America was, for fear that she would change her mind. "Tomorrow," I said.

"Very well," she said. "I will prepare some maize for you to eat along the way."

Next day, October 14, 1958, I left my home in the village of Mpale, in northern Nyasaland, East Africa. I had only the clothes I wore, a khaki shirt and shorts. I carried the two treasures I owned: a Bible and a copy of *Pilgrim's Progress*. I carried, too, the maize my mother had given me, wrapped in banana leaves, and a small ax for protection.

My goal was a continent and an ocean away, but I did not doubt that I would reach it.

I had no idea how old I was. Such things mean little in a land where time is always the same. I suppose I was 16 or 18.

My father died when I was very young. In 1952, my mother listened to the words of the missionaries of the Church of Scotland (Presbyterian), with the result that our family became Christian. From the missionaries, I learned not only to love God but also that if I was ever to be of value to my village, my people, my country, it would be necessary for me to have an education.

At Wenya, eight miles away, was a mission primary school. One day when I felt I was ready to study, I walked there.

I learned many things. I learned I was not, as most Africans believed, the victim of my circumstances but the master of them. I learned that, as a Christian, I had an obligation to use the talents God had given me to make life better for others.

Later, in high school, I learned about America. I read the life of Abraham Lincoln and grew to love this man who suffered so much to help the enslaved Africans in his country. I read, too, the autobiography of Booker T. Washington, himself born in slavery in America, and who had risen in dignity and honor to become a benefactor of his people and his country.

I gradually realized that it would be only in America that I would receive the training and opportunities to prepare myself to emulate these men in my own land, to be, like them, a leader, perhaps even the president of my country.

My intention was to make my way to Cairo, where I hoped to get passage on a ship to America. Cairo was over 3,000 miles away, a distance I could not comprehend, and I foolishly thought I could walk it in four or five days. In four or five days, I was about 25 miles from home, my food was gone, I had no money, and I did not know what to do, except that I must keep going.

I developed a pattern of travel that became my life for more than a year. Villages were usually five or six miles apart, on forest paths. I would arrive at one in the afternoon and ask if I could work to earn food, water and a place to sleep. When this was possible, I would spend the night there, then move on to the next village in the morning.

It was not always possible. Tribal languages change every few miles in Africa; often I was among people with whom I could not communicate. This clearly made me a stranger to them, perhaps an enemy; they would not let me into the villages, and I had to sleep in the forests, eating herbs or wild fruit.

I soon discovered that my ax sometimes gave people the impression I had come to fight or to steal, so I bartered the ax for a knife I could carry unseen. I was actually defenseless against the forest animals I dreaded, but although I heard them at night none of them approached me. Malaria mosquitoes, however, were constant companions, and I often was sick.

But two comforts sustained me: my Bible and my *Pilgrim's Progress.* Over and over again I read my Bible, particularly finding confidence in the promise *Trust in the Lord with all thine heart, and lean not unto thine own understanding. . . . Then shalt thou walk in thy way safely, and thy foot shall not stumble.* *

By the end of 1959, I had walked 1,000 miles to Uganda, where a family took me in and I found a job making bricks for government buildings. I remained there six months and I sent most of my earnings to my mother.

In *Pilgrim's Progress,* I read many times of the tribulations of the Christian who wandered through the wilderness seeking God, and I compared this to my own wanderings toward the goal I believed God had put into my heart. I could not give up, any more than the Christian had given up.

One afternoon at the USIS library in Kampala, I unexpectedly came upon a directory of American colleges. Opening it at random, I saw the name of Skagit Valley College, Mount Vernon, Washington. I had heard that American colleges sometimes gave scholarships to deserving Africans, so I wrote Dean George Hodson and applied for one. I realized that I might be refused but I was not discouraged: I would write to one school after another until I found one to help me.

Three weeks later, Dean Hodson replied: I was granted a scholarship and the school would help me find a job. Overjoyed, I went to the American authorities, only to be told that this was not enough. I would need a passport and the round-trip fare in order to obtain a visa.

---

* Proverbs 3:5, 23

I wrote to the Nyasaland government for a passport but it was refused because I could not tell them when I was born. I then wrote to the missionaries who had taught me in my childhood, and it was through their efforts that I was granted a passport. But I still could not get the visa at Kampala because I did not have the fare.

Still determined, I left Kampala and resumed my trip northward. So strong was my faith that I used my last money to buy my first pair of shoes: I knew I could not walk into Skagit Valley College in my bare feet. I carried the shoes to save them.

Across Uganda and into the Sudan, the villages were farther apart and the people were less friendly to me. Sometimes I had to walk 20 or 30 miles in a day to find a place to sleep or to work to earn some food. At last I reached Khartoum, where I learned that there was an American consulate and I went there to try my luck.

Once again I heard about the entrance requirements, this time from Vice-Consul Emmett M. Coxson, but Mr. Coxson wrote the college about my plight. Back came a cable.

The students, hearing about me and my problems, had raised the fare of $1,700 through benefit parties.

I was thrilled and deeply grateful; overjoyed that I had judged Americans correctly for their friendship and brotherhood. I was thankful to God for His guidance and I pledged my future to His service.

News that I had walked for over two years and 2,500 miles circulated in Khartoum. The Communists came to me and offered to send me to school in Yugoslavia, all expenses paid, including travel, and a subsistence during my studies.

"I am a Christian," I told them, "and I could not be educated into the kind of man I want to be in your godless schools."

They warned me that, as an African, I would have racial difficulties in the United States, but I had read enough in American newspapers to feel this was a diminishing factor. My religion had taught me that men are not perfect, but as long as they strive to be they will be pleasing to God. The

American effort, I felt, was why the land was so blessed.

In December, 1960, carrying my two books and wearing my first suit, I arrived at Skagit Valley College.

In my speech of gratitude to the student body, I disclosed my desire to become prime minister or president of my country, and I noticed some smiles. I wondered if I had said something naïve. I do not think so.

When God has put an impossible dream in your heart, He means to help you fulfill it. I believed this to be true when, as an African bush boy, I felt compelled to become an American college graduate. This is to become true in June when I will graduate from the University of Washington. And if God has given me the dream of becoming president of Nyasaland, this too, will become true.

It is when we resist God that we remain nothing. When we submit to Him, whatever the sacrifice or hardship, we can become far more than we dare dream.

A Prayer for Fulfillment

Make my mortal dreams come true
With the work I fain would do;
Clothe with life the weak intent,
Let me be the thing I meant;
Let me find in Thy employ
Peace that dearer is than joy;
Out of self to love be led
And to heaven acclimated,
Until all things sweet and good
Seem my natural habitude.
  John Greenleaf Whittier
  from Andrew Rykman's Prayer

One of America's leading businesswomen tells how a 25-cent investment changed her life.

The Promise of the Daffodils

by PATRICIA MURPHY

I CAN still see the little bouquet of daffodils, just as it sat on a battered table in a rented room on Henry Street in Brooklyn in the autumn of 1929. What a time for a 17-year-old girl to arrive in New York! I'd come from the tiny fishing village in Newfoundland where I'd grown up—with all the romantic ideas that a country girl weaves around the big city— just as the Depression was getting under way. Men were appearing on street corners selling apples. Help-wanted columns were measured in inches instead of pages.

I think I might have panicked in those days if it weren't for the daffodils. My only income came from coloring picture-postcards by hand; it earned me enough to pay my rent, but there wasn't much left over for food. Breakfast many days consisted of a glass of water.

And still, more often than not, my room had a gay bunch of daffodils on the table. I had been raised in a convent where the message preached day and night was: seek *first* the kingdom of God. I think this is what I was trying to do each time I bought flowers. For it involved a real choice: I had to make up my mind which I wanted more, lunch or daffodils, for they cost the same—25 cents—and I could not afford both. Whenever I was feeling especially pinched and closed in by the Depression I discovered I could shake my fears by deliberately "choosing first" and buying flowers.

By evening, of course, on the days when I chose daffodils, I was ravenous. I would leave the rooming house and walk down Henry Street to a basement restaurant where I knew

273

I could get lots of good Italian food for practically nothing.

But one evening when I arrived at Mr. Anthony's restaurant, the lights were out and the door locked. I knocked but no one answered. By now I'd gotten to know the Anthonys personally. I was worried and began to pound on the door until at last it opened and Mr. Anthony's drawn face appeared.

"Oh, it's little Miss Murphy. I'm sorry. There's no supper tonight. We've gone out of business." Perhaps the long, meal-less day showed in my face, because he suddenly held the door wider. "Have a cup of coffee, anyway, with some bread and butter."

So we went back to Mr. Anthony's kitchen and sat down under a naked light bulb while he told me the same woeful depression tale I had now heard so often. Nobody had money, he couldn't charge his customers enough to meet his bills, his creditors were after him, he was closing down one step ahead of bankruptcy.

Mr. Anthony kept talking. But I wasn't hearing him. The thought that was racing through my head drowned out all others. All my schoolgirl years I'd had one ambition: to be hostess in a restaurant.

There was a lull in the good old man's monologue, and I blurted it out. "Do you think there'd be any chance at all of my taking over your business?"

Mr. Anthony stared at me, dumbfounded. "My young colleen," he said at last, "how much capital do you have?"

"Sixty dollars."

"Why, you'd need almost half that for a single week's rent." He looked at me more closely in the harsh light. "How old are you?"

"Eighteen," I said proudly, very conscious of the birthday just behind me.

"You're an 18-year-old girl from the country, you've got 60 dollars to your name, you're living in the heart of the worst depression this country's ever seen; three times this year experienced businessmen have tried to operate this restaurant and each one has failed. And you still want to try?"

"Yes."

Mr. Anthony just shook his head. "Well I hope you've got a secret."

I did have a secret, and when I returned to my room and saw those yellow flowers laughing from the dingy table, I knew that the secret was a good one. If by "choosing first" with my daffodils I had been able to dispel the tight, pinch-penny fears of the Depression, couldn't I do the same through my restaurant?

Mr. Anthony watched skeptically as I prepared for the opening of my restaurant. I made a careful round of all the shops in the neighborhood, checking food prices to see how much it cost a housewife to prepare a meal. I wanted to keep my charges close to her budget. But then I wanted to give her the one thing she probably didn't get at home that year: that "feel of plenty," that taste of God's own abundance which was the answer to the poverty of 1930.

I spent a long time plotting ways to bring about that feel on a tiny budget. Relish trays. I could heap raw cauliflower wedges and celery curls on a tray—the heap was the important thing. Piping hot popovers passed round again and again; flour was cheap and I loved to bake. A coffee cup filled as you sat down and kept full throughout the meal. Really fresh linen. Candles, everywhere there would be candles. And—of course —daffodils, least expensive and loveliest of flowers.

I was counting on those little extras. There were plenty of restaurants that year devoted to feeding men's stomachs. But I knew from my own experience that there was another kind of feeding equally important.

Opening day. I scurried from kitchen to pantry and back again, tasting, adding, fretting. My chef was a student from Columbia University; the waitresses and busboys were students too.

As evening approached they circulated the neighborhood with a box of cookies in one hand and a sample menu in the other. It was time for me to dress. I went to my rented room and put on the evening gown I'd brought from Newfoundland, with such different dreams of the city, a long black dress edged with gold lace—a dress for a ball. It was almost time to open the doors.

Mr. Anthony, who had helped set the tables, was folding the last napkin.

On the sidewalk above us we heard footsteps. People were coming! I started up the steps, then, half way, knelt down and asked God's blessing on the restaurant. Then, with a smile that I hoped hid my stagefright, I opened the door.

Thirty-five years have passed since that night, and I have been in the restaurant business all that time. Just the other day I climbed into a plane at an airport near New York City and started flying south. Below I could see one of my restaurants, the Westchester Candlelight, set in a 10-acre park surrounded by gardens and greenhouses. Upwards of 10,000 people, I knew, would eat there on this one day alone. In the city were five other restaurants I had started; I was now on my way to still another one in Florida.

In the plane I stopped to count up the number of meals I have served in those 35 years and the figure came to over 50 million! I thought, as I often do when these figures startle me, that the principle we uncovered in the heart of the Depression has proved valid in prosperity, too. "Seek ye first the kingdom of God," Christ said. Afterwards, He promised, a real abundance would follow.

Hans lived in a make-believe world—or so it seemed.

The Boy Who Never Grew Up

by Sister M. Dominic

HANS was a pale, thin lad. Other children in his village of Odense, Denmark, often made fun of the gangling boy in wooden shoes and patched clothing.

"The boy will go the same way as his grandfather," some of the adults predicted. This grandfather was the village character. He had no trade, but carved strange little figures for the children who followed him in droves. Once, though, Hans had seen some older boys chasing him down the street, pelting him with stones and shrieking, "Madman!"

Hans' father was a shoemaker by profession, a dreamer by nature. The two did not go well together, so the little family of three was always poor. But Hans' hard-working mother kept their single room spotless and put meals on the table out of an almost barren cupboard. When the shoe trade was slow Hans' father read to his son from the *Arabian Nights*, taught him how to make puppets and a tiny theater, showed him how to cut silhouettes out of paper: feathery shapes of trees and flowers and animals. But insanity claimed this gentlehearted shoemaker as it had his father before him, and he died when Hans was eight.

Hans fitted into the work-a-day world no better than his father and grandfather. The first time he was caned in school he picked up his books and walked out. His mother enrolled him in another school, but the first day he heard a girl whisper to her companion, "He's going to be crazy, like his grandfather," and he would not go back. At a third school he told a story to a group of boys about enchanted birds and talking trees. But the boys threw sticks at him and he ran home in tears.

After that Hans spent his days beneath a gooseberry bush in his mother's garden. With her long apron over it, the bush was a tent—a private, secret world where he could spin his joyous daydreams. He got lost in his stories; he walked around the streets seeing only the visions in his own mind. Who could blame sensible people for tapping their heads and saying the family malady was upon him?

Next, his mother tried to apprentice him to a trade. She bonded him three times: three trades, three failures. Only in his inner world was Hans not a failure. He made up stories in which faith in God and simple goodness were rewarded and he acted them out in his puppet theater. To anyone who asked him what he was going to be, he answered, "Famous."

Confirmation time came and from somewhere his mother got him a pair of real leather boots. She also cut down his father's only suit for him. But the boots were the best. Hans was so proud of them that he tucked the trousers inside. The boots squeaked as he walked up the aisle, while he felt that everybody in the church, including God, looked admiringly at his boots. He never put on wooden shoes again. He wore those boots long after he had to curl his toes to get into them and bathe blisters where the soles were gone.

At 14 he announced that he was going to Copenhagen. His mother was bewildered.

"But what will you do there?" she asked.

"I shall be famous."

"How?"

The child knew. "First you suffer terrible things," he said, "and only then you get to be famous. God has told me."

The town was shocked. Let a boy like that, without a trade, without an education, without money, go by himself to a big city! Madness!

How he existed those first three years, nobody knows. He roomed in a windowless cupboard in a boarding house in the worst section of town. In vain he tried to find work in the theater: dancing, reciting, acting. But mostly he wrote, begging for enough to live on, reading his stories to anyone who would listen, until at last he attracted the attention of a man with influence at court. Hans was offered a royal grant, with the condition that he be a bona fide student.

And so at 17 Hans entered school again, competing with boys who barely reached his elbow. Desks were too small, teachers delighted in humiliating the ugly, awkward youth who steadfastly maintained that he would become famous. Certainly not as a writer, they assured him, when he persistently failed both grammar and classical composition. One teacher's assessment of the young man's talent:

"His verses will rot in a bookseller's attic and he will end his days in a madhouse."

His mother's death of delirium tremens when he was 24 plunged Hans into a despairing frenzy of writing, as though by sheer volume of words he could create a world where he could bear to live. He tried everything: plays, poetry, novels. But for himself, in the long winter evenings, he went back to the fairyland of his childhood, setting down on paper the tales he had spun under his mother's gooseberry bush.

And then one of his novels sold, and people began to seek out the bleak garret where the young man lived. There someone found the fairy tales. Hans was astonished that anyone else should be interested in them: they were not his "work," they were only the thoughts that popped into his head when he was too tired to work.

Lonely as his life had been, Hans did not know that other men, too, have a child deep inside them, that real life for everyone falls short of the dream. A couple of the fairy tales were printed, and the world clamored for more. And so Hans shared with everyone the princes and princesses, elves and fairies that populated his secret world.

Like the ugly duckling in one of his own stories who grew into a beautiful swan, the shabby son of the shoemaker became a wealthy and respected writer—yes, and famous, too, as he had always said. But he never really grew up—never lost his child's heart and his child's faith. After all, he wrote, "Every man's life is a fairy tale written by God's fingers."

He was 70 when he died in 1875, but each year he is young again, as a new generation discovers *The Fir Tree, The Snow Queen, The Red Shoes, The Steadfast Tin Soldier, The Princess And The Pea, The Nightingale, The Little Match Girl, The Emperor's New Clothes* and all the rest. We read them, and the child in all of us laughs for joy, because Hans Christian Andersen took the broken things in life—the discarded, the sad, the unwanted—and wove them into magic.

*The odds against this woman achieving her goal were
prohibitive, but she never gave up—and therein is the
story.*

A Dream in My Heart

by DOROTHY L. BROWN, M.D.

WHEN I was five, several of us children living in the same
orphanage in Troy, New York, were taken to a hospital for tonsillectomies. If I had any fears I lost them the moment I was struck by the sights and sounds and smells of the
hospital. Somehow I knew even then that this wondrous world
would be my world, that this was the kind of work I would do
when I grew up.

For a child in my position this was the wildest dream I
could have had. I had been born out of wedlock. Soon after
my birth my mother left me with friends in Troy, but they
couldn't care for me and so they placed me in the orphanage,
where I spent the next 12 years of my life. I grew up knowing
that I would probably have to go to work at an age when other
girls were entering high school, but even this could not shatter
my dream of some day becoming a doctor.

As soon as I could speak after my operation I started telling
people that I was going to become a doctor. I kept saying so as
I grew up, receiving in return either patient smiles or impatient frowns and the advice that I should start being realistic.

I think now that I have always been realistic. A lonely child
learns early to fend for herself, whatever confronts her. She
soon discovers that her life will be only what she makes of it.

For example, as I grew older I also grew aware that nobody
was coming to see me. I was about eight when one day I said
to the superintendent, "I want to know why I don't have any

visitors on visitors' day." I wasn't complaining; I just didn't understand.

Unknown to me, this good man reported our talk to friends at his Presbyterian church, and the next visitors' day my heart leaped when I heard myself being summoned to the lounge on the public-address system. Not knowing and not caring who it might be, I hastily put on my best dress and rushed to the visitors' room. It was a white family—Mr. and Mrs. Frank Coffeen and their daughter Janet, 16, a college sophomore.

Now I could be like the other children. I could brag about my visitors—one of them a college student—who were coming to see *me*. I experienced identity for the first time. I became of value to myself. When I told the Coffeens that I wanted to be a doctor and they approved, I felt as though I were already licensed.

I felt, too, that I had made a marvelous discovery about life: any problem could be overcome by making a decision and taking action. Eventually I learned that this was particularly true of dreams. And I now believe that God meant it to be that way.

One day, again answering a summons to the lounge, I was approached by a woman who said, "I am your mother." I wasn't prepared for that. I hadn't known my mother was alive. We sat there, the two of us, staring at each other, scarcely speaking. She didn't reach out for me and I didn't know how to reach out for her, and when she went away I was lonelier than ever.

When I was 13, my mother took me to live with her in Troy. She supported us as well as she could by cleaning homes, which meant that I was usually alone, living in what amounted to a Negro ghetto. And for the first time I experienced the despair with which so many Negroes viewed life. We weren't supposed to have much of a chance. We were expected to resign ourselves to a world against us.

I couldn't accept that. At the orphanage, I was one of six Negroes among 250 children, and we had all been treated the same. And it had evidently made no difference to the Coffeens that I was black. Why should it make a difference now? Why should I give up my dream because people now said the odds were against me? Unhappy, I ran away from home three times, always heading for the orphanage, but each time I was brought back.

At 14, I had to quit school and go to work as a maid for a family that had some children my own age. My room was on the top floor, the walls lined with books, and I spent every free moment poring over them. I told my employer that I intended to become a doctor, which sometimes amused her and her guests, but when I convinced her that I was serious she helped me by teaching me how to budget my $14 weekly salary.

In two years I saved $500—enough to start, I felt. I also believed that becoming a doctor would be a good thing, something God would approve, perhaps something He even wanted. "With Your help," I prayed, "I am going to make it." I had no idea how much help He was ready to give, and now looking back my heart is full of gratitude for all the help He did give.

The day I registered for high school I had no job, no home, and when the registrar asked for my address I said, "I don't have one, but I'll find a room this afternoon and give you the address tomorrow."

After I explained my circumstances, the principal said he knew a Christian Negro couple who might let me live with them, and he telephoned them. Immediately they invited me into their home, and with that I acquired a family of my own. I grew to call them Grandma and Grandpa. They were poor; Grandpa worked for a road construction company, but somehow he always managed to earn enough to feed me and other children who were welcomed into the house.

At one time, there were a dozen of us. More important, there was always more than enough love for all of us. I insisted on paying for my room and board, and when my $500 ran out Grandma told me, "This will always be your home. All we'll ever want is for you to stay in school and be a good girl."

In 1937, on graduating from high school, I returned to maid's work to earn money for college. One day I figured that, at the rate of my income, it would take me 11 years to earn enough for college. With hopes of cutting the time I took extra jobs, one in the home of Mrs. Charles E. Smart, who was active in the women's group at her Methodist church.

As I did with everyone, I told Mrs. Smart that I was going to become a doctor. She asked me if I were serious about college; when I assured her I was, she said, "Our group at church is thinking of sponsoring a girl at Bennett College in North Carolina. I want you to meet my friends, and if they approve, you may get the scholarship."

They approved. In September I became a college student. As in high school, I took all the science courses I could, preparing for medical school. Later I learned that the Methodist women expected me to become a school teacher and work in the missions for a few years. I explained to them that I was willing to work the rest of my life in the missions—but as a doctor, and I feared that would be the end of their support. Instead, they helped me finish at Bennett and said I should keep in touch with them as I proceeded through medical school.

My first problem was to get into a medical school. In 1941 I faced a familiar problem: no money. Then World War II created a man-shortage and the Army turned to women with science backgrounds to work as inspectors in ordnance depots. In two years, by living at home with Grandma and Grandpa, I saved $2,000, and though I knew this was far from enough I also knew I couldn't wait any longer. I entered Meharry Medical College in Nashville. When my funds ran out, the Methodist women again came to my aid. I received my medical degree in 1948; after internship in New York I returned to Meharry for five years training in surgery, and since 1954, in addition to teaching at Meharry, I have been in practice in Nashville.

Not a day has passed without the realization that I am now living the dream which entered my heart when I was five years old. And I have come to believe that just as God gives each one of us our special talent, so does He give us our dreams to make us aware of the talent.

Nor does it matter how farfetched or unattainable the dream may seem. If we remain steadfast, if we have enough faith in God and in ourselves to go to work and to stay at work making the dream come true, then God puts into our lives the people who, out of their love for Him and us, will do for us what we cannot do for ourselves.

Looking back on my life I know that this is true. These days I devote my life to assuring the young that no matter what they are, or what their early years may have done to them, they *can* dream. But I also tell them that they must *do*—and then their dreams will come true.

Tell this fellow—one of America's most popular story-tellers—that he was a disadvantaged boy and you will hear about his "rich" childhood.

Mama and My $9 Violin

by SAM LEVENSON

AT a party my wife, Esther, and I attended recently, a woman remarked of a successful author, "He certainly had a privileged childhood."

"So did I," I added quickly. The others laughed, knowing I grew up in the slums of New York. But I was serious, for I was privileged. I had wise parents who loved me and told me so.

Our poverty may have kept me from most luxuries as a boy, but Mama and Papa always found money for the essentials. Just what the essentials were was not always clear to me, but Mama knew. One seemingly impractical purchase she made fascinates me to this day. It was a used violin—a $9 violin. To realize what an outlay this was, one must know how poor we were.

I was the eighth child of eight children, seven boys and one girl, born to Hyman and Rebecca Levenson, immigrants to America from White Russia. Papa worked as a tailor in a sweatshop when he worked—which was about seven months out of 12. We lived in a four-room tenement apartment where three in a bed was private, four in a bed semi-private.

We didn't seem to be any worse off than people around us. Everyone else ate the dark pieces of chicken too. (The bony dark pieces were the cheapest, and I must have been 20 years old before I knew a chicken had white meat.)

When Papa was out of work, we were lucky to have anything to eat. But somehow Mama managed and didn't complain. My older brothers helped with the family finances. By the time I was old enough to remember, Joe, the oldest, was through medical school and had begun to practice. The same was true of Jack who was a dentist.

How did they find money enough to go to school? They worked. With Dad in the sweatshop, selling papers, running errands, anything.

The same kind of ingenuity that got them through school figured in the violin episode. I was eight when Mama decided it was time for me to begin music lessons. She chose the violin because there was already one in the family. The fact that it was full-size never entered her mind. When I went for my first lesson to the settlement house on 105th Street, the teacher just shook his head.

Reconstructing the picture, I realize why. I was a sight: from my oversize shoes to my ill-fitting hand-me-down pants to my home-scissored hair-cut. Barbering was another of Mama's talents. (She didn't use a bowl, but a sieve.) However, the real problem centered around my arms; they didn't reach the end of the violin.

I trudged home and sadly reported the news.

"*Oiy*," Mother responded. (That's Jewish for "Oh my.") "But blessed are they who have arms—long or short." She always had a verse—real or imagined—from the Bible.

I watched with great interest as Mama met this crisis head-on. Her resourcefulness and stubbornness in refusing to give up when the odds were so great always amazed me.

For the next three months, she concentrated all her energy on finding me a junior-size violin. She toured the pawn shops, watched the advertisements in the papers, put music teachers on the trail of an instrument we could afford (which would have been free). Finally she located one for $9.

Conferences were held in whispers as Mama and Papa inventoried the family finances. When brothers Joe and Jack visited, Mother talked in hushed tones with them. (I'm sure they contributed to the cause.) Though I yearned for a violin with all my heart, I couldn't imagine how she could even consider paying that much money for one when we had been eating off the same soup bone for a week. Actually there were many weeks when Papa didn't earn $9, but that didn't discourage Mama. By saving a nickel here, a dime there, the sugar bowl bank grew.

Then one day when I came home from school, Mama and Papa put on a little ceremony as they made the presentation. Mama's round face was one big smile. She nervously brushed her gray hair away from her forehead as she waited for my reaction. When she saw my excitement, tears of pride came to her pretty blue eyes. Papa blew his nose.

"Make a joyful tune unto God all ye blessed," Mama said, quoting one of those Psalms I've never been able to find. But right then I could only stare at the violin in awe. This experience was the highlight of my childhood. But that wasn't the end of this gift.

Violin lessons cost money: 25 cents a week. Somehow Mama always was able to put her hands on a quarter for violin lessons. I know she went without food herself.

Now I didn't play very well, but I played in earnest. The violin was my liberation; my identity. Whenever there was a special occasion I was invited to play the violin—at home, at school, at synagogue.

Every teacher I had told me, with fingers in their ears, "Sammy, the violin is not for you." At my high school graduation in 1929, Jacques Wolfe, composer of *Shortnin' Bread* and *Glory Road,* accompanied me on the piano. After I had finished butchering the Slow Movement of *Mendelssohn's Concerto,* he advised me, "Sammy, go to college and study history." Mr. Wolfe didn't particularly like history, but he loved music and figured I belonged to the opposition.

Almost everyone told me to quit but Mama. To her my music was a little piece of heaven. I can remember her head dreamily swaying with each sweep of the bow when I played at home.

Once when I hit one of those "cat's-tail-in-the-door" notes, she counseled reverently, "God speaketh in whispers, Sammy, whispers."

Eventually, after I had become established as a comedian, I put aside my violin and let Jascha Heifetz have the field to himself. But you can't put aside a memory as rich as this. It warms me now as I tell you about it.

Today, Esther and I have two children of our own—Conrad, 20, and Emily, 12. They are happy kids with many friends and a wide scope of interests. We have tried to let them choose their course, often waiting to see a bud of interest, then encouraging them to go to it.

Though world conditions have changed a great deal since I was a boy, the responsibility of parenthood is still the same: staggering. Kahlil Gibran knew what he was saying when he wrote, "You (parents) are the bows from which your children as living arrows are sent forth."

Mama and Papa never read Gibran, but their bows were true—full of love and encouragement. No parent can give a child more. That's why I can picture a small boy cradling the world's most valuable violin and say, "I was a privileged child."

Keep a Place Apart

Hold fast your dreams!
Within your heart
Keep one still, secret spot
Where dreams may go,
And sheltered so,
May thrive and grow—
Where doubt and fear are not.
Oh, keep a place apart
Within your heart,
For little dreams to go.
                    Louise Driscoll

Are Your Dreams Big Enough?

A five-way test to measure and evaluate your goals in life.

DEEP in your heart is there an unfulfilled dream? Perhaps you feel guilty about it—you think somehow that the dream is selfish. But you're not really sure.

The Spiritual Workshop this month will explore the subject of dreams—those deep desires in all of us which move some people to great achievement, and others to frustration, even tragedy. In the book *I Will Lift Up Mine Eyes* by Glenn Clark, there is a chapter which provides a series of tests to help discover whether or not our dreams are right for us; whether they are self-centered or a part of what God wants for us.

HOW TO BEGIN

Make a list of your deepest desires. Be specific and thorough. If you want a certain job, indicate the exact kind of job you think you want. If you want a new house, try to put down the kind of house, the location, etc. If you want a trip to Europe, list the countries you want to see—and why.

If you want a college education, what college and what courses? What capacities do you desire in yourself? For example, would you like the ability to speak well in public? Or greater concentration? Or more ability to make friends? Do you wish for better health?

What sort of ideas do you want? What spiritual graces would you like to ask God for? What gifts? What kind of insights from Him?

Do not be afraid of being this specific, for remember that

you are going to submit this list to a series of checks to amend, change, and correct. Don't show your list to anyone, though; this is between you and your God.

FIVE TESTS

Having made your list as complete as you can, now you are ready to begin applying God's tests to see whether or not your desires are true "soul's sincere desires."

FIRST TEST: *Are the desires which you have put down true to your own nature?*

One way of getting at this question is to trace your steps back to childhood. Go back in memory as far as you can. What were your sincerest ambitions then? Put these down exactly as you remember them, no matter how silly they may seem now.

Here, for example, are the chidhood ambitions of one woman:

To be a beautiful lady with plenty of perfume.

To be a great writer.

To be a great musician.

In analyzing these little-girl dreams 18 years later, the woman found that "the beautiful lady" and the "plenty of perfume" represented a normal desire for beauty, for fragrance and expressed an innate femininity. At the heart of the "great writer" was the love of ideas, a soul-satisfaction in trying to get those ideas on paper as well as possible. The woman did, in actual fact, become a writer. The "great musician" desire was at base the need for self-expression, but her musical ability turned out to be mediocre.

The point is—if you are frail and uncoordinated, don't dream of great athletic accomplishments. What a waste it would have been for a great scientist like Thomas Edison to have dreamed of becoming a novelist. What if Shakespeare had spent his life trying to be a painter?

SECOND TEST: *Is it an honest dream?*

Ask yourself if your dream is an attempt to imitate anyone else. Or to please someone else? (Parents, for example, sometimes try to force *their* dreams upon their children.)

Is there any backwash of envy, pride, ("I'll show them!")
or jealousy in your dreams? To the extent that this is so, then
these are not honest dreams.

Have you thought through what really would happen to you
if your dreams were granted tomorrow?

One man who dreamed of being elected to a political office
had his dream come true, only to discover that, by nature,
he totally disliked the pressures it brought to his daily life. A
sensitive introvert he was miserable in the achievement of his
dream.

Am I honestly willing to pay the price to realize my dream?

A girl dreams of becoming an opera singer. Is she willing
to pay the price: dedication to her music, almost total concentration of time and energy in practice, practice, practice;
the letting go of a myriad of other pleasures?

Think through carefully the unglamorous aspects of your
dreams; the toil, the added responsibilities, the pressures.

Go over your list of dreams and rigorously apply the "honesty test" to each one. Remove some items from the list or add
others.

THIRD TEST: *Is it in line with basic justice?*

Go over each dream on your list and ask yourself:

Do these dreams meet the test of absolute justice to my
fellow men?

Will what I am asking take something that rightfully be-
longs to another?

Will I encroach on anyone else's privileges, property, or
personality, in asking this of God?

Am I overlooking any debt (not just money!) which I owe
another?

FOURTH TEST: *Is it pure?*

Ask yourself if you are trying to use anyone else as a means
to the end you want?

For example, as a means to better yourself at someone else's
degradation or expense?

Would anyone else have to lower his ideals in order for your dream to come true?

Be honest with yourself and with God here. Amend your list accordingly.

FIFTH TEST: *The Test of God's Greatness.*

If your prayers appear to go unanswered, it may be not because you are asking for too much, but because "your God is too small." Very often our vision is limited and our requests petty and lacking in beauty. So here is a joyous test to apply:

Do your dreams meet the test of God's beauty and harmony?

God's work in nature as in man's nature always is beautiful. A snowflake is beautiful. A maple leaf is beautiful, and also it is true to its own pattern and design.

Do not be afraid to ask for beauty in your life, only be sure it is real beauty.

Are your dreams *big enough* to have God's blessing?

A woman prayed for help for her partially-deaf child in learning to read. As it turned out, God's answer was not only help for this child, but through her for all the deaf children in that particular school district.

In other words, lift your eyes from yourself to take a long look at God's big horizons. Where do your small dreams fit into God's dreams for all His children?

CONCLUSION

You have before you your "soul's sincere desires"—sifted, tested—undoubtedly a somewhat different list from the one with which you began. So now we suggest that you do something that may make no sense to you—we ask you to relinquish your dreams into God's hands. Here is a prayer you may want to use:

Lord, I know that You love me and want my life to be creative, happy and of meaning to others. Here is a list of my heart's desires. To the best of my knowledge, I believe they can be Your dreams for me as well as my own. So I leave them with You now, realizing that You can accomplish nothing through me without work, discipline and prayer on my part. Thank You, Lord, for helping me to see that it is not wrong to dream big—that I go wrong only when I dream without You.

With this act of relinquishment, do not worry about your dreams or even pray about them again for the next few weeks. For by this act, you are planting your dreams in the soil of the Kingdom of God. And remember—do not keep digging up the seeds you have planted—or they will die. You can have absolute faith that where tulips have been planted, tulips will come up. We do not have to plead that four plus four equals eight ... or for the tides to come in.

Keep your list. What joy it will be in the future to go back over it and recall how and when God fulfilled this dream, and that one!